HOW TO SOLVE
CROSSWORDS

A HANDBOOK

HOW TO SOLVE
CROSSWORDS
A HANDBOOK

Abbott Wainwright

Copyright © 2014 by Abbott Wainwright

ISBN: Softcover   978-1-4931-4324-5
             eBook   978-1-4931-4325-2

All rights reserved. No part of this book may be reproduced or transmitted in any form or by any means, electronic or mechanical, including photocopying, recording, or by any information storage and retrieval system, without permission in writing from the copyright owner.

This book was printed in the United States of America.

Rev. date: 12/13/2013

To order additional copies of this book, contact:
Xlibris LLC
1-888-795-4274
www.Xlibris.com
Orders@Xlibris.com
143428

to Ronnie

Acknowledgments

There were two reviewers of earlier editions of this handbook: Evelyn Helmick Hively, scholar and author, and Sally Brown Lackey, who can answer those TV quiz-show questions faster than most of us can even digest the question. Others have helped with individual portions: Benita and Paul Vassallo with the "Spanish" and "Italian" sections, respectively, and Lisa Wainwright with the "Art and Architecture" section. The author is grateful for their contributions and reminds readers that any errors are his own.

Carolyn Plotke, the very amiable proprietor of Desert Secretarial in Scottsdale, Arizona, prepared this volume (as well as its five predecessors) for publication. It would not have seen the light of day without her.

All of us who enjoy crosswords are indebted to the many constructors and their editors who give us such pleasure every day. Our lives are greatly enriched by them and they show us what a wonderful legacy we have in the English language.✢

Contents

Dedication

Acknowledgments

Introduction 1
    Methodology 1
    Definitions 2
    How to Use This Book 2

Strategy 3
    Themes 5
    Contractions and Abbreviations 6
    Variants 6
    Slang 7
    Hyphens, Spaces, and Punctuation 7
    Nonletter Characters 7
    Trade or Brand Names, Including Cars 7
    Noun, Verb, or Adjective? 9
    Synonym, Generic, or Specific? 9

Tactics 13
    General Clues 13
        Plurals 13
        Tense 14
        Parts of Speech 14
        Comparatives and Superlatives 14
        Prefixes, Fillers, and Suffixes 15
        Miscellaneous General Clues 16

Foreign Languages 17
    French 19
    Spanish (and Portuguese) 31
    Italian 38
    Latin 41
    German 49
    Greek 52
Mythology 55
The Old Testament 65
Literature 69
Poetry 82
Classical Music 89
Roman Numerals 100
Sports 102
    Baseball 104
    Football 110
    Soccer 113
    Basketball 113
    Ice Hockey 115
    Golf 117
    Tennis 119
    Volleyball 121
    Boxing 121
Entertainment 123
    Comics 123
    Movies 128
    Television 153
    Popular Music 162
Art and Architecture 169
Geography 177

- Miscellaneous Subjects 182
  - Typography and Editors' Marks................................183
  - Card Games and Chess 184
  - Travel and Transportation..186
  - Nautical Terms 186
  - Mathematics and Geometry 189
  - Metric System 191
  - Noble Gases and Other Elements............................192
  - Other Scientific Terms..193
  - Computers, Software, and the Web 195
  - Currency 198
  - Schools, Colleges, and Universities 199
  - Native Peoples 200
  - Olio 201
  - Initials 202
  - A Glossary of Special Words 202
  - British Words 205
  - Scottish Words 206
  - Hawaiian Words and Places 207
- Lists 208
  - Rulers of England and Their Dates of Accession................208
  - U.S. Presidents and Their Dates in Office 211
  - States and Their Capitals..212
  - Birthstones 214
  - Signs of the Zodiac..215
  - U.S. Military Officer Ranks 216
  - Hebrew Alphabet 217
  - Hebrew Months 217
  - (Note Concerning Other Lists) 218

Introduction

Welcome to the wonderful world of crosswords, with its own rules, customs, and quirks. The subject matter of crosswords spans the ages, from the myths of history to last night's TV sitcom. Serious or silly, anything is grist for the puzzle.

This handbook is designed to be of help to puzzle solvers of all abilities. Although experienced solvers do not need much help, the sections titled "Foreign Languages," "Mythology," "A Glossary of Special Words," and "Lists" contain names, words, and expressions that may not immediately come to mind.

There are two main sections. The first, titled "Strategy," provides some crossword conventions and broad, overall guidelines, such as how to approach a puzzle; the second, titled "Tactics," is focused on discerning what the clues are attempting to elicit. As with strategy and tactics in any field, there may be some overlap between them.

To parallel the format of crossword puzzles, this handbook generally uses regular type for clue words and capital letters for their solutions. There are some exceptions, however, such as when both the first and last names of a person or character serve as clues *and* answers, such as the "Superman" character Lois Lane, where "Lois" could be clue or answer and "Lane" could also be clue or answer. In such a case, regular type is used for greater readability.

Methodology: This volume is the result of notes made while solving puzzles from a variety of sources, primarily the *New York Times*, for a period of over ten years, ending on October 31, 2013. Therefore, this handbook is current and is empirically based; it is not the result of the author's opinion, but rather of actual puzzles solved. Since the author has done few puzzles from other countries in the English-speaking world, this handbook may not be as helpful to puzzle solvers in those countries.

Definitions: In this handbook, *area* is part of a puzzle, such as the upper right, or northeast, corner; *square* is the smallest unit in a puzzle, which usually contains a single letter or other character (although it can contain multiple letters on occasion); *clue* is that which is to be solved; and *entry* (or *answer* or *solution*) is the word or other string of characters that solves the clue. (Professionals use the first term, "entry.")

How to use this book: First, this book is meant to be read; it is only secondarily a reference. It will not help you solve puzzles unless you first know what is in it; this means more than simply scanning the "Contents" pages and then using it only as a reference. You do not have to read every word; rather, familiarize yourself with the contents by reading (1) all of the "Introduction" and "Strategy" sections, (2) all of the "Tactics" section, except its included lists, such as baseball players, but you should know that these lists can be found there, and (3) all the captions in the "Lists" section so that you know what it contains. In this way, you will discover the subject areas where this handbook will help you and where it will not.

Examples of this last point: U.S. presidents and their dates in office are listed, but not U.K. prime ministers. The reason for inclusion or exclusion of a list is that puzzle makers (professionals use the term "constructors") have preferences, and those preferences are the subject of this book. This does not mean that David Cameron or the Sun King, Louis XIV, or a certain Chinese dynasty are never mentioned in puzzles; each will be found now and then, but their frequency does not merit a separate list here. Thus, knowing what is in this book and what is not is essential to using it effectively.

The same principle concerning inclusion or exclusion applies to other subjects in the "Tactics" section. For example, the more popular Latin-based languages are included (as well as German and Greek), but not the Russian language; boxing is included, but not wrestling. Similar to the above, this does not mean that "nyet" and "da" and sumo wrestling are never mentioned in puzzles, because they are. But the same reason cited above applies here: constructors have preferences, and they are the subject of this handbook.

The reader should also know that this handbook makes no mention of cryptic crosswords or acrostics; it concerns only traditional crosswords, such as those found in daily newspapers. ✦

Strategy

Until a few decades ago, crosswords did not include many of the subjects found today, especially those related to popular culture. More traditional topics found in puzzles include literature, poetry, the Old Testament, mythology, classical music, art, geography, and foreign languages. More about each of them will be found in the "Tactics" section, along with such subjects as comics, movies, and television.

With respect to foreign languages, the reader who has knowledge of French will have an advantage, as that is the most common one in puzzles. Other languages found are Spanish, Portuguese, Italian, Latin, German, and Greek. In addition to providing the opportunity to learn foreign words and expressions, puzzles give us an enjoyable way to increase our English vocabulary, too. For example, we all know who Tonto is, but who knows what tontine means? (That word was once in a puzzle.) How many other pastimes allow us to learn new words so easily? By the way, "tonto" in Spanish means "silly" or "foolish" and "tontine" refers to a specific type of investment plan.

Roman numerals are often mixed with regular letters, such as ACTI (Act One), EDWARDVIII (Edward the Eighth), PARTIII (Part Three), and LEOVII (Leo the Seventh). On several occasions, the solution to a puzzle even required Arabic numerals, which would be a surprise to anyone in solving a puzzle. More on solving clues with Roman numerals, such as converting from Arabic numbers, will be found in the "Tactics" section. One may be led astray, however, in seeing such symbols as M (1,000), L (50), and XL (40); the foregoing letters in one clue were clothing sizes, not Roman numerals. Also, the letter X can represent the word "cross," as in "crosswalk" (XWALK) or "crossing" (XING). And keep in mind that the letter "I" can represent the number "1," as in IAM (for one o'clock) or USI (the eastern north-south route number).

Dare to guess! It is essential to "think outside the box," as the management gurus say. Always look for the not-so-obvious meaning in a clue, and do not be afraid to follow far-fetched hunches. There are many examples of double meanings, such as pad for lodging; tube for TV; heat for police; lock for hair; wheels for car (and wheel for cheese); handle for name; bean, noodle, dome, attic, or noggin for head; lemon for dud; Eagle for boy scout; and pump, mule, brogue, or Oxford for shoe.

Then there are Hampshire for pig; diamond as a referent for baseball; ice and rock for diamond (the gem); ring for boxing; pot for poker; hands for cards or clock; Joe and mud for coffee; ticker for heart; dogs for feet; juice for electricity; compact for car; stir, joint, cooler, jug, can, brig, slammer, clink, calaboose, hoosegow, or pokey for prison, cellblock, jail, or pen; piece, heater, gat, rod, hardware, Colt, Magnum, or Roscoe for revolver or pistol; and bread, dough, lettuce, and many other terms (see "Currency" section) for money.

The number "12" can refer to months of the year, the Zodiac, the number of great gods in the Norse pantheon, the tribes of Israel, or an hour on the clock (such as MIDDAY or NOON); the number "9" to baseball, the Valkyries, the Muses, or the U.S. Supreme Court; the number "8" to the planets (as of August 2006), but not including the three dwarf planets; the number "7" to the days of the week, the seven dwarves, the seven seas, or the seven continents; the number "13" to the original American colonies; the number "23" to the classical Latin alphabet (see "Latin" section); the number "26" to the English alphabet; the number "24" to hours, karats, the Greek alphabet (see "Greek" section), or "The Iliad" (its number of cantos); the number "50" to the United States (for its component states); the number "64" to checkers or chess (the number of squares on the board); the number "100" to the U.S. Senate; and the number "4" to the seasons or compass directions, so be open-minded.

"Love" and "court" can refer to tennis and "suit" to card games. On one occasion, a clue beginning with "Silver" referred not to the element silver, but to the Lone Ranger's horse, and on another, a clue beginning with "Trigger" referred not to a gun, but to Roy Rogers's horse. A clue starting with "Boy" was not for just any boy, but referred to Tarzan's son, Boy, and a clue beginning with "Havana" referred to a cigar. "Penguin" in a clue once referred to Batman's nemesis. And "John" may not be a man's name at all, but a LOO or LAV. Puzzle makers sometimes help us with these plays on words and other devices by placing a "?" after the clue, but just as often do not. If a "?" does follow a clue, one can be sure the solution is going to be a bit tricky.

Themes. It is not unusual for an answer to have as many as five words. Where there is a long string of letters resulting in a phrase, look for a pattern, or theme, which could be just about anything, such as (1) a strangely inserted letter (or letters) in one word of the phrases that creates a pun, for example, the homophone W*H*INE when the clue points to WINE, or T*HY*ME when the clue points to TIME, (2) where the same word is hidden in longer words, such as TOM or MOB in AUTOMOBILE, (3) where words have the same repeating letters, such as the "M"s in MERMAID and MINUTEMAN, (4) where the entry extends beyond the grid, or (5) where theme lines read backward (right to left) and/or upward (from bottom to top). These are just a few examples; the possibilities here are nearly infinite.

On birthdays of famous people or on holidays, and even on days of national elections or the equinoxes or on April Fool's Day, and on the date of issuance of a postage stamp, look for a theme related to them. If you absolutely know that your answer is correct, but does not fit all of the squares, you should suspect that something is tricky. In that case, look for clues that refer to the theme of the puzzle (if there is one) to see if that will help.

Many puzzles that do have themes are not titled as such; rather, one discovers the theme by solving the crossword. The ones in the *New York Times* have no titles, except on Sunday. If you are working on a puzzle that has a title, read it carefully and think about it as you work on the puzzle, as it can be helpful in the solution. For puzzles that do not have titles, the theme is typically elicited in the longest phrases, which sometimes have nothing in common but their construction, as mentioned above.

Some "themes" are not really themes, but quotations, slogans, or quips that may run through the puzzle; Yogi Berra has been the source of many of these, as have Mae West and Will Rogers. For example, a puzzle in September 2005 had four sayings as its theme, each one of three words, the middle of which was the same verb. The reason that themes can be especially helpful in solving a puzzle is that they provide a circumscribed "environment," as mentioned above. But because they are typically the longest entries, that can also make them more difficult. In the author's opinion, the "thematic" factor outweighs the difficulty of their length because once you have solved one or two of the themed entries, you likely know the pattern for all the others.

If you have correctly completed one of the "themed" lines, circle the clues of the others. For example, if the first themed entry is on the third line of a puzzle, circle that clue, the one for the line in the center, and the one for the third line from the bottom, and there may be others as well (look for the long entries). In some puzzles, you will find both horizontal and vertical theme entries, but they are usually only the former, and on three, four, or five lines. But a puzzle in May 2003 had six "across" and six "down" entries that each went the length or width of the puzzle (15 squares).

Consider what may be significant in the entry you have solved; it is generally something that stands out. Some themes can stretch the imagination and provide much pleasure when they are completed. A word of advice to those who may have advanced to the Friday and Saturday puzzles in the *New York Times*: unlike those during the rest of the week, they are usually "themeless." In the *Times* on Sunday, there are usually six to eight theme entries.

Contractions such as ARENT (aren't) are used in puzzles. Contractions in clues nearly always require a contraction in their solutions. Also see "Poetry" in the "Tactics" section, as poetic contractions such as OER (over) are popular. *Abbreviations* follow a similar pattern; for example, if "mo." (month) is in a clue, then APR (April) or another abbreviated month may be in the solution. On occasion, such a clue will end with "Abbr." Other keys to abbreviations are the clue formations "___, briefly," "___, quickly," "___, in ads," "___, for short," and "Short ___." However, keep in mind that clues that are *not* abbreviations can result in answers that *are*, such as "Sandwich" (clue) and BLT (solution). On some occasions, the answer desired is only initials. The most obvious type of clue here is "___, initially."

Variants are also common, and are seldom marked as such. Examples are ADZ and ADZE; AGA and AGHA; AMEBA and AMOEBA; ENROL and ENROLL; EON and AEON; ERN and ERNE; MYNA and MYNAH (and also MINA); RANI and RANEE; SARI and SAREE; TIPI, TEPEE, and TEEPEE; and EMIR, EMEER, AMIR, and AMEER; plurals like DWARFS and DWARVES; and verb forms like DREAMED and DREAMT. A word common in puzzles is TSAR, but one will occasionally come across the variants CZAR, TZAR, and CSAR. Other types of variants are words such as INTRO, REVUE, and PREVUE. Sometimes these are clued by the construction "___, informally."

Slang is sometimes used, and if a clue is slang, its solution nearly always is slang, also. A simple example is a clue such as "Croc relative," the answer being GATOR; other such clue-answer pairs might be "Spud" for TATER, and "Snaps" and "Fotos" for PIX. However, not all clues having an answer that is slang are themselves slang. A simple example might be "True" in a clue, with LEGIT as the entry.

Keep in mind that *hyphens, spaces,* and *punctuation* are typically ignored in crossword entries, for example, SIDEA (side A of a recording), PLANB (plan B, a fallback strategy), ATEAM (A-team), BMOVIE (B movie), TBONE (T-bone), and TREX (T. Rex). Other examples are APLUS (A-plus), AONE (A-one), and ONEA (One-A); the last two are quite common in puzzles. Some more are QANDA (Q and A, or "question and answer"), BSIX (the vitamin), DIALO (Dial O for operator), TENK (10-kilometer race), and ITEN (Interstate I-10). Based on the above, it is obvious that answers need not always be words.

Also, be aware that on occasion there are blank spaces or *non-letter characters*, such as asterisks, ampersands, dots, and such instead of letters in the squares. As mentioned above, the author has solved several puzzles requiring Arabic numbers in several of the cells. On occasion, blank squares will make a symmetrical pattern; ampersands can also make a pattern, as well as stand for the word "and." These are often around the center of the puzzle and can be helpful in the solution, as the blanks or characters often have symmetrical opposites, so you can guess where they might be. Generally, though, these non-letter characters can also appear throughout the puzzle, without any pattern.

As mentioned earlier, if you absolutely know the answer, and it just does not fit the space, you might expect that something more (or less) is needed. Mark this area in the puzzle and work around the space; you may be pleasantly surprised. For example, a square may contain two or more letters. Related to such puzzles are those that are printed with an "X" in some of the squares. If you should come across one of these, be aware that the "X" may stand for a word or portion of a word.

Trade or brand names are common in puzzles, especially those with more vowels than consonants, such as AETNA, ALCOA, ALEVE, AMANA, EUREKA, NOKIA, OREO (whose 100th anniversary was celebrated in puzzles on March 6, 2012), and OXO, a kitchen-tool brand. Also, the makes and models of automobiles are frequent, especially AUDI, IMPALA, TOYOTA, and the SUVs named TAHOE and UTE.

And if a clue begins with "Seville," wouldn't you think of Spain? No, the answer was a CADILLAC in one puzzle.

"Legend" can be a clue for ACURA; "Odyssey," "Accord," "Insight," "Passport," "Pilot," and "Civic" for HONDA; "Quest," "Stanza," "Frontier," and "Pathfinder" for NISSAN; "Trooper" for ISUZU; "Sidekick" for SUZUKI; "Eclipse" for MITSUBISHI; "Alero," "Cutlass," "Aurora," and "Omega" for OLDSMOBILE or OLDS; "Century" for BUICK; "Sable," "Mystique," "Mariner," "Lynx," and "Topaz" for MERCURY; "Aura," "Vue," and "Ion" for SATURN; "Aries," "Intrepid," "Ram," "Dart," "Caravan," "Dakota," and "Omni" for DODGE; "Cherokee" and "Wrangler" for JEEP; "Quattro" for AUDI; "Mustang," "Explorer," "Escort," "Focus," and "Pinto" for FORD; "Avalon," "Corolla," "Legacy," "Solara," "Paseo," "Tacoma," "Tundra," and "Sequoia" for TOYOTA; "Blazer" for CHEVROLET; and "Equinox" for GMC. Conversely, "Chevrolet" has been a clue for COBALT, IMPALA, RODEO, MALIBU, and AVALANCHE. Be careful of Chevy, though, as it sometimes refers to Chevy Chase.

Clues beginning with "Gremlin," "Hornet," and "Javelin" have referred to AMC vehicles, and there are also Colts, Cougars, and Jaguars. "Outback" and "Forester" can be clues for SUBARU; "Sedona," "Soul," "Optima," "Spectra," and "Sportage" for KIA; and, in a reversal, "Renault" for CLIO. One puzzle referred to Corsairs and Pacers in a clue, but you have to be of a certain age to remember the ill-fated EDSEL. It was also once clued by its pushbutton "Teletouch Transmission." A popular car in puzzles is the REO, made by Olds, a passenger car that lasted until 1936, but lives on in puzzles. Such a list could go on and on; the point is to be aware of all the possibilities when you come across what could also be the name of a car.

Some trade or brand names are everyday words, such as Ivory, Dial, Caress, Zest, and Dove (bath soaps), Tide, All, Era, Cheer, Dash, Gain, and Surf (detergents), Comet (a bath and kitchen cleanser), Life and Total (cereals), Promise (a margarine), Glade (an air freshener), Raid (a pesticide), Reach (dental cleaning products), Apple (a computer), Budget, Enterprise, National, and Alamo (rental cars), Omega (a watch), Royal (a typewriter), Subway (a fast-food restaurant), Joy, Obsession, Passion, and Persuasion (scents or perfumes), Ban, Sure, and Secret (deodorants), Equal (a sugar substitute), Bazooka, Eclipse, and Orbit (chewing gums), Mars and PayDay (candy bars), Lay's and Wise (potato chips), Waterman (a pen), Crest (a toothpaste), Aim (a tooth gel), and "Camel" and

Parliament," both cigarettes, so keep this in mind when you come across them in a clue.

Because these brand names are typically the first word in a clue and thus capitalized, there is no way to be sure they are being used as brand names. And do not overlook the names of magazines in this respect, such as *Time, Life, Seventeen, Ebony,* and *People*; as the first word in a clue, they are capitalized, and can lead one astray. The same applies to colleges and universities: Auburn, Bishop, Brown, Butler, Rice, Temple, and many others can easily throw you off.

One of the most common and confusing elements in a clue is whether it (and thus the solution) is a *noun* or a *verb*. If puzzle makers would simply add "to" before an infinitive, our task would be greatly simplified, but that would take some of the fun out of it (in any case, this is never done). An example is the word "study," which can mean either the verb "to study" or the noun "study," a room in a house, such as a den (as well as other nouns); "lobby," "skirt," "table," "lodge," and "charm" are other such words. Adverbs can be a source of confusion, too, for example, the verb "(to) close," the noun "close," as in the land containing a cathedral, and the adverb "close," as in "near."

Although the noun-verb problem is common, there is also the situation of a noun or verb or *adjective*. Think of the word "stiff." It is generally an adjective, but can also mean the noun "corpse" or the verb phrase "to not tip," as in tipping a server in a restaurant. And then there are homophones, such as "altar" and "alter," "hangar" and "hanger," "dual" and "duel," and "arc" and "ark," so look closely at the clue. "Mimic" can be the verb "(to) ape" or the noun "aper."

And sometimes the tense of a verb, such as "lay," must be determined. Example: "(to) lay low" (infinitive) means "(to) HIDE," but "(he) lay low" (past tense) means HID or HIDOUT, i.e., "(he) hid" or "(he) hid out." "Put," "let," "set," "hit," "hurt," "read," and "cut" are other examples, as they can be the present, the past, or the past participle. ("Put" is the most frequent in puzzles.) The English language is replete with such vexations, and the puzzle solver must know the language well enough to differentiate between verbs and nouns in cases like "(to) come back" (verb) and "comeback" (noun). Also see "Tense" in the "Tactics" section.

Another common and confusing problem in a clue is whether a word is a *synonym, generic,* or *specific*. Crosswords would be quite simple if the clues led only to synonyms, but that is seldom the case, and would be boring, in any event. Take the clue "souvenir"; a synonym might be "memento" or "token" or "keepsake." Assume that the puzzle maker wants the answer to be CURIO. Such a word might not come to mind, as a souvenir could even be a T-shirt, which for most readers could not be construed as a curio. (Actually, TEE is quite popular in crosswords as a souvenir, and TSHIRT has also appeared.) However, *some* souvenirs are indeed curios. Therefore, a curio in this case is specific, as it is a member of the class "souvenir," for the purpose of the puzzle, that is.

But let us suppose the *clue* is "Curio," which may be defined as a "curious or unusual object." The answer might be SOUVENIR, where "curio" in this case is generic and "souvenir" is specific, opposite to the case above. There is probably no limit to what could be called a curio (or a souvenir, for that matter), so in such a case, one would need a few crossing letters to determine what the puzzle maker is seeking—a synonym, a generic, or a specific.

Also related to generics and specifics, the reader should be aware that the sites of things such as monuments, mountains, seas, and rivers present the possibility of more than one solution. For example: the Arc de Triomphe is indeed in PARIS, but the solution could be ETOILE, RIGHTBANK, FRANCE, or even EUROPE. A clue concerning a building needed its location; it was certainly in the city of New York, but the answer was EASTSIDE.

In several cases the name of a city was wanted, but the number of squares was two more than the city needed; the answer, it turned out, included the state abbreviation as well, as in SALEMOR (Salem, Oregon). In other cases both the city and entire state name led to the solution: OREMUTAH (Orem, Utah) and AMESIOWA (Ames, Iowa). This might be the place to mention that definite and indefinite articles ("the," "a," and "an") as well as prepositions (usually "in" or "at") are sometimes attached to their related nouns. Examples are THELIBERTYBELL (the Liberty Bell) and INNYC (in NYC). The point of this paragraph is that if you are sure of the entry, consider how else it might be expressed to make it longer or shorter to fit the space.

For the close of this "Strategy" section, the following practical suggestions may be helpful in addition to the above:

1. Use either a soft pencil with an eraser or an erasable pen; if you are a novice there will be many erasures. Novices will also benefit from books of easier puzzles; these are available, with the level of difficulty usually indicated on the back cover. For example, there

are Monday *New York Times* puzzles (the easiest), Tuesday puzzles (which are somewhat more difficult), etc.

2. Be sure you are relaxed, in a quiet place, and have plenty of time. None of these factors are necessary for the experienced puzzle solver, but will probably help the novice. Look at (and take time to even admire) the pattern created by the constructor, which should be symmetrical. The crosswords in newspapers are typically 15x15 squares on Monday through Saturday and 21x21 squares on Sunday. Although some puzzle solvers take satisfaction in speed, others do not. Rather, for them the pleasure is thinking about the puzzle and its clues and possible answers—over hours, or even days.

3. Look at the third line across (usually numbered in the teens or 20s) and try to ascertain the theme of the puzzle (assuming there is one) just to get an idea of what the clue is trying to elicit. Do not try to fill it in; simply look at the length, and think about what it might be.

4. If the first area that you attempt seems difficult, go to another one, and branch out from there; many people start at "1-Across" and "1-Down" just because that is where we begin reading a page. Or do the short words and/or small areas first. If you do select an area, work on the shortest direction first, whether it is across or down; start with the shortest words and work up to the longest ones. If some words in the area still remain blank, take a look at the letters you have written and see if you can guess some of the others to make a word. If this "area" solution does not work, run down all the "Across" and "Down" clues and fill in the answers that you are completely sure of. In other words, do anything to get a start, and then try to fill in some of the intersecting words. Also, since most English plurals end in "s," look for plural clues and insert an "s" in the last of the relevant squares. Sometimes this will also be the first letter of another answer, which can be a great help.

5. If you are at a standstill, come back to the puzzle later; this "refresher" has helped the author solve many a puzzle. You will be surprised at what this can accomplish. Various writers have commented on this phenomenon, most of them suggesting that the brain "thinks" about a problem when it rests. That may be, but the author believes that simply being away from a puzzle and doing something else clears the brain so that it is fresh when

it returns to a puzzle. Somehow, this break rids the brain of its prior blind spots accumulated while doing a puzzle. Whatever the reason, it works. A helpful hint: when you do return from a break, do not look at the clues; instead, look at the puzzle without regard to the clues. In many cases, you will see some obvious words or phrases that you can complete.

6. Read and also use as a reference the "Tactics" section of this book until it becomes familiar. This handbook covers the most common crossword devices, which will soon become second nature.

7. Use references if you like, even though the best puzzlers do not need any. For the novice, the only references in addition to this handbook and a comprehensive dictionary that you might need are a current almanac, which is full of information for crosswords, and a world atlas, for all those places no one has ever heard of. A copy of the complete plays of Shakespeare is also helpful, especially the list of characters (dramatis personae) on the first page of each play. And in this modern world, doesn't everyone use a search engine? There are no rules, and do not feel as if you must complete every puzzle. Do whatever gives you pleasure; after all, that is what crosswords are for.

Generally, the more white space, the more difficult the puzzle. If you are a novice, you may not want to become frustrated in solving a puzzle in which first three lines and last three lines across (and, perhaps, one or more in the center) contain no black squares at all. As a final suggestion, do lots of puzzles, and do them every day, as there is no substitute for experience. Begin with easy ones and progress to more difficult ones if you are a novice.

Be aware that, in some newspapers, such as the *New York Times*, puzzles become more difficult as the week progresses, that is, Monday's puzzles are typically the easiest, while Saturday's are the most difficult. In some other newspapers, there is no change in the level of difficulty. As for the Sunday puzzles, Will Shortz, who is the well-known puzzles editor of the *New York Times*, has said that, although longer, they average "only Thursday-plus in difficulty." ("Endpaper," the *New York Times*, April 8, 2001.)

Tactics

The "Strategy" section provides some overall advice on what to expect in crosswords and some of the customs used in creating them, such as themes. This "Tactics" section is much more detailed, and the next several pages, titled "General Clues," include some conventions you need to know. There are actually several rules in crosswords. Some of these are: (1) a singular clue will have a singular answer and a plural clue will have a plural answer, (2) the tense of a clue will be the tense of an answer, and (3) the answer will be the same part of speech as the clue. These and other topics immediately following in "General Clues," along with the "Strategy" section, provide a comprehensive guide to solving puzzles, so it is important to get this basic information first.

Following "General Clues," you will finally get to the meat of this handbook, namely, the actual and sometimes elusive words that fill the squares in a puzzle. Until you become familiar with the location of the topics in this book, use the "Contents" pages to lead you to the ones you need.

GENERAL CLUES

Plurals

If a clue is obviously plural, the end of the answer is frequently "s." If it is, you also have part of an intersecting word, as mentioned in the "Strategy" section. However, many English plurals do not end in "s," and some words are indeterminate, such as "fish," "fruit," and "deer," which can be either singular or plural. Other indications of a plural are clues such as "___ and others," "___ and family," "___ et al.," or "They ___."

Tense

Clues using verbs in the present tense require an answer in the present tense. Although English is a difficult language, forming the present tense of verbs is quite easy, as only the third person singular takes an ending ("s"). Thus a synonym for the clue "gives" might be DONATES. If a clue meets this criterion, lightly write in an "s" at the end of the entry. And if the present participle ending "ing" is in the clue, the answer may end in ING, also.

Likewise, clues using verbs in the past tense require an answer in the past tense. This simple statement belies the complexity of the solution, however. The past tense of many verbs takes "ed," but as mentioned in the "Strategy" section, many English verbs form their past tense in other ways; examples are "spoke," "swore," "fought," and "lent." In the first two examples, the past participles are "spoken" and "sworn," while the last two, "fought" and "lent," do not change to form the past participle. And then there are verbs like "swim," "swam," and "swum." So look at the clue very carefully to realize all the possibilities in the solution.

Parts of Speech

The part of speech (noun, verb, adjective, adverb, etc.) in a clue is sometimes obvious. When it is, the answer should be the same part of speech as the clue; if there is any rule in crosswords other than the ones above, this is it. You can take it for granted that the part of speech of the answer is the same part of speech as the clue. Many English adverbs end in "ly" and many adjectives end in "y," so write them in on a trial basis, perhaps looking at the intersecting word to see if it might be a help. A tricky case: clue words themselves can stand for the answer. For example, take the clue "Skating or skiing." One could rack one's brain for an answer, but the answer is GERUND, since both words are gerunds. A gerund is a verb form ending in "ing" and used as a noun, sometimes called a verbal noun.

Comparatives and Superlatives

English is rather consistent in its use of the word endings "er" and "est" to denote comparatives and superlatives. Thus, if a clue is "More ___" or "Less ___" or "Most ___" or "Least ___" (or a phrase of equivalent meaning), the answer will usually end in ER or EST. Other indicators of such endings are clues like "Comparatively ___" and "Superlatively ___." For example, assume the clue is "More simple." Think of a synonym for "simple" and turn it into the comparative; one solution is EASIER.

Prefixes, Fillers, and Suffixes

There are many clue words that elicit beginnings and endings of words, some of which are tricky. Examples of the *prefix* clues are "intro," "introduction," "introducer," "preceder," "predecessor," "start of," "onset of," and "left of" (usually followed by a noun), "start to" (usually followed by a verb), "opener," "opening," "head," "heading," "beginning of," "debut," "first," "front," "entrance," "leader," "lead-in," and variants thereof. Example: "Sphere preceder," one solution being HEMI (for "hemisphere"). The word "attachment" in a clue usually refers to a suffix, but on occasion has instead referred to a prefix.

Filler means to add letters between two other letters of the alphabet, such as "RV filler" or "R-V filler," the solution being STU, that is, those letters between "R" and "V" in the alphabet. One sees how the associated term "RV" confuses, as "recreational vehicle" comes to mind. Another popular one is "LP filler," where one naturally thinks of a long-playing record (if you are over a certain age, that is); the answer here is MNO. The clue word "filler" gives away the solution immediately. Other terms that have been used for fillers are "tie," "string," "bridge," "hookup," "center," "insert," "interrupter," and "go-between." Still another clue is "interior," as in "KO interior," where the answer is LMN.

Not fillers, but also of three (or four) consecutive letters, are the letters on telephones, which are sometimes related to the number in a clue. An example of such a clue might be something like "Letters seen next to a 6." Thus (on modern telephones), 2=ABC, 3=DEF, 4=GHI, 5=JKL, 6=MNO, 7=PQRS, 8=TUV, and 9=WXYZ (no letters are associated with 1). The three-letter combinations are sometimes referred to in puzzles as "trios."

Closely related to fillers are *links* (also called *fragments, partials, connectors, connections,* or *fill-in-the-blanks*). A link is a word or words between two given clue words, for example, "Fit-fiddle link," the answer being ASA (or "fit as a fiddle"). Because these are so easy, they would not typically be found in a difficult puzzle.

Some of the *suffix* clues are "follower," "end," "conclusion," "closing," "finish," "finale," "extension," "add-on," "additive," "ending," "ender," "end of" and "right of" (usually followed by a noun), "chaser," "wrap-up," "queue after ___," "attachment," "back," "back side," "stub," "tail," "trailer," "terminal," "tack-on," "addition," "tip," and, on one occasion, "butt." Also in the suffix category is something like the clue "String after J," the answer being KLM. And a VW follower has nothing to do with cars; it is simply XYZ.

Miscellaneous General Clues

If the clue consists of a verb and linked preposition (sometimes called a "phrasal verb"), such as "looks after," the answer will often be in the same form, in this case, "sees to." Both terms mean "to take care of." Another example is "corresponds to" (clue) and "agrees with" (answer). It may be difficult to keep miscellaneous clues like this in mind, but with practice it will become easier.

If the clue is "First name in ___," the *first* name of the person who satisfies the clue is wanted in the answer. A simple example might be "First name in mass production of automobiles," the answer being HENRY (Henry Ford). This is done with last names as well. Also, if the clue is the name of someone associated with the name in the answer (such as a partner, spouse, or other relation), then the answer will match whichever name (first or last) is in the clue. An example might be the clue "Garland's daughter," the answer being MINNELLI. And likewise its alternate: the clue "Judy's daughter" results in LIZA. On a few occasions, both first and last names are in an entry; these are usually short names, such as MELOTT (Mel Ott), TYCOBB (Ty Cobb), or UTHANT (U Thant).

If a clue contains a foreign word or expression, then the answer usually will, also. An example might be the clue "faux pas," with the answer being GAFFE, both meaning "blunder," among other definitions.

Puzzle makers make us laugh when they use clues like "Capital of Campania" or "Leader of Liberia." Instead of scratching your head, simply see if the first letter of the country, in this case the letter "C" (which becomes CEE in the entry) or the letter "L" (which becomes ELL in the entry) fits the space. A favorite is the clue, "Capital of Zambia," with the entry ZEE. Going back to "Campania" above, a puzzle in 2011 might have had you wondering, as there were five squares for the entry. It turned out to be HARDC (hard C). (And HARDG occurred in a puzzle early in 2013, so do not think this a rarity.) The "Strategy" section includes the reminder to look at all possibilities when you know the answer.

Quite popular are "partner," "mate," "counterpart," or "companion" clues, which are as easy as the "link" clues, mentioned above. Examples are "to and fro," "on and off," "flora and fauna," "beck and call," "kith and kin," "yin and yang," "alas and alack," "life and limb," "mortise and tenon," and "peanut butter and jelly." The clue will be something like "Flora partner" in the case of FAUNA, for example.

If the clue points to *someone* who does something, the answer may very well end in ER; the simplest, most general example might be DOER. And as mentioned above, another indication to add ER at the end of a word is when the comparative is required, such as in the clues "Less ___" or "More ___."

At the opposite end of the word, the beginning, the reverse of ER may be said to occur, namely, RE. The clue for RE at the beginning of a word is usually "Changes ___," "Repairs ___," "Regains ___," "Fixes ___," "Checks ___," "Switches ___," "Alters ___," "Freshens ___," "Works on ___," "Double-checks ___," "Turns into ___," "Brings back ___" or "Going back to ___." An example might be "Fixes brakes," with the answer being RELINES. Another could be "Changes the clock," with the answer being RESETS.

Some RE clues have the *second* and following words of the clue as the trigger for this construction; these are "___ again," "___ another," "___ over again," "___ over," "___ anew," "___ as it was," "___ for more," and "___, not for the first time." If the clue is something like this, you can feel confident about writing RE as the first part of the entry, even though the remainder might stay unknown for a while.

Also related to the beginning of a word, of all its letters, the first is the most useful in solving clues. If you are having trouble with the meaning of a clue, try to solve the crossing entry that includes the first letter of the problem entry.

Foreign Languages

As mentioned in the "Strategy" section, having a knowledge of one or more foreign languages is helpful in solving puzzles. The most common of these, far and above the others, is French. Illustrative of this point was a puzzle in August 2000 with two French words, three Spanish words, two Italian words, two Latin words, and two Roman names. And in March 2012 a puzzle had three French words, three Spanish words, two Portuguese words, and one each from Italian and German. But the puzzle that takes the cake for foreign words appeared in September 2004, in which there were 13 foreign words from four languages. In all the languages, however, the words tend to be simple and/or short nouns. Many foreign words and expressions are already known to English speakers because they have entered our language, such as "angst," "ennui," "mesa," "virtuoso," and "alma mater." If you do not think there are many foreign words in puzzles, just take a look at the list that begins a few pages from this one.

If the clue contains a foreign word, then a foreign word is usually needed for the answer. Example: If the German spelling, "Rhein," instead of the English "Rhine" or the French "Rhin," is in a clue, the answer will also be in German. Typically, the answer would be the German spelling of a city on that river, such as KOLN (Köln, or Cologne to us). If the clue does not contain a foreign word, but a foreign word is to be the answer, then the clue usually contains an abbreviation of the language needed, such as "Fr.," "Sp.," "Italian-style," etc. However, this is not always the case, as one puzzle contained the answer TETEATETE (tête-à-tête); the clue made no mention of its being a French expression, although the term can be said to have entered our language.

On occasion, a clue will be simply "French___" or "Spanish___"; in this case, it is quite obvious that the answer is simply the French or Spanish correlate of the clue word. Example: "French wine," the answer being VIN. (This way, you do not have to search your brain for all the possible French wines.) An example of a more interesting construction eliciting a foreign word is "It's pretty in France," where JOLI or JOLIE is the answer. (It could be good, bad, or ugly, too.)

Another common clue for a foreign word or expression is "___, overseas," "over there," or "___, abroad." The only problem with this form of a "foreign" clue is that it gives no indication of which language is needed, but it is usually French. Sometimes you will see "___, there," where the blank stands for the name of a city in English; in this case, the desired answer is the name of the city in its own language. A simple example: "Florence, there" as the geographical clue and FIRENZE as the answer. Somewhat related to this is a clue in a foreign language needing an answer in the same language. Example: "Of Venezia locale," the answer being ITALIA.

Some of the helpful hints listed in the French section immediately below, such as the use of alliteration in clues, also apply to other languages. Occasionally a word will be encountered from a language other than one listed below; examples are "da" (yes), "nyet" (no), and "mir" (peace) in Russian and "hai" (yes) and "iie" (no) in Japanese. Although these instances are uncommon, "DOMO arigato," or "Thank you very much," has been in puzzles, where the clue was "___ arigato." KARIOKE, IKEBANA, and SAYONARA have also been entries. By the way, the Japanese bourse makes its way into puzzles: TSO (for Tokyo Stock Exchange). The Chinese word for water has also been needed (SHUI), as has the Swahili expression for "Thank you" (ASANTE) and the Mongolian word for ocean (DALAI). Not unusual in puzzles is IBN, Arabic for "son of"; and the related Hebrew BNAI (b'nai) has also appeared; it means the same thing.

French

Clues containing French proper names such as Antoine, Camille, Claude, Colette, Émile, Fifi, François and Françoise, Giselle, Guillaume, Héloise, Henri, Jacques, Jules, Louis, Marc, Marie, Maurice, Mimi, Pierre, René and Renée, Simone, and Yves and Yvette are indications that a French word is the solution. Example: "Street, to Pierre," the solution being RUE. Titles and honorifics are also used in this way, for example, "Monsieur's hat," the solution being CHAPEAU. Others are "Mme" (Madame), "Mlle" (Mademoiselle), and "St" and "Ste" (saints masculine and feminine). By the way, the use of "Mademoiselle" is no longer used in France (as of early 2012), much as "Miss," "Mrs.," and "Fraülein" have lost favor.

Notice that the French do not use periods after abbreviations that end with the last letter of the word they represent; American writers do, while the English generally do not. The French do use a period, however, if the abbreviation does not end in the last letter, for example, "M." (with a period) for "Monsieur." This parenthetical note is of little use in doing crossword puzzles, but the author could not write "M.," "Mme," and "Mlle" here (and "St Lô" and "St Tropez" below) without someone's raising an eyebrow and assuming there was a typo. A careful constructor will follow these conventions.

Cities and regions of France and other French-speaking entities like Québec are also used to elicit French answers. Common examples are

"Seine sight," the solution usually being ILE (island); "Nice night," the solution being NUIT; and "Dijon day," the solution being JOUR. Notice the *alliteration* of the two clue words in the examples; this is also common for clues in other languages. Other French-speaking cities used in this way are Arles, Avignon, Bordeaux, Brest, Cannes, Chartres, Isère, Lyon, Montréal, Nancy, Nantes, Paris, Toulouse, Tours, Verdun, and Versailles. Be aware that Nice and Tours, being capitalized as the first word in a clue, can lead you astray if you assume they are English words, which they almost never are in puzzles. One simple example of the former is the clue "Nice man," the answer being HOMME.

Regions of France frequently used in clues are Normandy and the Riviera. Sites from the former (nearly always answers) are sometimes the code-named wartime landing beaches of GOLD, JUNO, OMAHA, SWORD, and UTAH; the neighboring towns of STLO (St Lô) and CAEN are also used as answers, and several puzzles required one to know that St Lô is the capital of the Manche Département of France. For the Riviera, Nice as a clue is by far the favorite, for obvious reasons, but Cannes and St Tropez are used, too.

Some other French words found as answers in puzzles are listed below, classified first by the number of letters, and then alphabetically. Where adjectives are different due to gender agreement, both are given (there are only two genders in French), for example, BLANC in the five-letter column and BLANCHE in the seven-letter column. *Note:* In French and in all the languages below, diacritical marks are ignored for words in capital letters. In some cases, they completely change the meaning of words, but their English translations below are the most common in puzzles.

Where two words below constitute an expression, like "bon mot" and "déjà vu," they are classified below by their total number of letters, e.g., BON MOT and DEJA VU. Especially for the longer ones, part of the expression is often a clue, as in "___fixe," where the other part, or answer, is IDEE (idée). Where an expression contains punctuation, such as a hyphen or apostrophe, the actual expression follows in parentheses. An example of this below is BIEN AIME (bien-aimé).

ALA (à la) (in the style of, with, like, according to)
AME (soul)
AMI (male friend)
ANE (ass, donkey)
BAL (dance)
BEL (beautiful, fair, fine)
BIS (twice, again; in a street address, half)
BLE (wheat)
BON (good)
CAS (case)
CES (these and those)
CIE (abbreviation of "Compagnie)
COU (neck)
CRI (shout)
CRU (vineyard, as well as several other meanings)
DUC (duke, earl, nobleman)
EAU (water)
ELU (chosen)
FEU (fire)
FIL (thread)
FIN (end)
FOI (faith)
GAI (cheerful, merry)
GRE (pleasure, liking, taste)
ICI (here)
ILE (island)
JEU (game, sport)
LAC (lake)
LIS and LYS (lily)
LOI (law, statute)
MAI (May)
MAL (bad)
MER (sea)
MOI (me)
MOT (word)
MOU (soft)
NEE (born)
NEZ (nose)
NOE (Noah)

NOM (name)
NON (no)
OIE (goose)
OUI (yes)
PAS (no, not, a ballet step)
PEU (a little or a few)
ROI (king)
RUE (street)
SEC (dry)
SEL (salt)
THE (tea)
TON (tone, also the smart set)
VIE (life)
VIN (wine)
VUE (sight)

A BAS ___ (down with ___)
ABBE (priest, friar, cleric)
ALLO ("Hello")
ALPE (alp)
A LUI (his, its)
AMIE (female friend)
A MOI (mine)
ANGE (angel)
ANIS (anise)
ANSE (handle)
AOUT (August)
ARME (weapon)
A TOI (yours)
AVEC (with)
BAIN (bath)
BANC (bank)
BEAU (beautiful, fair, fine)
BOIS (wood)
CHER (dear)
CIEL (sky)
CITE (city)
COUP (blow, strike)
CROC (hook, tooth, fang)

CUIR (leather, skin, hide)
DEJA (already)
EGAL (same, equal, alike)
ELAN (verve, dash, vivacity, zest for life)
ELLE (she, her)
EPEE (fencing sword)
ETAT (state)
ETES (are)
FILS (son)
FINI (done, finished, ended)
FOIE (liver)
GOUT (taste)
GRAS (fat)
GROS (big, bulky, stout)
HAUT (high)
HIER (yesterday)
IDEE (concept, notion, idea)
JETE (ballet leap)
JEUX (games, sports)
JOIE (joy)
JOLI (pretty)
JOUR (day)
KEPI (military cap or hat)
LAIT (milk)
LIEU (place, stead)
LOUP (wolf)
MAIS (but)
MARI (husband)
MERE (mother)
MIDI (noon)
MONT (mountain)
NAIF (artless, ingenuous, guileless, naive)
NOIR (black)
NUIT (night)
OEIL (eye)
OEUF (egg)
ONDE (wave, billow)
OURS (she-bear)
PAIX (peace)

PARC (park)
PATE (paste)
PAYS (country, region)
PERE (father)
PLIE (in ballet, a knee-bend)
PNEU (tire, as on a wheel)
PONT (bridge)
PRIX (price, prize)
QUOI (what)
RECU (received)
REVE (dream)
RIEN (nothing)
ROTI (roast)
SANS (without, lacking)
SEUL (alone)
SOIR (evening)
TETE (head)
TOUS and TOUT (all)
TRES (very)
TROU (gap, hole)
UNIS (united)
URNE (urn, ballot box)
VERT (green)

ADIEU (good-bye, farewell)
ALORS (then, as well as an interjection)
ANNEE (year)
APRES (after)
AROME (aroma, flavoring)
ARRET (stop)
AU JUS (with juice, in juice)
AUSSI (also)
AUTRE (other)
AVANT (before)
AVION (airplane)
AVRIL (April)
BARRE (ballet railing)
BIJOU (jewel)
BLANC (white)

BOMBE (frozen dessert)
BONNE (maidservant (n.) and good (adj.))
BONTE (kindness)
CARRE (square)
CARTE (menu, map, card)
CHERE (dear)
COMME (as, like)
COMTE (count or earl, county or earldom)
CONTE (tale)
CREME (cream)
CROIX (cross)
DANSE (dance)
DENIS or DENYS (patron saint of France; also the first bishop of Paris)
ECALE (shell, pod)
ECLAT (brilliance)
ECOLE (school)
EGALE (same, equal)
ELEVE (pupil, student)
ENCRE (ink)
ENNUI (boredom)
ENTRE (between)
ESSAI (essay)
ETAGE (story, as in the level of a building)
ETAPE (military halting place, warehouse, a day's march)
FEMME (woman, wife)
FILLE (girl, daughter)
FLEUR (flower)
FRANC (former unit of currency)
FRERE (brother)
GARDE (keeper, watchman, care, custody, guardianship)
GELEE (frost, jelly)
GENOU (knee)
GESTE (gesture, motion, movement)
GLACE (ice)
HAUTE (high)
HEURE (hour, time)
HOMME (man)
JEUDI (Thursday)

JOLIE (pretty)
LAPIN (rabbit)
LECON (lesson)
LIVRE (book, also pound)
LOUPE (magnifying glass, jeweler's tool)
LUNDI (Monday)
LYCEE (high school)
MARDI (Tuesday)
MATIN (morning)
MERCI ("Thank you")
MINET (pussycat)
MOINE (monk, friar)
MONDE (world, society)
MUSEE (museum)
NOIRE (black)
NOTRE (our, ours)
ONCLE (uncle)
OUTRE (bizarre, outlandish)
PACTE (agreement, covenant)
PASSE (past, gone by)
PERDU (lost, hidden)
PESTE (plague)
PETIT (small)
PLUME (pen, feather)
POILU (hairy, shaggy; French soldier in World War I)
PORTE (door, gate)
REINE (queen)
RENTE (income)
REPAS (meal)
ROMAN (novel)
ROUGE (red)
SALUT (safety, salvation; also a greeting)
SANTE (health)
SECHE (dry)
SENAT (senate)
SOEUR (sister)
TABAC (tobacco, store selling tobacco)
TANTE (aunt)
TASSE (cup)

TOLLE (hue and cry)
VALSE (waltz)
VERTE (green)
VOILA (there is, there are, and loosely, "There!")

AGENCE (agency, office, bureau)
A LA FIN (at last, finally)
ANANAS (pineapple)
APERCU (glimpse, also outline or summary)
BON MOT (a witticism)
BON TON (taste, good form)
BROSSE (brush)
CLOCHE (woman's hat)
DEJA VU (already seen)
DE MODE (in fashion)
DE RIEN ("It's nothing," "Forget it")
DE TROP (too much, excessive)
ECHECS (the game of chess)
EGLISE (church)
ENCORE (again)
ENFANT (child)
ENNEMI (enemy)
ESPRIT (spirit)
ETOILE (star)
FLACON (flask, bottle)
GARCON (boy)
GATEAU (cake)
GROSSE (big, bulky, stout)
MAITRE (master)
MENAGE (house-keeping)
MILIEU (environment)
OEUVRE (work)
PALAIS (palace)
PETITE (small)
POIVRE (pepper)
POUPEE (doll)
SAISON (season)
SAMEDI (Saturday)
SOIGNE (well-groomed, carefully finished)

TOUTES (all)
TRISTE (sad)
VIANDE (meat)

AUBERGE (inn)
BIEN SUR (of course)
BLANCHE (white)
BONJOUR ("Hello")
BONSOIR ("Good evening")
BRIOCHE (sweet roll)
CAP A PIE (from head to foot)
CHANSON (song)
CHAPEAU (hat)
CHEMISE (short jacket)
CHEVEUX (hair)
DERNIER (last)
ETAGERE (what-not rack or shelf)
FAUX PAS (false step, blunder)
GAVOTTE (a baroque French dance)
MALAISE (uneasiness, discomfort)
MINETTE (pussycat)
NOUVEAU (new)
PARFAIT (perfect)
PAS ALLE (simple dance step)
PENSEUR (thinker)
PLAISIR (pleasure)
POISSON (fish)
POULARD (hen)
QUI VIVE (on the alert)
SEMAINE (week)
SOUPCON (small quantity, dash)

AU GRATIN (with cheese)
BALLONEE (in ballet, a bouncing step or jump
    on one foot as the other leg is extended)
BIEN AIME (bien-aimé) (beloved)
COQ AU VIN (chicken cooked in wine)
CUL DE SAC (blind alley)
DERRIERE (back)

ENTRACTE (entr'acte) (intermission)
IDEE FIXE (obsession)
MAL DE MER (seasickness)
NOUVELLE (new)
PAR AVION (by plane, by air)
PARCE QUE (because)
PEUT ETRE (peut-être) (perhaps)
PINCE NEZ (eyeglasses)
PIS ALLEZ (last resort)
PRIE DIEU (kneeling bench for prayer)
PRIX FIXE (fixed price)
TRES BIEN (very well)
TRES CHIC (very smart, stylish)

APRES MIDI (afternoon)
AU COURANT (up-to-date, "with it")
BEAU GESTE (handsome gesture, noble act)
BEAU IDEAL (epitome)
BETE NOIRE (someone disliked or to be avoided)
BIEN AIMEE (bien-aimée) (beloved)
BON VIVANT (jolly good fellow)
CEST LA VIE (c'est la vie) (such is life)
COUP DE FEU (gunshot)
ENTRE NOUS (just between us)
ETATS UNIS (United States)
GARDE ROBE (garde-robe) (closet, wardrobe)
HAUT MONDE (fashionable people)
PAS DE DEUX (in ballet, a duet)
RECHERCHE (choice, select, in demand)
RIS DE VEAU (sweetbreads)
ROBE DE BAL (evening dress)
SACRE BLEU (an interjection, such as "Heavens!")
SANS SOUCI (carefree)
SOI DISANT (soi-disant) (so-called, self-styled)

AVANT GARDE (ahead of the times)
DERNIER CRI (latest style)
FER DE LANCE (spear-head, tropical viper)
FLEUR DE LIS (lily or iris)

JEU DESPRIT (jeu d'esprit) (witty remark)
NOM DE PLUME (pen name, pseudonym)
PEU DE CHOSE (a trifle)
PIED A TERRE (a small, occasional lodging)
TABLE DHOTE (table d'hôte) (the meal available)
TRICOULEUR (the French flag)

AMOUR PROPRE (self-esteem)
A VOTRE SANTE ("To your health!")
CHEMIN DE FER (railway)
FRUITS DE MER (seafood)
HORS DOEUVRE (hors d'oeuvre) (appetizer)
IDIOT SAVANT (someone having extraordinary skills in some areas, but who is deficient in more common ones)
LESE MAJESTE (an affront)
MISE EN SCENE (design aspects of a production)
NE PLUS ULTRA (acme)
PRET A PORTER (ready to wear)
RAISON DETRE (raison d'être) (reason for being)
ROTI DE BOEUF (roast beef)
SAVOIR FAIRE (skill, tact)
TOUR DE FORCE (impressive achievement)
TOUT LE MONDE (everyone)
TROMPE LOEIL (trompe l'oeil) (illusion)

AVANT DERNIER (penultimate)
CAUSE CELEBRE (famous happening)
FAIT ACCOMPLI (accomplished fact)
HORS DE COMBAT (out of action)
HOTEL DE VILLE (city hall)
JE NE SAIS QUOI (I do not know)
LES ETATS UNIS (les États-Unis) (the United States)
LETAT CEST MOI ("L'état c'est moi," from Louis XIV)
NOUVEAU RICHE (upstart)
POMMES FRITES (French fries)
RONDE DE JAMBE (ballet position)

MERCI BEAUCOUP ("Thank you very much")
POUR AINSI DIRE (so to speak)
PATE DE FOIS GRAS (goose-liver pâté)

It is also helpful to know the verb "to be," which is ETRE, and the verb "to have," which is AVOIR. Sometimes these are clued as "French 101 verb." The latter's present participle, AYANT (having), has also appeared. An expression that is helpful to know is R.S.V.P. (Répondez s'il vous plaît); typically, the answer is SIL. *All the words listed above were found in puzzles; none were added by the author, as is also the case for the languages below.* If you are unfamiliar with French, a basic French dictionary might be helpful.

Some other subjects are points of the compass (NORD, EST, SUD, and OUEST), the seasons (PRINTEMPS, ETE, AUTOMNE, and HIVER), the definite articles LE, LA, and LES, the indefinite articles UN, UNE, and DES, and the pronouns IL(S) and ELLE(S) ("he," "she," "it," and "they"). French possessives have also been encountered; some of these are MON, MA, and MES (my), TON, TA, and TES (your), SON, SA, and SES (his, her, or its), and LEUR and LEURS (their). The demonstrative pronouns also appear: CE, CET, CETTE, and CES. The reason that the two-letter words are listed above is that they could be useful for a French phrase, such as the overworked "La plume de ma tante"; they would never stand alone in a puzzle. For the French cardinal numbers, see the end of the "Latin" section below.

Spanish (and Portuguese)

As in the other languages, clues eliciting a Spanish answer often include Spanish first names, such as Alfonso, Angel, Carlos, Carmen, Cesar, Charo, Eduardo, Hernando, Jose, Juan, Juanita, Luis, Manuel, Mateo, Muñoz, Pablo, Pedro, Ricardo, or Tomás. Sometimes a Spanish explorer's name is used, such as Coronado, Cortés, or Pizzarro.

Another indication of a Spanish answer is the use of a Spanish city, as in "___, in Barcelona" (or Granada or Leon or Madrid or Segovia or Seville or Toledo, etc.), or a Mexican city or state, as in "___, in Acapulco" (or Chiapas or Chihuahua or Juárez or Nogales or Oaxaca or Taxco or Tijuana, etc.). Still another is an expression such as "south of the border" or "down south" following a word or phrase. Be aware that puzzle makers make no distinction between Spanish as spoken in Madrid, say, and the language used in Argentina or Mexico or the American West. At the end of this Spanish section, you will find some words from the western hemisphere that are quite common in crosswords.

Spanish words in puzzles are usually short, such as most of those in the list below. Keep in mind that the definitions given here are brief and that there may also be other meanings; and as in French, a single diacritical mark can completely change the meaning of the word. The definitions below reflect what is found in puzzles, not necessarily all the synonyms you will find in a Spanish dictionary.

ANO (year)
ASI (so)
DIA (day)
DON (gift, talent, also a masculine Spanish title)
ESA and ESO (that)
HOY (today)
MAR (sea)
MAS (more, most)
MES (month)
MUY (very)
OJO (eye)
OLA (wave, surge)
OLE (a cheer)
ORO (gold)
OSA (she-bear) and OSO (bear)
PAN (bread)
PAZ (peace)
QUE (what, which, that, who)
REY (king)
RIA (estuary)
RIO (river)
SAN (male saint)
SER (being, essence, life (n.); to be (v.))
SOL (sun)
TIA and TIO (aunt and uncle)
UNA and UNO (one, someone)

AGUA (water)
AIRE (air)
ALMA (soul, spirit)
ALTA and ALTO (high, upper, top)
AMOR (love)
ARTE (art, knack, skill)
ASNO (donkey)

BAJA and BAJO (low, under, short, humble)
BEBE (baby)
BESO (kiss)
BOCA (mouth, speech, taste, flavor)
BOLA (ball, marble, bowling)
BUEN (good)
CAPA (cape, cloak)
CASA (house)
CENA (supper)
CINE (movies)
COMO (how)
COSA (thing)
DAMA (lady)
DIOS (God)
ELLA (she, her, it)
ENTE (fellow)
ESTA and ESTO (this, this one)
FLOR (flower, blossom)
FRIA and FRIO (cold)
GATO (cat)
HIJA and HIJO (daughter and son)
HOLA (hello)
HORA (hour, time)
ISLA (island)
JEFE (boss, chief)
LOBO (wolf)
LOCO (crazy)
LOMA (small hill)
MANO (hand)
MAYO (May)
MESA (table)
NADA (nothing)
NENA, NENE, and NENO (baby, dear)
NINA and NINO (child)
OTRA and OTRO (other)
PASO (step, pace, gait)
PERO (but)
PESO (weight, also unit of currency in some countries)
PURA and PURO (pure, sheer)

RICA and RICO (rich, dear)
SALA (living room)
SANA and SANO (healthy, sound)
SERA (will be)
TAPA (lid, cover, top, cap)
TORO (bull)
TREN (train)
UNAS and UNOS (some)

ABRIL (April)
ADIOS ("Good-bye")
AHORA (now)
ALAMO (poplar)
AMIGA and AMIGO (friend)
ANCHA (broad, large)
ANGEL (angel)
AVISO (advice, counsel, warning)
BANCO (bench, bank)
BESAR (to kiss)
BUENA and BUENO (good)
CALMA (calm, serene, peaceful)
CHICA and CHICO (little girl and little boy)
CIELO (sky)
COSTA (coast, shore, price)
ELENA (Helen)
ENERO (January)
ESTAS and ESTOS (these)
HASTA (until)
JULIO (July)
JUNIO (June)
JUNTA (meeting, council)
LECHE (milk)
LIBRO (book)
LLANA and LLANO (plain, simple, clear)
MADRE (mother)
MANTA (blanket, heavy shawl)
MUCHA and MUCHO (much, a lot of)
MUNDO (world)
NOCHE (night)

NO MAS (no more)
OSADA and OSADO (bold, daring)
OTONO (autumn)
OTROS (others)
PADRE (father)
PASEO (leisurely stroll, walk, promenade)
PLATA (silver)
PLAYA (beach, shore)
POBRE (poor)
POLLO (chicken)
QUESO (cheese)
RATON (mouse)
REATA (rope for animals, such as a lasso)
REINA (queen)
RENTA (income)
RIOJA (a wine region in northern Spain)
SALUD (health)
SANTA and SANTO (saint (n.) and holy (adj.))
SENOR (Mr.)
TAPAS (appetizer)
TARDE (late, also afternoon or early evening)
TEDIO (ennui, boredom)
USTED (you)
VIEJA and VIEJO (old woman and old man)

ARRIBA (up, above)
ARROYO (stream, brook, gutter, street)
BODEGA (grocery store)
CUANDO (when)
DE NADA ("It's nothing," "You're welcome")
DIABLO (devil)
DINERO (money)
ESPOSA and ESPOSO (spouse)
ESTADO (state)
FAJITA (little sash, grilled strips of meat)
FIESTA (celebration, holiday)
FRIJOL (bean)
FUTBOL (soccer)
GUERRA (war)

HOMBRE (man)
HUEVOS (eggs)
MANANA (tomorrow)
MANCHA (spot, stain)
NOMBRE (name)
PICARO (rogue, schemer)
POR QUE (why)
PUEBLO (people, town)
PUENTE (bridge)
PUERTA (door)
PUERTO (harbor, port)
SABADO (Saturday)
SEMANA (week)
SENORA (often abbreviated to SRA) (Mrs.)
SERAPE (shawl)
SIESTA (nap)
TAL VEZ (maybe, perhaps)
TESORO (treasure, treasury, valuables)
TONADA (song)
TORERO (bullfighter)

A LA MANO (at hand, nearby)
ALAMEDA (shaded walk)
CARRERA (race, run)
CHORIZO (sausage of pork and paprika)
CORRIDA (bullfight)
DOMINGO (Sunday)
FAMILIA (family)
GRACIAS ("Thank you")
HIDALGA and HIDALGO (noblewoman and nobleman)
OTRA VEY (again)
PAISANO (fellow countryman)
QUE PASA ("How's it going?")
TURISMO (touring)
VAQUERO (cowboy)

ANO NEUVO (new year)
CALIENTE (hot)
ENCIERRO (confinement, prison)

MUCHACHA and MUCHACHO (girl and boy)
POR FAVOR (please)
SENORITA (often abbreviated to SRTA) (Miss)

CABALLERO (gentleman, knight, horseman)
COMO ESTAS ("How are you?")
COMPANERA and COMPANERO (companion)
MAS O MENOS (O.K., so-so)
ORO Y PLATA (gold and silver, Montana's motto)

CALENDARIO (calendar)
HASTA LUEGO ("So long," "Good-bye")
POR EJEMPLO (for example)

FELIZ NAVIDAD (Merry Christmas)

ARROZ CON POLLO (rice with chicken)
COMO ESTA USTED ("How are you?")

With respect to "toro," be careful if it is capitalized in a clue, as it sometimes refers to a brand of lawn machine. The most frequent Spanish answer by far is the shout or cheer OLE, the clue often relating to fiesta, corrida (bullfight), Pamplona, a bull, or bullring.

The definite articles are EL, LA, LOS, and LAS and the indefinite articles are UN, UNA, UNOS, and UNAS. As in French, the points of the compass sometimes appear: NORTE, ESTE, SUR, and OESTE. On occasion, the verbs ESTAR (to be), SER (another verb "to be") and TENER (to have) are needed, as they are in the other languages, but the most frequent verb in Spanish to be found in puzzles is HABLAR (to speak). For the Spanish cardinal numbers, see the end of the "Latin" section below.

A few words from the American West and Central and South America are as follows: CHALUPA (a small canoe; also a fried tortilla dish); CHARRO (a Mexican cowboy), GAUCHO (good horseman, cowboy of the South American pampas, especially Argentina), and LLANO (large, grassy South American plain). (The last, llano, is in the preceding list in its adjectival meaning.)

Note: If a *Portuguese* explorer or territory or city or a Brazilian city is in a clue, a Portuguese word is the answer. Except for explorers, such as

Vasco da Gama or Vasco Nuñez de Balboa, the only words the author has encountered in the answer are (1) SAO (saint), which is often in the name of places, such as São Luis, São Paulo, and São Tomé, (2) the titles DON (Mr.) and DONA (Mrs.), (3) ALO (hello), (4) ARTES (arts), (5) REI (king), and (6) SENHORA (lady).

Italian

Italian, the primary language of music notation (see "Classical Music" below), is not as strongly represented in crosswords as French and Spanish, but, like them, clues containing Italian names and places indicate that an Italian answer is needed. Examples of names are Antonia and Antonio, Carla and Carlo, Enrico, Enzo, Giovanna and Giovanni, Guido, Luigi, Maria and Mario, and Romeo; and typical places are Capri, Florence, Milan, Pisa, Ravenna, Rome, Salerno, Sorrento, Tivoli, Turin, and Venice.

Unlike the case in Spanish for titles, the author has seldom come across their Italian correlatives, namely, "signore," "signora," and "signorina." The informal CIAO ("Hello" or "Good-bye") is one of the most popular Italian words in puzzles due, no doubt, to its having three vowels out of four letters. And ARRIVEDERCI ("Good-bye") has five vowels. The former currency of Italy often appears: LIRA (sing.) and LIRE (pl.).

The only Italian words the author has encountered (except those related to music) are as follows:

BLU (blue)
CHE (that (conj.) and what, which, and who (pron.))
DIO (god)
MIA and MIO (mine, my)
NEI (in the)
NOE (Noah)
NOI (we, us)
ORA (hour, now)
PIU (more)

A DUE (together)
ARPA (harp)

ARTE (art)
BENE (good, well)
BRIO (gusto, zest)
CAPO (head)
CARA and CARO (dear)
COSI (thus, so)
DUCE (captain, leader, chief)
ESSA and ESSO (she, he, it)
GITA (excursion, trip, outing)
IERI (yesterday)
LAGO (lake)
MENA and MENO (less)
OSSO (bone)
OSTE (innkeeper)
POCO (little or a little)
SERA (evening)
UOMO (man)
VOCE (voice)

AMARE (to love)
AMICA and AMICO (friend)
AMORE (love)
BASTA ("Enough!")
BECCO (beak)
BOCCE (bowling)
CITTA (city)
COTTA and COTTO (cooked)
DENTE (tooth)
DOLCE (sweet, soft)
FIORE (flower)
GATTO (cat)
GENTE (people, folk)
ISOLA (island)
LENTE (lens)
LENTI (eyeglasses)
LIBRO (book)
MOLTO (much, very)
MONDO (world)

NOTTE (night)
ONERE (burden)
OPERA (work, labor)
PAESE (country, town)
PASTO (meal)
POETA (poet)
PONTE (bridge)
RESTA (pause)
SANTA and SANTO (saint (n.) and holy (adj.))
SCOPA (broom)
SCUSA (excuse, apology)
SOAVE (soft, sweet)
SOGNO (dream)
SOTTO (under, below)
SPOSA and SPOSO (spouse)
TORRE (tower)

AVANTI (ahead)
ATTORE (actor)
GIORNO (day)
GIUOCO (game)
MINUTO (minute, small)
NIENTE (nothing)
OMERTA (code of enforced silence in criminal organizations)
STRADA (street, road)
TAVOLA (table)

AL DENTE (cooked firm but not hard)
FONTANA (fountain)
PISTOLA (pistol)

BUONA SERA ("Good evening")
SOTTO VOCE (in a quiet voice)

The verb "to be" is ESSERE and the verb "to have" is AVERE. For the Italian cardinal numbers, see the end of the "Latin" section immediately below, and for many more Italian words, see the "Classical Music" section.

Latin

It is difficult to think of Latin apart from those who used it, especially in the last years of the republic and through the years of the emperors. The name of Rome's greatest orator, CICERO, a contemporary of Julius Caesar, is sometimes found in crosswords, due not only to the works attributed to him, such as "De Amicitia," but also perhaps because of the three vowels out of six letters in his name. Later, during the Augustan period, Virgil and Horace (the latter known for his odes, especially "Ars Poetica"), who were near contemporaries, were so popular that they are referred to in puzzles and elsewhere as the poets laureate of Rome. Virgil (sometimes "Vergil," from the Latin "Vergilius") is especially known for his epic AENEID, with its wandering hero, AENEAS. The "Aeneid" was once clued as being "Tale in dactylic hexameter." This clue is an example of a case where a constructor wanted to make a puzzle difficult; there are much easier ways to arrive at "Aeneid."

Following Virgil and Horace were Livy and Ovid (the latter exiled, which is sometimes a clue), also near contemporaries (they died within a year of each other). Ovid is also sometimes clued by his "Metamorphoses," "Ars Amatoria," or "Tristia." On one occasion, his full name was needed: Publius Ovidius NASO. After Livy and Ovid, the greatest writers (in chronological order) were Seneca (a Stoic and Nero's tutor, which are both clues), Quintilian, Martial, Pliny (naturalist is a clue), Tacitus, and Juvenal. To Seneca is attributed the saying, "What fools these mortals be!" The works of all these men have been immortalized down through the ages by many writers and are perhaps best known to us through Dante, Shakespeare, Bacon, and the English poets, especially Milton.

The Latin words and expressions found in puzzles are rather basic, limited, and predictable. The clues typically elicit them by using "___, in Rome," "Centurion's ___," or "___, at the Forum," or one of the names mentioned above or another Roman, such as "___, to Claudius" or to his successor, Nero (Claudius's adopted son as well as the grandson of Germanicus), or to Cato the Elder, called the Censor as well as the Wise and the Ancient. A statesman who became a general, he is known as the author of the first Latin history of the Italian towns, especially Rome.

The most popular Roman in puzzles is NERO, and it helps to know the following: Nero's wife was OCTAVIA; Julius Caesar's first wife was CORNELIA, his second was POMPEIA, and his third was CALPURNIA; Tiberius's mother was LIVIA; Augustus died at NOLA; the Colosseum was completed under TITUS; CASCA was the first to stab Caesar; and the symbol of Rome was the EAGLE. A common forename for the emperors ("praenomen" in Latin) was GAIUS (also CAIUS).

It is convenient to have the names of the early Roman emperors at hand. The first 14 of these were, beginning in 27 B.C.E. and ending in 138 C.E., as follows:

Augustus	Vitellius
Tiberius	Vespasian
Caligula	Titus
Claudius	Domitian
Nero	Nerva
Galba	Trajan
Otho	Hadrian

In several puzzles, Nero was clued as the last of the Julio-Claudian emperors. In the year 69 C.E., the year of Galba's assassination by Otho, there were four emperors: Galba, Otho, Vitellius, and Vespasian.

Be aware that constructors take liberties with Latin, especially regarding case and declension. For example, in the list below, ANNUS is defined as year, but in Latin (and in other languages that have genders and cases and declensions for various parts of speech), there are many endings, depending on a word's use in the sentence; examples are "anno domini" and "per annum." So keep this in mind for Latin nouns, and just write in the stem and go with the flow for the rest if you are not sure.

Concerning the nouns in the list below, they have all been converted to the singular in the nominative case, regardless of how they appeared in a puzzle. Keep in mind, too, that Latin words often have several meanings, depending on the context. For example, the word ARS below can mean (1) a work of art, (2) profession, (3) theory, (4) manner of acting, and (5) cunning or artifice. But the definitions listed below are the ones typically found in crosswords. For expressions of more than one word, such as "ad hoc" and for footnote references, legal terms, and parts of the body, consult the paragraphs following the list below. Entries have included the following:

ALA (wing or wing-like structure)
ARS (art, skill)
AVE (a greeting, "Hello")
CUM (with)
DEA (goddess)
EGO (I, myself)
HIC (here)
IBI (there)
IRA (anger, wrath)
LEX (law)
MEL (honey)
NAM (for)
NOS (we)
PAX (peace)
PER (by, through, during, according to)
PES (foot)
QUA (how, where, by what means)
RES (thing, and often, legal matter)
REX (king)
SED (but)
SIC (thus, so)
SOL (sun)
UBI (where)
VAS (vessel or duct)
VIA (way)
VIR (man, male)
VIS (power, strength)
VOX (voice)

ACTA (acts, chronicles, record)
AMOR (love)
ANSA (handle)
ANTE (before)
AVIS (bird)
DEUS (god)
DIES (day)
ECCE ("Lo," "Behold," "Look," "Here is")
EHEU ("Alas," "Woe")
ERGO (thus, therefore, consequently)

ESSO (he, it)
GENS (clan, tribe, family)
GULA (throat, appetite)
HOMO (man, human being)
IDEM (same)
IDES (midmonth)
IPSE (itself)
ITER (road, route, or highway, as well as journey, aqueduct, and anatomical canal)
LUNA (moon)
MARE (sea)
MONS (mountain)
NISI (unless)
NOLO (to not wish)
NUNC (now)
OLEA (olive)
ONUS (burden, load, affliction)
OPUS (work)
OVUM (egg)
POST (after, behind)
RUGA (wrinkle, furrow)
SINE (without)
SPES (hope, joy)
URSA (she-bear)
UXOR (wife)
VALE ("Good-bye")

AGNUS (lamb)
ANIMA (breath, soul, life)
ANNUS (year)
CALOR (heat)
CANIS (dog)
CAUDA (tail)
CIRCA (about, around)
CURIA (senate in ancient Rome)
CUTIS (skin)
ETIAM (likewise, too)
FORUM (market, the forum in Rome)
LICIT (it is allowed)

LOCUS (place)
MATER (mother)
MODUS (mode, manner)
NIHIL (nothing)
NOMEN (name)
NONES (a specific day in the Roman calendar)
OSTIA (the name of a port of old Rome)
PATER (father)
PINNA (feather, wing)
SAETA (bristle) (sometimes shortened to SETA)
SALVE (a greeting, "Hello")
SINUS (hollow inner part)
STOLA (long upper garment)
SUPRA (above)
TENSA (ceremonial Roman chariot or wagon)
TERRA (land, earth)
URSUS (bear)

ABOLSA (woolen cloak of ancient Rome)
ANTRUM (chamber or cavity, esp. of the body)
ASTRUM (star, constellation, sky)
ATRIUM (central court in a Roman villa)
CLARUS (bright, distinct)
DICTUM (saying, maxim, decree)
DORSUM (back)
FERRUM (iron)
FESTUM (holiday)
GLOSSA (tongue)
GRATIS (free)
HAERES (inheritor, in law)
LINGUA (language, speech)
MENSIS (month)
MUNDUS (world)
NULLUS (not any)
OSTIUM (entrance or doorway, mouth of a river)
PASSIM (here and there)
PATRIA (fatherland)
STILUS (writing instrument)
UBIQUE (everywhere)

AVERNUS (in myth, entrance to the underworld)
LACRIMA (tear)
PATELLA (small dish, kneecap)
PRAETOR (Roman magistrate)

VIA SACRA (the main street in ancient Rome)

MARE NOSTRUM (our sea, namely, the Mediterranean)

For greater readability, the entries below are not presented in their usual capital letters. These expressions are as follows:

ab ovo *or* ab initio: from the start
ad hoc: to the side
ad rem: relevant(ly)
alter idem: exact duplicate
a priori: from cause to effect
ars gratia artis: art for art's sake; MGM's motto
ars longa, vita brevis: art is long, life is short
bona fide(s): in good faith
carpe diem: seize the day (a saying of Horace)
caveat emptor: let the buyer beware
curia romana: papal offices
de facto: in reality
de novo: anew, again
dona nobis pacem: give us peace
ecce homo: behold the man
ecce signum: look at the proof
ex tempore: immediately
festina lente: make haste slowly (a saying of Augustus)
in esse: actually existing, at heart
in hoc signo vinces: in this sign conquer
in medias res: in the middle of a series of things
in re: about, concerning
in situ: unmoved, as found, as originally placed
in toto: as a whole, entirely
in utero: unborn
in vivo: living
ipso facto: by the fact itself

mala fide(s): bad faith
mea culpa: my fault, a formal apology
non compos mentis: not of sound mind
non grata: unwelcome
nota bene: note well
ora pro nobis: pray for us
per aspera ad astra: to the stars with difficulties
per diem: by day
per se: of, in, or by itself or oneself; intrinsically
pro forma: as a matter of form or procedure
pro tempore: for the time being
quid pro quo: an equal exchange
rara avis: rare bird
semper fidelis: always faithful (the Marine's motto)
semper idem: always the same
sine die: without assigning a specified day
sine qua non: indispensable condition or element
sub rosa: confidentially, secretly
sui generis: unique
tabula rasa: blank slate
terra firma: firm ground
vox populi: voice of the people

There are many more everyday Latin expressions, but these are the ones that have been found in puzzles.

Some word combinations are: "amo, amas, amat" (first, second, and third person present indicative of the verb "to love," sometimes referred to in puzzles as a Latin trio); "Veni, vidi, vici" ("I came, I saw, I conquered," from Suetonius, in quoting Caesar at his victory at Zela in 47 B.C.E.); "Iacta alea est" ("The die is cast," also from Caesar, in crossing the Rubicon, according to Suetonius); "Cogito ergo sum" ("I think, therefore I am," from Descartes); "Omnia vincit amor" ("Love conquers all"); and "Quod erat demonstrandum," or "Q.E.D." ("which it was necessary to demonstrate," from Euclid's *Elements*). Then there are "hic, haec, hoc," three forms of the demonstrative adjective "this." The combination appears in puzzles with the clue being two of the three; the entry is the one remaining.

In addition, there are the college honors, namely, "cum laude" (with praise), "magna (great) cum laude," and "summa (highest) cum laude."

Then there are footnote references, such as "et alia" (neuter), "et alii" (masculine), and "et aliae" (feminine), or "et al.," "ibidem" or "ibid.," "idem" or "id.," "id est" or "i.e.," "exempli gratia" or "e.g.," "loco citato" or "loc. cit.," "opere citato" (or alternately, "opus citatum") or "op. cit.," "et sequens" or "et seq.," "vide infra," "sic," "passim," and others. The most popular footnote reference in crosswords is the first one in this sentence, which is typically rendered as "et alia."

Clues in crosswords also often elicit the Latin names of anatomical parts, especially bones, which are OSSA (OS is the singular and OSTEO is frequently a prefix). These include ULNA, ILIUM (this is also another name for Ilion, the ancient name of Troy), SACRUM, TIBIA, RADIUS, HUMERUS, and FEMUR, as well as their plurals, namely, ULNAE, ILIA, SACRA, TIBIAE, RADII, HUMERI, and FEMORA. Sometimes a clue will ask for an adjoining bone, such as in the example "___ neighbor," where, say, a "humerus neighbor" is ULNA.

From several puzzles, we learn that, in the mouth, the UVULA dangles in the VELUM and that those bumps on the sides of the ankle (TALUS) are MALLEOLI. STRIA has appeared, with the clue being "muscle fiber," as has ILEA, with the clue being "intestinal sections." The change in one letter of "ilea" results in ILIA (see paragraph above), which are hipbones. A part of the eye, or OCULUS, is not uncommon in crosswords: this is the UVEA, which is where the iris is. And then there are FOSSA, an anatomical cavity; BURSA, an anatomical sac; NASUS, the nose; GLOSSA, the tongue; CONCHA, the bowl part of the ear; SEPTUM, a divider; SCAPULA, a shoulder bone; and MALAR, relating to the cheek or jaw. Before leaving these body parts, it is helpful to know that a term from prescriptions, TER, stands for "thrice," as in, say, "three times a day."

And legal terms are sometimes used; examples are "mens rea," "mandamus," "in camera," "in rem," "de jure," "ipse dixit," "onus probandi," "nihil dicit," "sui juris," "pro bono," "stare decisis," "ex parte," "nisi," "certiori" (usually abbreviated to CERT), "res judicata," "nolle prosequi," "nolo contendere," "res gestae," and "habeas corpus." The longest Latin word to appear as an answer was APOSTERIORI, for the clue word "Empirical."

The list of cardinal numbers through ten below, in Latin and in the romance languages of Italian, Spanish, and French, illustrates their similarity:*

Latin	Italian	Spanish	French
unus	un(o)	un(o)	un
duo	due	dos	deux
tres	tre	tres	trois
quattuor	quattro	cuatro	quatre
quinque	cinque	cinco	cinq
sex	sei	seis	six
septem	sette	siete	sept
octo	otto	ocho	huit
novem	nove	nueve	neuf
decem	dieci	diez	dix

*From *Latin*, by Frederic M. Wheelock. (New York: Harper & Row, Publishers, Inc., 1963.)

German

When German words occur in crosswords, they are usually one of several forms of the definite article "the" in the nominative case, namely, DER (m.), DIE (f.), DAS (n.), and DIE (pl.). The indefinite article "a" or "an" in the nominative case is also used: EIN (m.), EINE (f.), and EIN (n.). The indefinite plural "some" is EINIGE, which has also appeared.

The cardinal numbers up to 12 are sometimes encountered, and are as follows:

EINS	SIEBEN
ZWEI	ACHT
DREI	NEUN
VIER	ZEHN
FUNF	ELF
SECHS	ZWOLF

As in the other languages, clues wanting a German word as an answer are usually names of cities, such as Berlin, Bonn, Frankfurt, Munich, or Potsdam, but for alliteration, lesser-known cities are also used for this purpose. Example: "Magdeburg mister," the answer being HERR. And one will also encounter his mate, FRAU. The industrial city of ESSEN and the coal-producing region of the SAAR are popular in puzzles, more so than any other German places.

As with other languages, proper German names are also typically clues, such as Emil, Franz, Fritz, Georg, Hans, Heinrich, Hermann, Karl, Philipp, Werner, Wilhelm, or Wolfgang. (Puzzle makers must not know the names of any German women, as none have appeared to the author.)

A few other short words in German (nouns are always capitalized, not that it makes any difference in puzzles) are the following, where nouns are listed only in the nominative case and adjectives only in their simplest form:

ACH (an interjection)
ALT (old)
AUS (out)
GUT (good)
EIS (ice, ice cream, sherbet)
ICH (I)
IST (is)
MAI (the month of May)
MIT (with)
NEU (new)
NIE (never)
NUR (only)
OMA (grandmother)
PIZ (peak)
REH (deer)
SEE (lake, sea)
SIE (you, and also she, her, they, or them)
TAG (day)
TOD (death)
UHR (hour, time)
UND (and)
VON (of or from)

ABER (but)
ALTE (old person)*
BAHN (road, railroad)
BIER (beer)
ECHT (genuine)
EDEL (noble)
EIER (eggs)
ENTE (duck)
ERDE (earth)
ESEL (donkey)
HAUS (house)
KIND (child)
KLAR (clear)
MEER (ocean, sea)
NEIN (no)
OBER (waiter (n), upper (adj.))
SEHR (very)
SEIT (since)
SIEG (victory)
TOPF (pot)
UBER (over, above)
WAHR (true)
ZEIT (time)
ZIEL (goal)

ALLES (everyone)
BEIDE (both)
BITTE (please)
DAMIT (therewith)
DANKE ("Thank you")
ESSEN (meal (n.), to eat (v.))
GEHEN (to go)
KUNST (art)
NACHT (night)
PFERD (horse)
PFUND (pound)
SAUER (sour)
SELIG (blissful)

STADT (city or town)
WARUM (why)

JAWOHL (yes, of course)
KINDER (children)
PROSIT (a toast)

ACHTUNG (a warning)
GESTALT (unified whole that is inseparable)
PFENNIG (penny)
SEHR GUT (very good)
STRASSE (street)

VERBOTEN (forbidden)
WIE GEHTS ("Wie gehr's?") ("How are you?")

ACH DU LIEBER (an exclamation)

Compass directions also appear; they are NORD, OST, SUD, and WEST.

*Der ALTE often refers to the late Chancellor of Germany, Konrad Adenauer.

Greek

Ancient and modern Greek are brought together in crosswords, and the clues invariably use ancient names such as Socrates and his pupil, Plato, as well as Plato's pupil, Aristotle, and other philosophers to elicit a Greek word for the answer. Speaking of Socrates, his wife, XANTHIPPE, has been an answer, as has HERODOTUS, clued as "father of history." The Athenian statesman, lawgiver, and poet SOLON appears in crosswords, and the philosopher DRACO has also been cited, once clued as "unmerciful Athenian lawgiver"; he is the source of our word "draconian."

In Greek, the name for Greece is ELLAS (Ellás), which has been required in puzzles. Typically, the only city used as a clue is Athens, although SPARTA, located in Laconia and a member of the Achaean League, and the ancient Greek colony of IONIA have been answers, as well as NEMEA, site of the Nemean games after 573 B.C.E., and SAMOS, the birthplace of Epidaurus. The most popular Greek words in puzzles seem to be as follows:

AGON (contest)
ANTA (architectural pier, pilaster)
MINA (ancient Greek weight and unit of money)
OSSA (the name of a mountain peak in Eastern Greece, north of Thessaly)
STOA (covered walk, promenade, portico, or colonnade)

AGAPE(E) (love, affection)
AGORA (market, gathering place)
DEMOS (populace)
ELENI (Helen)
HELOT (a class of serfs in ancient Sparta)
ILION (Troy, to the Greeks)
ODEUM or ODEON (theater)
STELE (upright engraved stone used as a monument)

KRATER (bowl for mixing wine and water)
LYCEUM (hall)

If Pindar is in a clue, ODE is invariably the answer; and if Zeno (of Citium) is in a clue, STOIC is usually the answer. (He is not to be confused with an earlier philosopher, Zeno of ELEA.) The famous Athenian tragedians of the 5th century B.C.E. will be encountered from time to time: Aeschylus, Sophocles, and Euripides. The most popular of Euripides's plays in puzzles is MEDEA but you may also come across "Hippolytus" and "The Trojan Women" in clues.

One of the plays of Aeschylus that appears in puzzles is "The ORESTEIA," with its five vowels; another is "The Persians." Two plays of Sophocles have appeared: "Ajax" and "Antigone," which are among his Theban plays. In them, Oedipus can be a clue or answer in puzzles. The other Theban play is "Oedipus at Colonus." A bit younger was the Athenian comedian, Aristophanes. Some of his plays include "Lysistrata," "The Frogs," "The Birds," "The Wasps," and "The Clouds." Nineteen plays of Euripides survive, 11 for Aristophanes, and only seven each for Aeshylus and Sophocles. (The number of plays is adapted from *The*

Classical Tradition, by Gilbert Highet [New York: Oxford University Press, 1961] and other sources.)

If a clue is "fraternity letter," "sorority letter," or "sweater letter," then a Greek letter is wanted (if it is three letters, it is often ETA); on occasion, the clue is "key letter" (for Phi Beta Kappa). The Greek alphabet appears below; its beginning and end, "alpha" and "omega," are often referred to together, similar to our "A to Z," and they will sometimes be called opposites in a clue. A device sometimes used by puzzle makers is to have the clue contain a Greek letter, whereby the letter preceding or following it is to be the answer, for example, "Pi follower" is RHO (for some reason, this is the most popular combination). Rho is also the scientific symbol for air density.

On several occasions, clues related to a trident or a pitchfork, and the answer was PSI, as the Greek letter does look like them (Ψ or ψ); it is also a symbol for Neptune. The letter "tau" looks like a cross (T or τ), a capital "omega" looks like a horseshoe (Ω), a capital "eta" looks like our capital letter H, and "rho" looks like our P. All of these have been in puzzles, with the Greek letter names clued by the letters of our alphabet. Much more concerning ancient Greece will be found in the "Mythology" section below.

The 24 letters of the Greek alphabet are as follows:

ALPHA	NU
BETA	XI
GAMMA	OMICRON
DELTA	PI
EPSILON	RHO
ZETA	SIGMA
ETA	TAU
THETA	UPSILON
IOTA	PHI
KAPPA	KHI (or CHI)
LAMBDA	PSI
MU	OMEGA

Mythology

The number of gods, goddesses, and other beings in mythology seems to be infinite. However, crossword puzzles are largely limited to the Greek and Roman deities and, to a lesser extent, those from northern Europe, generally leaving to rest in peace the Hindu deities BRAHMA (referred to as the creator), SHIVA (or SIVA) (associated with destruction), his son GANESH (or GANESHA), the god of wisdom and depicted with the head of an elephant, and VISHNU (or VISNU). Brahma, Shiva, and Vishnu are referred to as the "Vedic trinity," or "triad." The goddess DURGA has 18 arms and is clothed in red. Lord RAMA, who has been clued as blue-skinned and as a hero, is the seventh incarnation or avatar of Vishnu, and very popular among Hindus.

More frequently, you will come across one of the ancient Egyptian deities, such as OSIRIS, adored throughout Egypt, who has been clued as "king of the dead" or "god of the underworld"; the sacred bull of Memphis, APIS, is an embodiment of Osiris. Other deities are his wife and sister ISIS, who holds a flail and a crook and who has been clued as "horned" or as "cow-headed" or as "fertility goddess" or as "goddess of creation"; PTAH (or PHTAH), the Egyptian god of creation and patron of artisans, who was the chief deity of Memphis; HORUS, a god of the sun, the son of Osiris and Isis and who is hawk- or falcon-headed; and SET, originally a warlike god and the symbol of darkness or evil and enemy of Osiris; one of his forms is as a hippopotamus.

Other Egyptian deities are ATON or ATEN, a god of the sun; THOTH, the god of reason, wisdom, magic, and the moon, and who is ibis-headed (the ibis was a sacred bird in ancient Egypt); and the child-god AMEN, also known as AMON, AMMON, or AMUN, a chief Theban deity and god of life and reproduction, having the head of a ram. Sometimes his various names are followed by RA or RE, so if six or seven squares are to be filled, use one of these alternatives such as AMONRE (Amon-Re). Another symbol of power in ancient Egypt was the ASP.

Of the many Norse and Teutonic divinities, the most frequent in crosswords is ODIN, also known as WODEN, WODIN, or WODAN (and as WOTAN in Richard Wagner's music-drama, "The Ring of the Nibelungs"). He is sometimes clued as one-eyed. His wife is FRIGG (anglicized as FRIGGA), and in "The Ring" is called FRICKA. He rides on his eight-legged steed, SLEIPNER, and lives in his great hall, VALHALLA, which is within ASGARD, the capital city of the realm of the Norse gods. It is accessible only by a rainbow bridge, BIFROST (or Bilröst), which connects it to Midgard, the middle world.

One will also encounter THOR, often clued as the god of thunder, who was Odin's eldest son, and FREYA, usually identified with Frigga (above), and in "The Ring" is her sister, FREIA. Then there are the nine virgin VALKYRIES, daughters of Odin and Erda, who were Odin's messengers and warrior-maidens. ERDA is often referred to as the earth goddess.

A mythological character useful for crosswords (it is short and has two vowels) is LOGI, and in Wagner's "Ring" is LOGE, the personification of fire. Close in construction, but an entirely different character, is the crafty LOKI, associated with mischief, trickery, and magic.

Puzzles have required the Norse god of strife (or war), TYR (another son of Odin), and the Norse goddess of the underworld, who is HEL. (Another meaning of HEL is the underworld itself, for the dead not killed in battle.) As a group, the great gods of the Norse pantheon, who number 12, are referred to as the AESIR, which puzzle makers probably like because of its three vowels.

The source of the Norse and Teutonic tales may be found in the 13th century EDDAs, one in poetry and one in prose; they are sometimes referred to as the Icelandic sagas. In them we also meet the three NORNS (who decide fate), BALDUR (sometimes BALDER), another son of Odin and god of light, spring, peace, and joy, and the ELVES. Those familiar with Wagner's "Ring" will recognize the similarities and plots between those in the Eddas and his monumental work. Other European characters neither Norse nor Teutonic whom one may come across are the Celtic DRUIDS and MAB, the fairy-queen. It has helped to know that the tree sacred to the Druids was the OAK. (Not to confuse the issue, but in Wagner's "Ring," a sacred tree is the ASH.) And then, from English literature, there is the poem of BEOWULF, beset by the monster GRENDEL, who lives in a cave.

In *Bulfinch's Mythology*, the tales are classified into three groups: "The Age of Fable," "The Age of Chivalry," and "Legends of Charlemagne." The first group, containing the Greek and Roman gods, the Egyptian and oriental deities, and the stories from northern mythology, is the most popular in puzzles. The second contains the tales of ARTHUR,

LANCELOT (or LAUNCELOT) and GUINEVER (or GUINEVERE), TRISTRAM and ISOUDE (or ISEULT), perhaps more familiar in German as "TRISTAN und ISOLDE," thanks to Wagner, and ROBINHOOD (Robin Hood), his companion Allen-a-DALE, and GALAHAD. Iseult has been clued as the wife of King Mark.

Galahad's mother has often been a clue, the entry being ELAINE (of Astolat); she died of love for Lancelot. Galahad's father, UTHER Pendragon, has also been found in puzzles, as has one of the roundtable knights, GARETH. You may also come across Sir KAY and Morgan le FAY; the former was a foster brother to King Arthur and the latter was a half-sister. And then there is Arthur's EXCALIBUR, the sword or, sometimes, lance. It helps to know that Arthur and the other heroes went to an island called AVALON, the isle of apples, when they died. In many of the tales, Morgan le Fay is also associated with Avalon. On several occasions, a clue was "Geraint's wife," the answer being ENID. She has also been clued as being patient and as "Camelot lady." Edith Hamilton, in her *Mythology*, used a different classification of the tales; both Bulfinch and Hamilton are excellent sources.

Concerning the Greek and Roman myths in crosswords, no clue is usually given as to whether the Greek or Roman form of the deity's name is wanted. Thus the answer (not capitalized here, for greater readability) could be Ares or Mars, Hera or Juno, Heracles or Hercules, Persephone or Proserpina (or Proserpine), each pair of an equal number of letters. Although the Romans appropriated the Greek divinities, usually giving them new or altered names, they also had some of their own, such as FLORA, POMONA, and the deity having two faces, JANUS. Two names of Roman household gods, PENATES and LARES, have occurred, as has JUTURNA, goddess of springs, fountains, and wells. Every Roman family had a LAR, who was the spirit of an ancestor, and several Penates, gods of the hearth and guardians of the storehouse. Where two names are given in the paragraphs below, the first is Greek, the second (in parentheses) is Roman.

But be aware that the two names do not represent the very same god or goddess and that they do not necessarily have the same attributes or characteristics. For example, Zeus is not Jupiter; Zeus's tales are pre-Homeric, and he was the subject of many stories, which changed down the centuries, long before the Romans acquired him and made him their own as Jupiter. Jupiter had his home in Rome, not on Mt. Olympus. One way to regard the Greek and Roman gods and goddesses with respect to each other is to think of them as being *identified* with or *analogous* to each other rather than being the same as each other. They are sometimes referred to in puzzles as "counterparts."

Another complication is that Zeus (Jupiter or Jove) had many wives and children; perhaps on this account the Greek mythical world seems to revolve around him. His parents (who were Titans) were Cronos or Cronus or Kronos (Saturn) and Rhea (Ops); both are associated with the harvest. Cybele, an Anatolian nature goddess and Phrygian state deity, was adopted by the Greeks and is sometimes identified with Rhea in the tales. Do not take any of this too seriously; in cases where sources differ, the author has used as referee Sir William Smith's excellent *Smaller Classical Dictionary*.

Zeus's grandparents were Ouranus (Uranus) (father of the Titans, Furies, and Cyclopes) and Gaea or Gaia or Ge (Tellus), who were the personification of Heaven and Earth, respectively. Among Zeus's siblings were Demeter (Ceres), Hera (Juno), Hades or Pluto (Dis), Poseidon (Neptune), and Hestia (Vesta). Although Athena, also known as Athene, Pallas, or Pallas Athena (Minerva), is said to have sprung directly from Zeus's (Jupiter's or Jove's) head fully armored (but see paragraph immediately below for a another account), he had other children born in a more customary way: with Hera (Juno), the queen of the gods, he had Hebe (Juventas), Ares (Mars) and his twin sister Eris (Discordia), and Hephaestos or Hephaestus (Vulcan); and with Leto (Latona), he had Apollo and Artemis (Diana).

And there are more: with Dione (one of the Titans), he had Aphrodite (Venus), whose son was Eros (Cupid(o) or Amor); other accounts have her being born of sea-foam. With Maia, he had Hermes (Mercury); with Semele, he had Dionysus, also known as Bacchus, the only god whose parents were not both divine; with Demeter (Ceres), he had Persephone (Proserpina or Proserpine); with Metis, he had Athena (but see paragraph immediately above for another account); with Themis, he had Irene (Pax); with Danaë, he had Perseus; and with Alcmena, he had Heracles (Hercules).

With Leda the Spartan queen, he disguised himself as a swan; she gave birth to an egg, from which the twins Castor and Pollux were born; and with him Leda produced another egg, from which Helen (later known as Helen of Troy) was born. Other accounts have Castor as the natural-born son of Leda and Tyndareus, king of Sparta. And that's not all: among Zeus's other children were the Muses, the Fates, and the Graces.

The arts are the domain of the Muses, and clues for the Muses often refer to the arts. The mother of the Muses, Mnemosyne or Mneme (Memory), is unlikely to be found in a crossword, but some of her children are (their father was Zeus). There were nine sisters, the most common in puzzles being Erato, associated with lyric and love poetry; her symbol is the lyre and she wears a wreath of myrtle and roses. The others were Calliope (epic poetry and eloquence), Clio (history, and perhaps second most popular in puzzles), Euterpe (lyric poetry and music), Melpomene (tragedy), Polyhymnia (sacred poetry, rhetoric, and song), Terpsichore (dance and sometimes song), Thalia (comedy and pastoral poetry), and Urania (astronomy). Urania and Thalia are next in popularity. Sometimes the clue for one of the muses will be the name of another, as in "Sister of ___." If a clue mentions a tenth muse, it relates to the fact that Plato referred to SAPPHO that way.

The Fates, Graces, and Furies each number three. The Fates (or "Moirae" in Greek) are Clotho, who spins the thread, Lachesis, who draws off the thread and thus determines a person's destiny (like a lottery), and Atropos, who snips the thread of life. The Graces (or "Charites" in Greek) are Euphrosyne (mirth), Aglaia (splendor), and Thalia (good cheer) (this is another Thalia, not the Muse), and the Furies (or "Eumenides" in Greek) are Tisiphone, noted for retaliation, Alecto, noted for jealousy, and Magaera, noted for anger.

It will probably be a cold day on the ferry with CHARON going across the river STYX encircling HADES when you will need the Fates, Graces, or Furies, but every now and then one of them appears. Another river in the netherworld is LETHE, from which the shades drank and forgot the past; thus it is sometimes clued as the "river of forgetfulness." On the way to Hades, there is a cavern called EREBUS. If you come across the word "Tartarus," this term was used by later poets to refer to Hades or the netherworld. And it helps to know that CERBERUS is the dog that guards the entrance to Hades; depending on the source, he might have 100, 50, or only three heads.

Below is a list of some of the characters in Greek and Roman mythology that the author has come across in puzzles, and what they were associated with. Keep in mind that, in most cases, the Greek and Roman characters shared the attributes listed below, but sometimes not. Also, the passage of time caused changes: Artemis was originally like a universal mother, associated especially with childbirth; only later did she acquire the attributes of hunting and chastity. If an asterisk follows a name below, that character is one of the 12 Olympian, or divine, gods or goddesses, and if a double asterisk follows, it indicates a lesser deity. Sources are generally but not always in agreement on the 12 Olympians, but even less on the so-called lesser deities. For example, some sources include Dionysus and leave out Hestia.

> Aphrodite (Venus)*—love, beauty, desire, and fertility; patroness of seafarers and war; most beautiful of the goddesses; also known as Cytherea and Cypris; mother of Eros; daughter of Zeus and Dione in the "Iliad," but later sources tell of her as springing from the foam of the sea; wife of Hephaestus, but she loved many men, especially Ares
>
> Apollo, Phoebus, or Phoebus Apollo (no other Roman name)*—sunlight, music, poetry, medicine and healing, beauty, law, prophecy, and archery; his instrument is the lyre; his symbol is the laurel; son of Zeus and Leto; twin brother of Artemis; a town sacred to Apollo was Delphi; Apollo is sometimes clued as the name of an historic theater in New York City's Harlem
>
> Ares (Mars)*—war and destruction; loved by Aphrodite; the vulture sacred to him; father of Deimos, who represents terror and dread, and Phobos, who represents fear and panic; son of Zeus and Hera; twin brother of Eris and half-brother of Heracles
>
> Artemis (Diana)*—hunting and the moon; childbirth and the young; chastity added later; she carries a bow and arrow and has a golden chariot; twin sister of Apollo; daughter of Zeus and Leto; slayer of the hunter, Orion, the lover of Eos; she changed the young hunter, Actaeon, into a stag, and he was felled by his own dogs
>
> Athena (also Athene) or Pallas or Pallas Athena, sometimes known as Alea (Minerva)*—wisdom, courage, law and justice, prudence, invention, agriculture, battle, arts (especially women's handicrafts); among her symbols are the owl, the olive plant, and the snake; daughter of Metis and Zeus, she sprang from his head fully armored (he had swallowed Metis to prevent the birth, but Athena had already been conceived); her statue was in the Parthenon
>
> Demeter (Ceres)*—agriculture (especially grains and corn), the harvest, fertility, marriage; mother of Persephone and sister of Zeus

Dionysus (Bacchus)**—wine, fertility, ecstacy; son of Zeus and Semele (or of Zeus and Persephone or Demeter)
Elpis (Spes)—hope
Eos (Aurora)—Titan goddess of the dawn; daughter of Hyperion; sister of Helios and Selene; in Homer, she is saffron-robed
Eris (Discordia)—strife and discord; twin sister of Ares; sister of Hephaestus, Hebe, Hypnos, and Thanatos
Eros (Cupid(o) or Amor)**—erotic love; son of Ares and Aphrodite; has golden wings; "archer" and "arrow" are clues and answers
Hades (originally Aïdes) or Pluto (Dis)**—death, wealth, god of the underworld, his wife Persephone; brother of Zeus, Hera, Poseidon, Demeter, and Hestia
Harmonia (Concordia)—goddess of harmony, wife of Cadmus, counterpart of Eris (Discordia)
Hebe (Juventas)**—youth, spring, cupbearer to the gods and goddesses, pardons and forgiveness; wife of Heracles; daughter of Zeus and Hera; sister of Ares, Hephaestus, and Eris
Hecate or Hekate**—sorcery, witchcraft, magic, crossroads, gates, entrances, and darkness
Helios (Sol)**—god of the sun; brother of Selene and Eos; frequently called Hyperion, his father's name; his mother's name is Thea (or Theia)
Hephaestus (Vulcan, Vulcanus, or Mulciber)*—metalwork, craftsmanship, technology, volcanoes, fire, and the forge; the only god who is ugly and lame; husband of Aphrodite; son of Zeus and Hera; brother of Ares, Eris, and Hebe
Hera (Juno)*—queen of the gods and goddesses and ruler of the earth, known for marriage, well-being of women, and her jealousy and vindictiveness; the peacock and cow sacred to her; wife and sister of Zeus; sister of Poseidon, Hades, Demeter, and Hestia
Heracles (Hercules)**—extraordinary strength; loved Iole; known for his twelve labors, or dodekathlon; slew the lion at Nemea; son of Zeus and Alcmene (or Alcmena)
Hermes (Mercury)*—thieves, physicians, and heralds; messenger of the gods; commerce, invention, trade, boundaries, gymnastics, shrewdness, cunning, and theft; patron of travelers and rogues; winged cap and sandals; carries the Caduceus, or magic wand, in his left hand; inventor of the lyre; conductor of the dead to Hades; son of Zeus and Maia

Hestia (Vesta)*—home and the hearth, fire, sanctuary, domestic life, agriculture, and architecture; her sacred animal the cow; sister of Zeus, Hera, Poseidon, Demeter, and Hades

Hypnos (Somnos)—sleep; twin brother of Thanatos

Irene or Eirene (Pax)—peace and spring; one of the Horae; daughter of Zeus and Themis; sister of Eunomia and Dike

Iris**—rainbow, communication, clouds, and rain; goddess of the sea and sky; like Mercury, a messenger of the gods; daughter of Thaumus and Electra

Momus—satire, laughter, mockery, and censure

Nemesis—an avenging goddess, she measured out misery to the proud and insolent

Nike (Victoria)**—victory, speed, strength; usually shown with wings

Pan (Faunus)**—fields, forests, flocks, shepherds, fertility, spring; his favorite residence Arcadia; son of Hermes and a wood nymph; represented with horns, snub nose, and goats' feet; clued as being hairy

Persephone (Proserpine or Proserpina)—vegetation, seeds, grain, spring; wife of Hades; daughter of Zeus and Demeter

Poseidon (Neptune)*—the sea, earthquakes, and streams; horses; carries the trident; brother of Zeus; husband of Amphitrite; his son, Triton

Selene (Luna)**—goddess of the moon; sister of Helios and Eos; daughter of Hyperion and Thea; wife of Endymion; later identified with Artemis

Thanatos (Mors)—death; brother of Hypnos, the god of sleep, and of Nemesis, the goddess who punished crimes

Zeus (Jupiter)*—king of the gods and goddesses and ruler of the heavens; thunder and lightning; law and order; his symbols are the eagle, bull, and oak; husband of Hera and others; son of Cronus and Rhea

The ancient myths often consist of pairings of characters. Listed below are some of these, at least one of the pair having a name consisting of seven or fewer letters (and thus more likely to be used in puzzles):

Acis and Galatea
Apollo and Daphne
Bacchus and Ariadne, daughter of King Minos

Baucis and Philemon
Castor and Pollux (twins born from an egg)
Cupid and Psyche
Damon and Pythias
Diana and Actaeon
Dido (founder and queen of Carthage) and Aeneas (hero of Troy)
Echo and Narcissus
Hebe and Ganymede
Hero and Leander (they both drowned)
Orpheus and Eurydice
Pegasus and Bellerophon
Perseus and Medusa
Psyche and Eros
Pygmalion and Galatea (he brought her to life)
Pyramus and Thisbe
Scylla and Charybdis
Theseus and the Minotaur
Venus and Adonis

Although Niobe, queen of Thebes and daughter of Tantalus (and possibly, Dione), was not a goddess, she is usually clued by the terms "weeping," "tears," or "stone." Her 14 children were slain by Artemis (Diana) and Apollo at the urging of their mother, Leto (Latona), in a fit of pique, and she was changed into stone. Electra is also associated with grief. Speaking of a liquid (tears), on several occasions it helped to know that ICHOR was the divine or ethereal fluid that took the place of blood in the Greek deities.

Some other mythological characters in puzzles are ENYO, the goddess of war who accompanied Ares in battle; MORPHEUS, the "dream god"; COMUS, the guardian of revelry; CALLIOPE, whose son was ORPHEUS and whose symbol is the lyre (Pindar referred to Orpheus as the father of songs); the titan ATLAS, who was the brother of PROMETHEUS (who stole fire); MOMUS, god of ridicule; and ADONIS, god of beauty and desire, a life-birth-death deity.

Others are ORESTES, Electra's brother; CREON, Antigone's brother; RHEA Silvia, daughter of Mars and a vestal virgin, who was the legendary mother of Romulus and Remus; CIRCE, goddess of magic who lived on the island of AEAEA; and INO, who was a mortal queen of Thebes and daughter of Cadmus and Harmonia.

And who can forget that Pandora's jar (or box) held ILLS or EVILS? Londoners and puzzle makers often mistake the Shaftesbury memorial fountain and statue of an archer in Piccadilly Square as Eros; in fact, it was intended to be Anteros, the younger brother of Eros, but if there are four squares, EROS is the answer.

The story of Jason and the golden fleece is another rich source for crosswords, including the huge, hollowed-out tree that served as his ship, the ARGO, which was named for its builder, ARGOS, a watchman having 100 eyes. Strangely, the Argo had a speaking beam. Many of Jason's sailors, or Argonauts, later became famous as heroes of Greece. On the way from Iolcus to the land of Colchis to claim the fleece, he married MEDEA, whose sorcery helped to overcome the many daunting obstacles to his quest. They eventually reached the coast of Thessaly and home.

The story of the Trojan War, especially as memorialized in Homer's "Iliad," can be said to begin when the shepherd Paris, who was tending his flocks on Mount IDA, had to decide who was fairest among three goddesses—Hera, Aphrodite, or Athena. He chose Aphrodite, and under her protection he sailed to Sparta and kidnapped HELEN, whose husband was Menelaus, king of Sparta, and carried her away to Troy. Daughter of Leda and sister of Castor and Pollux, Helen has been clued as "most beautiful woman." Other chiefs of the Greek cities joining Menelaus in rescuing Helen are Achilles (who killed Hector), her brother-in-law Agamemnon (whose father was Atreus), Ulysses, Patroclus, AJAX (a warrior also sometimes clued as a hero), and NESTOR (usually clued as wise).

Most notable on the Trojan side are Paris's father, King Priam; Priam's other son, Hector (sometimes referred to for his wisdom); Aeneas, born on Mt. Ida and the son of Anchises and Aphrodite; Glaucus; and several others (of longer names). A good and faithful friend of Aeneas was ACHATES. The deities help one or another of the combatants over the years, often changing sides, until Troy is defeated and King Priam is killed. Priam's wife, HECUBA, has also been an answer in puzzles.

Homer's other great epic poem, the "Odyssey," tells the story of the 20-year wanderings of Odysseus (Ulysses to the Romans), king of Ithaca, on his return home from Troy. In this great travelogue, he meets or is challenged by the Lotus-Eaters (who have been clued as listless), the Cyclopes (singular: Cyclops), Circe (sometimes referred to as enticer of Odysseus or as Homer's enchantress), the Sirens, the Monsters, the

Amazons, Scylla and Charybdis, Calypso, and others on his voyage. Again, as in the "Iliad," the deities intervene all along the way. His faithful dog ARGUS died from joy when his master returned home.

Before leaving this section, it may be helpful to mention three kinds of nymph: DRYAD, a woods and forest nymph, NEREID, a sea nymph (any of the 50 daughters of Nereus), and OREAD, a mountain nymph; the last is the most common in puzzles. Also needed from time to time are three dwarf planets of our solar system: CERES, ERIS, and PLUTO. (Pluto's moons are Nix, Styx, Hydra, Charon, and Cerberus, all names from the underworld).

The Old Testament

Of all the books of the Old Testament (listed at the end of this section), the very first, Genesis, is the source of most Bible-related clues and entries. In that book, EDEN is the most popular answer, with the clue often being "perfect place," "ideal home," "first home," "Utopia," "first garden," "idyllic place," "Shangri-La," "place of delight," or "fall site." Eden was watered by a river, and flowed from there into four "heads"; the only one to make it into puzzles is the PISON (Hebrew: Pishon). A "place of plenty" was GOSHEN, in Egypt, a "place of wealth" was OPHIR, and a site clued as an oasis was ELIM.

A place not so nice was SODOM; Abraham's nephew, LOT, whose home it was, survived its destruction by fire and brimstone because he did not look back; his wife PUH did, and she was turned into a pillar of salt. Another bad place was ENDOR, in Canaan, home to a witch, who was consulted by Saul. And a place of human sacrifice was TOPHET. The clues "Esau's land" and "Ancient Dead Sea kingdom" resulted in EDOM (which is in the Negev), as did "Ancient region near Moab." MOAB itself, north of Edom, was once clued as "Ruth's country," and Moab was once a clue for King BALAK's land. The Edomite capital was PETRA.

There are many names of Biblical characters in puzzles, the most frequent being the brothers CAIN (Adam and Eve's eldest) and ABEL (their second). Cain, a farmer, was expelled from Eden and went to NOD, which was EAST of Eden. Abel is sometimes referred to in clues as a shepherd or victim (of Cain) or as "Eve's second" or as "third man" (that is, Adam as the first and Cain as the second). The clue for their third son, SETH, is often something like "Adam's youngest," but even more frequent than Seth as an answer is Seth's own son, ENOS, whose clue may be "Adam's grandson," "Eve's grandson," "Son of Seth," "Biblical oldster," or "third-generation figure." (Enos is not to be confused with ENOCH, who was the eldest son of Cain and father of Methuselah.)

After the so-called "first family," the twin brothers JACOB and ESAU are next in popularity, sometimes with one twin as the clue. Esau is sometimes clued as being a hunter or being hairy or having a reddish complexion, or as being tricked by his brother out of his birthright as first-born (for a pot of lentils or, depending on the puzzle, lentil soup, lentil stew, or a bowl of red pottage), or as being the eldest child of Isaac, since he preceded Jacob into the world. Jacob was not far behind, as he grasped Esau's heel at his birth. Esau had three wives, but only ADAH, a daughter of Elon the Hittite, makes it into puzzles; their eldest son was Eliphaz, who has been a clue for Esau.

The parents of Jacob and Esau were ISAAC (his name in Hebrew is Yitzchat, which means "laughter") and REBECCA (or REBEKAH), and their paternal grandparents were ABRAHAM and SARAH. It has also helped to know that Rebecca's brother was LABAN, whose daughter was LEAH. Jacob is an extremely important person historically, as his 12 sons were the progenitors of the 12 tribes of Israel. Getting back to Sarah, one puzzle required you to know that she was jealous of HAGAR, her Egyptian maid, who had a son, ISHMAEL, by Abraham. He was Abraham's eldest son, which has been a clue.

Jacob and his first wife, LEAH, had among their six sons ZEBULUN (sometimes ZEBULON). Leah's younger sister, RACHEL, the second wife of Jacob, is also found in puzzles from time to time. Altogether, Jacob had 12 sons and one daughter, DINAH, but the sons to appear in crosswords are usually Joseph and Benjamin. One puzzle required you to know that the mother of Jacob's eighth son, ASHER, was Leah's maid, ZILPAH.

The story of the flood also makes its way into puzzles. Noah had three sons—Shem, Ham, and Japheth—with him on the ark, which alighted on Mt. ARARAT after 40 days and 40 nights. The ARK has been clued by its length: 300 cubits. Although Shem was the first-born, the birth order of the other two is in dispute; Shem's eldest son was ELAM. HAM has been clued as an ancestor of the Canaanites. The eldest son of Ham was CUSH, who had a son named NIMROD, who was a king of Shinar and a mighty hunter, the latter usually a clue to his name. SEBA was another son.

There are also the stories of Moses dividing the REDSEA (Red Sea), the burning bush on Mt. HOREB, and his receiving the Ten

Commandments on Mt. SINAI. It has also helped to know that he was found in bulrushes on the NILE as a baby. His elder brother AARON is sometimes called the first high priest, and Aaron's third son was ELEAZAR, once clued as an Aaronite, who succeeded him as high priest. Then there are the stories of DANIEL in the lion's den, cast there by Nebuchadnezzar, the Babylonian king, and JONAH and the whale. It has been helpful to know that Jonah prophesied repentance in NINEVEH, which was the capital of the Assyrian Empire.

It may be difficult to remember that NER, the father of ABNER, was a cousin of SAUL, the first king of the united kingdom of Israel, and that Saul was succeeded by DAVID, the father of SOLOMON, who was known for his wisdom. Other names that appear in crosswords are the Phoenician princess and queen of Israel, JEZEBEL, and her husband AHAB, a pagan king of Israel who allowed temples of the Phoenician god BAAL to operate there; Samuel's mother HANNAH and his teacher ELI, a judge and high priest, quite popular in crosswords; CALEB, a spy of Moses in the promised land of Canaan. A place mentioned is LEHI, where Samson killed 1,000 Philistines with the jawbone of an ass.

And more: OMRI, father of Ahab, was one of the ablest kings of the northern kingdom of Israel; HIRAM was a king of Tyre; Ruth's second husband was BOAZ and her mother-in-law was NAOMI, who renamed herself MARA, as she was bitter; the prophet NATHAN chastised King David, who had a daughter named TAMAR and a son named ABSALOM; ASA, father of Jehoshaphat, was the third king of Judah (Judea is a Greek and Roman adaptation of the name); Goliath's birthplace was GATH, and David slew him in the valley of ELAH; ESTHER became queen of Persia by her marriage to King Ahasuerus; ORNAN was a Jebusite; EZRA led the Israelites back to Jerusalem; ELIJAH (also ELIHA) was a son of Elam; NAHUM predicted the destruction of Nineveh; and ANAK was a son of ARBA. All these names have been found in crosswords.

Every now and then you will see a clue like "___, Biblical style." In such a case, the answer will be a word evocative of the 1611 King James Version (KJV) of the Old Testament. Examples are SMITE and SMOTE (for strike and struck); SAITH (for says); CANST (for can); DOTH (for does); HATH (for has); SEEST (for sees); SHALT (for shall); BEGET, BEGAT, and BEGOTTEN, etc. Measurements such as the CUBIT (based on the length of the forearm from the elbow to the tip of the middle finger, or about 18 inches) and numbers are used, too, such as SCORE for the number 20 (as in Lincoln's Gettysburg address). Also found in puzzles is the word SELAH, a psalmic pause or interjection. The term KINE has appeared; it usually refers to cows or cattle.

The word PENTATEUCH stands for the first five books of the Bible; in Judaism these are known as the TORAH or the LAW. The six books from Joshua through 2nd Kings (leaving out the book of Ruth) are sometimes referred to as the Former Prophets. The Latter Prophets are divided into the Major Prophets—Isaiah, Jeremiah, and Ezekiel—and the 12 Minor Prophets, beginning with Hosea. Daniel is considered one of the Major Prophets in the English Bible, but in the Hebrew canon, that book is part of what is called the "Writings."

One reason that the list of 39 books of the Old Testament below may be helpful is that Bible-related clues often ask for a book that precedes or follows another. These are listed below.

Genesis	Ecclesiastes
Exodus	Song of Solomon
Leviticus	Isaiah
Numbers	Jeremiah
Deuteronomy	Lamentations
Joshua	Ezekiel
Judges	Daniel
Ruth	Hosea
1 Samuel	Joel
2 Samuel	Amos
1 Kings	Obadiah
2 Kings	Jonah
1 Chronicles	Micah
2 Chronicles	Nahum
Ezra	Habakkuk
Nehemiah	Zephaniah
Esther	Haggai
Job	Zechariah
Psalms	Malachi
Proverbs	

LITERATURE

In this section and in "Poetry," which follows, authors are classified in the genre in which they are most popular in puzzles. For example, Shakespeare is known for his sonnets, but even more for his plays, so he is included only in this section, which includes playwrights. Other writers are more problematic, such as Joseph Addison, essayist, dramatist, and poet, whose name will be found here in this section, as well as Thomas Hardy, also a poet. On the other hand, John Dryden was a poet, dramatist, and critic, and he will be found in "Poetry," especially since he was a poet laureate. And Edgar Allan Poe will also be found there, in spite of his many tales, macabre and otherwise, because it is his poetry that most frequently appears in crosswords. Names of authors in this section are in bold type for quick recognition; the convention of capitalization for crosswords entries of authors is suspended for this and the "Poetry" section.

The most common "literature" answer in crosswords seems to be ELIA, Charles **Lamb**'s pseudonym for some of his works. They have been collected in two volumes: *The Essays of Elia* (1823) and *The Last Essays of Elia* (1833). In fact, if "essay" is in a clue, chances are the answer will be Elia. A word close in construction is Elea, the home of Zeno, the Greek philosopher; both Zeno and Elea have appeared as mutual clues and answers. (There was also another, but later, Zeno, who was from Citium.)

Speaking of the Greeks, **Aesop** appears in crosswords, usually clued by the term "fabulist"; his animal fables had MORALS as their lessons. About 600 years later lived **Plutarch**, a Platonist philosopher of Rome, who has been clued by *Private Lives*, also called *The Parallel Lives* as well as *Lives of the Noble Greeks and Romans*. The Anglo-Saxon monk and historian known as the Venerable **Bede** is also found in puzzles. He lived in the seventh and eighth centuries C.E. and is known for his *Ecclesiastical History of the English Nation*, written in Latin; he is sometimes referred to as Saint Bede. Beginning with the paragraph below, authors are listed in order of their dates of birth. This classification should help with clues such as "18th century author of ___."

About two millennia after Aesop, Don Miguel de **Cervantes**, the great Spanish poet, playwright, and novelist, was born in 1547. His famous novel, *Don Quixote*, a satire on chivalry, usually elicits the don's home, La MANCHA, his love, DULCINEA, or his horse,

ROCINANTE. His so-called squire, Sancho Panza, is his faithful but realistic companion, who rides a mule. Cervantes' contemporary in England, who died on April 23, 1616, the next day after Cervantes, was William Shakespeare.

Some of **Shakespeare**'s characters are quite common in crosswords: the villain IAGO, an ensign to Othello (who was a MOOR); Iago's wife, EMILIA; King LEAR, often referred to as tragic and usually clued as "Father of Regan," "Father of Cordelia," or "Father of Goneril," from the eponymous play (his loyal follower, KENT, also appears, as does one of his sons-in-law, ALBANY); and ROMEO, JULIET, and MERCUTIO with all their vowels. At least one puzzle required Romeo's family name of MONTAGUE, but Juliet's is more frequent: CAPULET.

Several other names from Shakespeare are Prospero's servant, ARIEL, from "The Tempest"; Prince HAL, who became King Henry V, from various plays; KATE (or more formally, Katharina), who is the shrew in "The Taming of the Shrew"; Sir TOBY Belch, from "Twelfth Night"; and Puck's master, OBERON, king of the fairies and spouse of TITANIA, from "A Midsummer Night's Dream." Hamlet's nationality is sometimes an answer: he was a DANE. Other characters from "Hamlet" are his mother GERTRUDE; the son and daughter of POLONIUS, namely, LAERTES and OPHELIA; and Hamlet's friend, HORATIO. And can you believe that, of all Shakespearean possibilities, several constructors asked us what Hamlet smelled: ARAT (a rat).

It helps to know that Macbeth was THANE of Cawdor and that he was haunted by the ghost of BANQUO, but who remembers that he was buried on the small island of IONA? Several actual Shakespearean settings have occurred, namely, VERONA ("Two Gentlemen from Verona") and PADUA ("The Taming of the Shrew"), as well as the fictional forest of ARDEN in "As You Like It." Speaking of the last, one of its characters, CELIA, the daughter of Frederick and the love of Oliver, appears in puzzles now and then. A very popular Shakespeare-related answer is AVON, for the river that flows through his birthplace, Stratford-upon-Avon. (And it has also helped to know that "avon" is the Celtic word for "river.") His contemporary, Ben **Jonson**, although living more than two decades longer, is sometimes clued by his play, "Volpone," or by his poem, "Song to CELIA." The latter is the source of the lyrics of the popular English song, "Drink to Me Only with Thine Eyes."

Moving to those born in the 17th century, Pierre **Corneille** is usually the clue for his tragic play, "Le CID," and another of his plays is "Horace." Jean Baptiste Poquelin **Molière** is usually clued by his comedies "Tartuffe," "The Misanthrope," "The School for Wives," "The Miser," or "The Bourgeois Gentleman." He not only wrote his plays, but acted in them. Born about a decade later was Samuel **Pepys**, with the obvious clue his diary; he has also been clued by the Great Plague, the Great Fire of London, and by two of his signature phrases, namely, "Up this morning . . ." and "And so to bed." Sometimes the latter phrase is clued by two of its words, leaving the other two to be solved. The third great French dramatist after Corneille and Molière was Jean **Racine**. He is clued by one of his tragedies, such as "Phèdre," "Andromaque," or "Athalie."

The novelist and journalist Daniel **Defoe** is clued by his castaway character, Friday, in *Robinson Crusoe*, as well as by *Moll Flanders*; he also wrote *Journal of the Plague Year*. Two near-contemporaries of Defoe were Jonathan **Swift**, satirist and poet, and Sir Richard **Steele**, founder and editor of "The Tatler." He later founded "The Spectator" with his friend and former classmate Joseph **Addison**, a politician, playwright, essayist, and poet. They were born in the same year, 1672. There have been obvious plays on Swift's name as the first word in a clue, but one of the answers associated with his name (since he was a satirist) is IRONY. He was the author of *Gulliver's Travels* as well as the two satirical essays, "A Modest Proposal" and "A Tale of a TUB."

Born about 13 years after Steele and Addison was John **Gay**, a poet and playwright, nearly always clued by "The Beggar's Opera," a ballad opera in three acts. But he himself has been the clue for his opera, POLLY. He also wrote the libretto to Handel's "Acis and Galatea." Samuel **Richardson** is usually the clue for *PAMELA*, considered by some as the first modern English novel. Although he was a prolific writer, François Marie Arouet **Voltaire** is found in crosswords only for his satire, *Candide*, and in it, only for Dr. PANGLOSS, Candide's mentor. He also wrote *The Philosophical Dictionary*.

As for those born in the 18th century, Henry **Fielding** is best remembered for his novels *Joseph Andrews* and *The History of Tom Jones: A Foundling*, as well as for his play, "Tom Thumb: A Tragedy." And his name has been the clue for his last novel, *AMELIA*, with its four vowels. The philosopher Jean-Jacques **Rousseau**'s novel, *EMILE*, is frequently found in puzzles, and it has helped to know that Rousseau was born in Switzerland.

Laurence **Sterne** is nearly always clued by his popular novel, *Tristram Shandy*, a precursor of later stream-of-consciousness novels, but another that has been used is *A Sentimental Journey Through France and Italy*. James **Boswell** is usually clued as the biographer of Samuel Johnson (*The Life of Samuel Johnson*), but he has also been clued as a diarist. Richard **Sheridan**, Irish poet and playwright, is known for his play, "The School for Scandal," but his name is nearly always the clue for his play, "The RIVALS," with its amusing character, Mrs. MALAPROP.

Sir Walter **Scott**'s *IVANHOE* and *WAVERLEY* are the novels needed most frequently for his crossword entries, but he also wrote *Rob Roy*, *The Lady of the Lake*, and *The Bride of Lammermoor*. It is helpful to remember that Ivanhoe's bride was ROWENA. One of the most popular characters in puzzles is Jane **Austen**'s EMMA Woodhouse, from the novel, *Emma*, followed in popularity, perhaps, by Mr. DARCY, from *Pride and Prejudice*; the heroine, Elizabeth BENNET, has also appeared. The author herself has been clued by these as well as by *Persuasion* and *Sense and Sensibility*. From the latter, the sisters are ELINOR and MARIANNE.

Stendahl, whose real name was Marie Henri Beyle, is nearly always associated in puzzles with Julian SOREL, his character in *The Red and the Black*. Mary **Shelley** will probably always be linked in puzzles with her novel, *Frankenstein*, and born in the last year of the century was Honoré de **Balzac**, who is usually associated with *Le Père Goriot* or *La Comédie Humaine*. Aleksandr **Pushkin**, perhaps Russia's greatest poet, is sometimes in crosswords for his poetry, but usually for his verse novel, *Eugene Onegin*, or for *Boris Godunov*, a drama written largely in blank verse.

Concerning writers born in the 19th century, the novelist Victor **Hugo**'s most popular character is the hunchback IGOR, from *Notre Dame de Paris*, known in English as *The Hunchback of Notre Dame*. He also wrote *Les Misérables*, for which the characters JEAN Valjean and JAVERT are the most frequent in crosswords. Alexandre **Dumas** (père) wrote *The Three Musketeers*, *The Count of Monte Cristo*, and *La Reine Margot*. The only Dumas character in puzzles has been ATHOS, a swordsman in several of his novels. Ralph Waldo **Emerson** appears now and then, and if the word "essay" is in a clue and the answer is seven letters long, it may well be EMERSON, the "Sage of Concord." One of his early essays was titled "Nature," on the philosophy of Transcendentalism; others were "Self-Reliance," "The Oversoul," and "Circles."

Nathaniel **Hawthorne** was born the year after Emerson, and most clues relate to *The Scarlet Letter* or to *The House of the Seven Gables*. In the former, it has helped to know that Hester Prynne's daughter was named PEARL and that Hester was required to wear a REDA (red A); in the latter, puzzles have required the setting, which is SALEM. Five years later Nicolai **Gogol**, founder of realism in Russian literature, was born. He is clued either by his novel, *Taras Bulba*, or by his satirical novel on political corruption, *Dead Souls*.

Harriet Beecher **Stowe** was the author of the most widely published book of the 19th century, except for the Bible; this was the antislavery novel, *Uncle Tom's Cabin*, first published in 1852. The character from the book that appears in crosswords the most is Little EVA, sometimes clued as "heroine" or as "Uncle Tom's charge"; other characters are ELIZA, TOPSY, Aunt CHLOE (Uncle Tom's wife), and the villain, Simon LEGREE. Another of her novels in crosswords is *Dred: A Tale of the Great Dismal Swamp*; the entry is always DRED. William MAKEPEACE **Thackeray** is usually clued by *Vanity Fair: A Novel Without a Hero*. Two of his other novels are *The Virginians* and *Pendennis*.

The many novels of Charles **Dickens** include such characters as PIP, TINYTIM (Tiny Tim), SMIKE, Mr. GUPPY, ABEL Magwitch, Mr. PICKWICK, AGEDP (Aged P. or Aged Parent), URIAH Heep (who was Mr. Wilkins MICAWBER's employer and a law clerk for Mr. Wickfield), SETH Pecksniff, the villain FAGIN, Barnaby RUDGE, Little Dorrit (whose name was AMY), Little NELL, DORA (the first Mrs. Copperfield), and AGNES (the second)—a very limited sample. It is helpful to remember that Bob Cratchit was a CLERK and that Ebenezer Scrooge's retort was BAH (if three letters) and BAHHUMBUG (Bah! Humbug!) (if nine letters). And Scrooge's nephew was FRED. Remember, too, that the ghost of JACOB Marley appeared to Scrooge. The character ADA, from *Bleak House*, also appears. Two bits of trivia that appear in puzzles: (1) Dickens's pen name for many of his works was BOZ (*Sketches by Boz*, 1833-1836, a collection of stories written originally for the newspaper and published in 1836 in two volumes) and (2) of his ten children, one was named DORA.

Charlotte **Brontë**'s *Jane EYRE* is frequently in crosswords; she is usually clued as a governess (to Adele Varens, both clue and answer), but has also been clued by her employer (and later, suitor), Mr. Rochester. Brontë's first novel has also appeared: *The Professor: A Tale*. And every now and then one of her sisters, Emily (who wrote *Wuthering Heights*) or Anne (who wrote *Agnes Gray*), also novelists and poets, are mentioned. Their brother, Branwell, has yet to be found in puzzles. Whenever **Turgenev** appears in puzzles, only his first name is needed: IVAN. His most famous novel was *Fathers and Sons*.

Herman **Melville**'s character, Captain AHAB (who has a peg leg), from *Moby-Dick*, is popular, sometimes clued as "Moby-Dick's foe" or "Whale's foe" and once as "Accursed white whale pursuer." The fact that he was employed by the captains Peleg and Bildad has also been a clue. Of the many other memorable characters in the novel, only the narrator and survivor, ISHMAEL, seems to make his way into puzzles, although Ahab's ship, the PEQUOD, has appeared. Melville's most popular novel for crosswords, however, is *OMOO*, with its predecessor, *TYPEE*, a close second. Two clues for *Omoo* are "South Seas" and "1847," its publication date. Rarely has Captain "Starry" VERE appeared, from *Billy Budd*.

George **Eliot**'s miserly SILAS Marner (his town of Raveloe is sometimes a clue) is her most frequent character, followed by the novel's foundling, his adopted daughter, EPPIE; other novels are *ADAM BEDE* and *MIDDLEMARCH*. Her first published collection of fictional stories, "Scenes from Clerical Life," also appears. Sometimes a puzzle will have her real name as clue or answer: Mary Ann(e) Evans.

Born in 1821, Feodor **Dostoyevsky** was the author of such novels as *Crime and Punishment* and *The Brothers Karamazov*; from the latter, IVAN is the most popular character. But in crosswords Dostoyevsky is best known for his novel, *The IDIOT*. Gustave **Flaubert**'s EMMA Bovary (from *Madame Bovary*) is a frequent entry. Jules **Verne** is sometimes referred to as the father of science fiction. His most well-known character is the skipper of the submarine "Nautilus," Captain NEMO (once clued as a megalomaniac), from *20,000 Leagues Under the Sea*. Other novels that serve as clues for Verne are *Journey to the Center of the Earth* and *Around the World in Eighty Days*. From the latter, PHILEAS Fogg and his valet, Passepartout, are pursued by FIX, a private detective.

The Norwegian playwright Henrik **Ibsen**'s most popular heroine in puzzles is NORA, the wife of Torvald Helmer, from "A Doll's House"; she is as well known in puzzles as Flaubert's Emma. Other clues and answers are Ibsen's home, OSLO, and "Hedda Gabler," "The Wild Duck," "Ghosts," and "Peer Gynt" (whose mother, ASE, has appeared in many puzzles). If a five-letter answer is ever needed from "Peer Gynt," try TROLL. Also from the same work is the Arabian princess, ANITRA. Leo **Tolstoy**'s most popular character is ANNA, from *Anna Karenina* (in English, sometimes shortened to *Anna Karenin*); her lover, ALEXEI, has also been found. The heroine NATASHA, from *War and Peace*, has appeared, and *The Cossacks* has been a clue for Tolstoy.

Lewis **Carroll** was the pen name of Charles Dodgson. Answers from *Through the Looking-Glass* are ALICE and the cat, DINAH. On occasion, the tea party from *Alice's Adventures in Wonderland* is in a clue; some of its participants were the HATTER, the March HARE, the Cheshire CAT, the white RABBIT (who has been clued by "I'm late") and the DORMOUSE. It has also helped to know the name of the illustrator, John TENNIEL. The author has been clued by his poem, "Jabberwock(y)."

The sisters in Louisa May **Alcott**'s *Little Women* are needed from time to time; they are JO, AMY, MEG, and BETH (the acronym JAMB, as in door or window jamb, is a useful mnemonic). It also helps to know that Meg is the eldest of the March girls, followed by Jo, Beth (Elizabeth), and Amy. Their mother MARMEE (Margaret) also appears in puzzles. The Mississippi River is sometimes in clues for Mark **Twain**'s characters: TOM Sawyer, HUCK(leberry) Finn, INJUN Joe, and DANL (Dan'l), the jumping frog. And Tom's Aunt Polly has been a clue for Twain's name, as has the novel *Pudd'nhead Wilson*. On occasion, Twain's actual name will be in a clue or answer: Samuel Langhorne Clemens. It has also helped to know that he is buried in ELMIRA, New York.

If California mining towns or gold-rush stories are in a clue, the answer is usually BRET or HARTE (Bret **Harte**). He is associated with the genre of local color and "The Luck of Roaring Camp" is his most frequent clue, but "The Outcasts of Poker Flat" is also well known. A very common clue and answer are **Zola** (Emile Zola, who defended Alfred Dreyfus) and his novel, *NANA*, which was the ninth of his 20-volume series, *Les Rougon-Macquart*. The seventh in the series, *The Dram Shop*, has also been a clue for his name. Zola was a proponent of naturalism in fiction.

Thomas **Hardy**'s TESS (from *Tess of the D'Urbervilles*) is very popular in crosswords; she has been clued as "Hardy's 'Pure Woman'" and as "Hardy's dairymaid," among others. She was seduced by ALEC, who has been clued as a villain; she later killed him. The only other Hardy character found by the author was JUDE (from *Jude the Obscure*), sometimes clued as "Hardy hero"; Jude's love interest was SUE. Joel Chandler **Harris** is usually linked with *Uncle Remus: His Songs and His Sayings*.

Looking ahead 30 years from the publication of *Uncle Remus*, the Nobel Prize for Literature was first awarded in 1901; and the first Pulitzer Prize for Fiction was awarded in 1916. The Nobel Prize is awarded to an author without regard to a specific work. On the other hand, a Pulitzer Prize cites a specific work; examples are William Faulkner's *A Fable* and *The Reivers*, which won Pulitzers in 1955 and 1963, respectively; he also won a Nobel in 1949. Because clues also often include the year of award, these additional data items make it somewhat easy to find the answer in various almanacs.

Oscar **Wilde**, the Irish-born novelist, playwright, and poet, is usually clued by his only novel, *The Picture of Dorian Gray*. Three of his plays that have appeared in puzzles are "The Importance of Being Earnest," "Salome," and "An Ideal Husband." His poem, "The Ballad of Reading Gaol," was his last one. Another of his poems that has appeared is "By the ARNO." Born two years later was the critic and playwright George Bernard **Shaw** (Nobel, 1925), also Irish; his plays include "Arms and the Man," "Pygmalion," "Major Barbara," "Man and Superman," and "Saint Joan." Of the Polish-born British novelist Joseph **Conrad**'s works, the most popular in crosswords is *NOSTROMO*, but *Lord Jim* and *Heart of Darkness* will also be encountered.

Several of ANTON **Chekhov**'s plays elicit his first name. These are "The Seagull," "Uncle Vanya," "Three Sisters," and "The Cherry Orchard." The last is sometimes a clue for one of its characters, the 17-year-old ANYA, and "Uncle Vanya" is sometimes a clue for the character ELENA, wife of Alexander. From "Three Sisters," the eldest, OLGA, appears in puzzles (the others are Masha and Irina). The anti-hero IVANOV, from the eponymous play, has also been an entry; it was Chekhov's first full-length play.

J.M. (James Matthew) **Barrie** is known for his novels and his play, "Peter Pan," whose eponymous character can fly and who never ages. Peter and his friend, WENDY, have many adventures on the island of Neverland. Another friend is Tinker Bell, a fairy. The dog NANA takes care of the children. The character SMEE, a sidekick of Peter's archenemy, the pirate Captain James HOOK, who sails on the Jolly Roger, is the most frequent crossword entry from the play; he has been described as a "baddie."

Edith **Wharton**, the American novelist, won a Pulitzer Prize in 1921 for *The Age of Innocence*. Also popular was *The House of Mirth*, but in crosswords she is best known for her novel, *ETHAN FROME* (both first and last names in crossword answers). William Sydney Porter, known as **O. Henry** for his short stories, was the author of "The Gift of the Magi" and "The Ransom of Red Chief." His only novel was *Cabbages and Kings*. The O. Henry Award is given annually for outstanding short stories.

Rudyard **Kipling** (Nobel, 1907) seems to be known in puzzles mainly for his novel about an orphan, *KIM*, but the hero, MOWGLI, the wolf-pack leader, AKELA, and the snake, KAA, from *The Jungle Book*, also appear, as does the snake's sound, SSS. Kipling's poem, "Gunga Din," has also been in puzzles, and it has helped to know that Gunga Din's burden was WATER (he was a water-bearer).

H.G. **Wells** is known for his science-fiction novels, such as *War of the Worlds*, *The Island of Doctor Moreau*, and *The Time Machine*; in the last are two post-human races, of which only the ELOI make it into puzzles (the other is the Morlocks). John **Galsworthy** (Nobel, 1932), novelist and playwright, is usually clued by his series of three novels, separated by two "interludes," known collectively as *The Forsyte Saga*. American novelist Frank **Norris**, who died at age 32, wrote *McTeague* and *The Pit*, both of which have appeared in puzzles.

The pen name of the British short story writer H.H. **Munro** is SAKI and the Irish poet and playwright John Millington **Synge** is nearly always clued by *The Playboy of the Western World*, but *Riders to the Sea* has also been a clue. Theodore **Dreiser** has been clued by *An American Tragedy* and by *Sister Carrie*; from the latter, the character Robert (Bob) AMES has been in puzzles.

WILLA **Cather**, a Nebraskan, wrote many novels of frontier life, and *One of Ours* won a Pulitzer Prize in 1923. Cather's other novels include the prairie trilogy, namely, *O Pioneers!*, *Song of the Lark*, and *My Ántonia*. Two others are *The Professor's House* and *Death Comes for the Archbishop*. SOMERSET **Maugham**, the British writer, is usually clued by his novel, *Of Human Bondage*. Gertrude **Stein**, an American writer and poet who spent most of her life in France, is usually associated with her famous statement concerning a ROSE, but *The Autobiography of Alice B. Toklas* is used as a clue to her name. Clues to the German novelist Thomas **Mann** (Nobel, 1929) nearly always relate to *Death in Venice*, *Doctor Faustus*, *Buddenbrooks*, or *The Magic Mountain*.

The German-born Swiss novelist and poet Hermann **Hesse** (Nobel, 1946) is usually clued by *Demian*, *Siddartha*, *Steppenwolf*, or *Magister Ludi*. The American writer and reformer UPTON **Sinclair** is nearly always clued by either *The Jungle*, a novel about exploitation by factory owners, or the stockyards of Chicago, but in one of his novels, *OIL!*, the family name of ROSS has been needed. A character from E.M. **Forster**'s *A Passage to India* is frequent in crosswords; she is ADELA Quested (the character on trial in the novel is Dr. AZIZ). *Howards End*, *A Room with a View*, and *Maurice* are also clues to FORSTER. Born in 1880 was the Irish playwright SEAN **O'Casey**, perhaps best known for his "Dublin Trilogy," composed of "Juno and the Paycock," "The Shadow of a Gunman," and "The Plough and the Stars."

A.A. (Alan Alexander) **Milne**'s *Winnie-the-Pooh*, who is a teddy BEAR, is common in crosswords; not as frequent is Pooh's friend, EEYORE, an old gray donkey, who has been described as gloomy. Others you may come across are Baby Roo, Kanga (his mother), Piglet, Tigger, Owl, Rabbit, Gopher, and Christopher Robin. They live in Hundred Acre Wood, sometimes a clue. "Oh, Bother!" has appeared in puzzles; it is one of Pooh's expressions. Two of Milne's plays, "The Great Broxopp" and "Mr. Pim Passes By," have also been in puzzles. In the former, the play was a clue to MILNE, while, in the latter, being absent-minded was a clue for Mr. PIM. As another clue to his name, Milne's autobiography has been cited: *It's Too Late Now*.

Virginia **Woolf** has been clued by her novels, *Mrs. Dalloway* and *To the Lighthouse*, as well as by one of her collections of essays, "A Room of One's Own." Franz **Kafka** was born the year after Woolf; clues to his name are usually one of his stories, such as "The Metamorphosis" or "In the Penal Colony," or one of his novels, such as *The Trial*, *The Castle*, or *Amerika*, the last of which was published posthumously by his biographer and literary executor, Max Brod. The heroine, OLGA, of *The Castle*, has appeared in crosswords. Sinclair **Lewis** (Nobel, 1930) is cited most often for his novels, such as *Main Street*, *Babbitt*, *Arrowsmith*, and *Elmer Gantry*. He was the first American to win a Nobel Prize for Literature.

The Danish author Baroness Karen Blixen, whose pseudonym was ISAK **Dinesen**, is frequently in puzzles. On several occasions the solution was not her pen name, but her given name. *Out of Africa* is most commonly cited, but one of her stories is also popular: "Babette's Feast." The British novelist D.H. (David Herbert) **Lawrence** is typically clued by one of his novels, such as *Sons and Lovers*, *Women in Love*, or *Lady Chatterley's Lover*.

The American novelist EDNA **Ferber** is popular in puzzles (especially her first name); she won a Pulitzer in 1924 for *So Big*, but other popular works were *Show Boat* and *Giant*. Her novel, *Ice Palace*, about Alaska, has also appeared in puzzles. The American playwright Eugene **O'Neill** (Nobel, 1936) wrote "Mourning Becomes Electra," "A Moon for the

Misbegotten," "Desire Under the Elms," "Beyond the Horizon," and "Long Day's Journey into Night"; the last won him his fourth Pulitzer in 1957. The character Willie OBAN, from "The Iceman Cometh," has appeared in crosswords. Many puzzles have required O'Neill's daughter's name, OONA; she became the fourth wife of Sir Charles Chaplin.

ENID **Bagnold** is usually in puzzles for her 1935 novel, *National Velvet*, about a girl named Velvet and her PIEBALD horse, who wins the Grand National steeplechase. Some may remember the characters more from the movie of the same name, with the young Elizabeth Taylor. Bagnold was also a playwright; two of her better-known plays are "The Chalk Garden" and "A Matter of Gravity."

The Russian novelist and poet Boris **Pasternak** (Nobel, 1958, which was declined) is represented in crosswords by his novel, *Doctor Zhivago*. The heroine LARA is the most frequent answer, but YURI, the protagonist of the title, also appears. Pearl S. **Buck** (Nobel, 1938) is usually linked to *The Good Earth* (Pulitzer, 1932), and her heroine OLAN is frequently an answer. Both the first and last names of the American screenwriter, playwright, and author Anita **Loos** are used as clues and answers; she adapted her novel, *Gentlemen Prefer Blondes*, into a film. The heroine of her stories that were published in *Harper's Bazaar*, Lorelei Lee, has also been a clue to the author's name.

J.R.R. **Tolkien**'s *The Hobbit* and its sequel, *The Lord of the Rings*, are found in puzzles. The most frequent answer is ENTS, which are usually clued as "Tolkien creatures" or "forest creatures"; they live in Fangorn Forest. The eldest and most prominent of the ents is TREEBEARD. FRODO is the protagonist in *The Lord of the Rings*; he was adopted by his cousin, BILBO Baggins, and has been clued as a ring-bearer. You may also come across ORCS, which are usually described in clues as baddies or villains or soldiers of Saruman. Zora NEALE **Hurston**, whose fiction and nonfiction concern the African-American experience in the South, needs only her middle name. If a clue is "U.S.A.," the author is John **Dos Passos**. F. SCOTT **Fitzgerald** is usually clued by one of his novels, such as *The Great Gatsby*, *The Beautiful and Damned*, or *Tender Is the Night*.

A character from William **Faulkner**'s (Nobel, 1949) *As I Lay Dying* has been needed on several occasions; this is ANSE, the patriarch of the Bundren family. Another Faulkner character is EULA Varner, sometimes clued as a femme fatale or as a vixen, from *The Hamlet* and other stories. If you come across anyone named Snopes in a puzzle, there are many of them in Faulkner's novels. One of his short stories, "A Rose for Emily," has also appeared. Federico **García Lorca**, the Spanish dramatist and poet, has been clued by two of his plays: "The House of Bernardo Alba" and "Blood Wedding."

C.S. **Lewis** is perhaps best remembered for his series of seven books for children, *The Chronicles of Narnia*, whose central character is the beneficent ASLAN, known as the "Greatest Lion." *The Allegory of Love* has also appeared. Ernest **Hemingway** (Nobel, 1954), usually needs only his nickname, PAPA, in puzzles. *The Old Man and the Sea* won a Pulitzer in 1953. Some other novels are *The Sun Also Rises* (the protagonist, JAKE Barnes, has been an entry), *A Farewell to Arms*, *For Whom the Bell Tolls*, and *A Moveable Feast*.

Vladimir **Nabokov** usually needs the title of his novel, *ADA*, although *PNIN* has also appeared. *Pale Fire* is a novel, but is written as a 999-line poem. *Lolita* is not that popular in crosswords, even with its three vowels. His autobiography has also been a clue: *Speak, Memory*.

The first of these authors to be born in the 20th century was John **Steinbeck** (Nobel, 1962). He is often clued by *The Grapes of Wrath* (Pulitzer, 1940); its hero, Tom JOAD, is sometimes an answer. *The Red Pony* has also been a clue, with the boy JODY the solution, and *Tortilla Flat* has been a clue for Steinbeck's name. Two characters from *East of Eden* are the brothers CALEB and ARON; another is Aron's love interest, ABRA, sometimes described as a temptress. ("Aron" is more frequently in crosswords, though, as the middle name of Elvis Presley, as that is the name in his birth records.) Sometimes a clue relating to Steinbeck results in OKIES.

Anaïs **Nin** is usually linked to her work, *The Diary of Anaïs Nin*, with DIARY the answer if the clue is her name, but she herself has been clued by *Delta of Venus*, *House of Incest*, and *Little Birds*. Contemporary with the three authors above, but not living as long, was the novelist and essayist George **Orwell**, whose birth name was Eric Arthur Blair; his clues are usually *Animal Farm* or *1984*. For the latter, OCEANIA has been in puzzles; the other two land areas are Eastasia and Eurasia. A British-born American, Christopher **Isherwood**, is usually linked to *CABARET*, a musical and then a film, based on *The Berlin Stories*, which consisted of two of his short novels: "Goodbye to Berlin" and "Mr. Norris Changes Trains." An earlier play and then a film, also based on *The Berlin Stories*, is "I Am a Camera," which also appears in puzzles.

The French philosopher Jean-Paul **Sartre**'s (Nobel, 1957, which was declined) clues are usually one of his plays, such as "No Exit," or one of his novels, such as *Nausea*. His autobiography (of a portion of his life) has appeared in puzzles: *Les Mots*, or *Words*. Samuel **Beckett** (Nobel, 1969) is best known for his play, "Waiting for GODOT." Others were "Krapp's Last Tape," "Endgame," and "Happy Days." Clifford **Odets** wrote plays and movie scripts on the subject of social justice, such as "Waiting for Lefty," "Golden Boy," "Sweet Smell of Success," and "The Big Knife."

William **Saroyan** wrote the short story, "The Daring Young Man on the Flying Trapeze," and the play, "The Time of Your Life" (Pulitzer, 1940, which he refused), as well as novels, such as *The Human Comedy*. EUDORA **Welty** wrote about rural southern life; *The Optimist's Daughter* won a Pulitzer in 1973. She has also been clued by her novel, *Delta Wedding*. James **Agee**'s autobiographical novel, *A Death in the Family*, won a posthumous Pulitzer in 1958. *Let Us Now Praise Famous Men* is about tenant farmers in the South. Sometimes clued as a critic, his name is extremely popular in crosswords.

Lawrence **Durrell** is typically clued by his series of novels, *The Alexandria Quartet*. They are *Justine*, *Balthazar*, *Mountolive*, and *Clea*; the character CLEA is his most frequent entry. The "playwright of the Midwest," William **Inge**, is clued by "Bus Stop," "Picnic," or "Come Back, Little Sheba." He won a Pulitzer for "Picnic" in 1953. Albert **Camus** (Nobel, 1957) has been clued by some of his novels, such as *The Plague* and *The Stranger*. He also wrote plays, nonfiction, short stories, and essays. Of the last, only "The Myth of Sisyphus" seems to appear in puzzles.

J.D. **Salinger** is best known for *The Catcher in the Rye*, with its protagonist, HOLDEN Caulfield. More popular in puzzles, however, is ESME, from his short story, "For Esmé—With Love and Squalor." She is usually clued as "Salinger girl." Also encountered are Franny and Zooey, the former from a short story and the latter from a novella; they were subsequently combined into a book titled *Franny and Zooey*.

Jack **Kerouac** is typically clued by the Beat Generation or his autobiographical novel, *On the Road*. Edward **Albee**'s "Who's Afraid of Virginia Woolf?" is usually a clue for his last name, but other plays are "The Zoo Story," "The Sandbox," "Three Tall Women," "Tiny Alice," "A Delicate Balance," and "The Lady from Dubuque." He won three Pulitzers: in 1967, 1975, and 1994. One of the most frequent 20th century names in crosswords is that of the essayist and novelist ELIE **Wiesel** (Nobel Peace Prize, 1986). TONI **Morrison** (Nobel, 1993) received a Pulitzer in 1988 for her novel, *Beloved*. Some others are *Sula*, *Jazz*, *A Mercy*, and *Song of Solomon*.

Another answer is ANON (for "anonymous"). More trivia, but necessary to know: the annual literary mystery award is the EDGAR, named for Edgar Allan Poe; it was first awarded in 1946, a clue. The sci-fi award is the HUGO and the romance writer's award is the RITA. Except for Aesop, Plutarch, and the Venerable Bede, the above is just a smattering from a period of about 400 years. Constructors give us such a small sample of our rich literature.

Poetry

For all their quotability, poetic lines seldom find their way into crosswords; this may be due to the limited space requirements of a clue. The earliest poem in a modern European language seems to be the epic "Beowulf." The protagonist was one of the warriors from the Baltic region who invaded England after the Romans left, in the early 6th century C.E. Likely written early in the 8th century, it combines history and legend. Beowulf's activities include slaying the monster GRENDEL, a giant cannibal living in a cave, as well as Grendel's dam (mother) and a fire-spitting DRAGON.

Except for the ancients, such as Homer, the earliest poet's name in puzzles seems to be OMAR **Khayyám**, of Persia, clued by his *Rubáiyát* ("A book of verses underneath the bough/ a jug of wine, a loaf of bread—and thou . . ."), but on occasion as "FitzGerald's poet," because of Edward J. FitzGerald's several translations (a sample is immediately above). It has helped to know that Khayyám was also an astronomer and mathematician (two clues to his first name).

Dante Alighieri, about 200 years later (1265-1321), is somewhat more popular in puzzles, and his clue is usually something related to "The Divine Comedy" or Virgil (his guide through Inferno and Purgatorio) or Beatrice (his guide through Paradiso). Each of the three is divided into CANTOs or canticles, 34 for "Inferno" and 33 for each of the others. Another clue for Dante is "La Vita Nuova," or "The New Life," written in a combination of poetry and prose. LETHE, the river in "The Divine Comedy," also appears. **Petrarch** (Francesco Petrarca) came along about 40 years later, and if the clue relates to an Italian sonnet form or to his "Canzoniere," you have the answer.

Geoffrey **Chaucer** was born about 35 years after Petrarch, and his clues and answers nearly always relate to his "Canterbury Tales," such as those of his pilgrims, some of whom are the FRIAR, the COOK, the

REEVE, and the MILLER. Some others are the MONK, the knight, the wife of BATH, the pardoner, the prioress, and the CLERK.

Edmund **Spenser** is usually clued by "The Faerie Queene," his epic but uncompleted poem in praise of Queen Elizabeth I, with its many characters, three of which are UNA (its heroine), ALMA, and ATE. IRENA has also appeared, clued by the villain, Grantorto. John **Donne** ("No man is an island . . .") has been clued as "Metaphysical poet," and "Twickenham Garden" has also been a clue for his name.

The poets above and below are listed in the order of their birth dates. John **Milton**, the first of those to be born in the 17th century, is sometimes clued by his blindness or by his epic poem, "Paradise Lost," and its sequel, "Paradise Regained," as well as by "Samson Agonistes," a tragedy, and "Lycidas," a pastoral elegy. His use of ancient language has also been a clue. Two early English poets laureate appear in puzzles: Nahum **Tate**, appointed in 1692, and Nicholas **Rowe**, in 1715. Alexander **Pope** has been clued by his epic poem, "The Dunciad," as well as by his translations of Homer. From "The Rape of the Lock," the head sylph, ARIEL, has been in puzzles.

As for those born in the 18th century, Thomas **Gray** is usually linked to his "ELEGY Written in a Country Churchyard." One of the trees mentioned in the poem has been in crosswords: the ELM. Johann Wolfgang von **Goethe** is typically clued by his dramatic poem, "Faust"; it is part poem and part play. William **Blake**, also an artist, is linked with "The Lamb" and with his poem that begins, "Tyger! Tyger! burning bright . . . ." His poems such as "The Marriage of Heaven and Hell" and "Songs of Innocence" are mystical.

Robert **Burns** is sometimes in a clue when a Scottish word is needed for an answer, such as BRAE, for "hillside." Conversely, "Auld Lang Syne" has been a clue for BURNS. Other poems are "To a Mouse," "To a Louse," and "A Red, Red Rose." Johann C.F. von **Schiller** has been associated with his poem "Ode to Joy," but he was also a dramatist and historian. (He and Goethe are recognized as the two giants of German literature.) William **Wordsworth**, poet laureate, has appeared with "Tintern Abbey" ("Lines Composed a Few Miles Above Tintern Abbey") as well as "I Wandered Lonely as a Cloud," which is also well known.

If his friend Samuel Taylor **Coleridge** is in a clue, the answer will usually be RIME, from "The Rime [Rhyme] of the Ancient Mariner." Another Coleridge-related answer is XANADU, from his poem, "Kubla Khan." Xanadu's sacred river is the ALPH. George Gordon (Lord

Byron) is known especially for "Don Juan," "Manfred," "The Prisoner of Chillon," and "Childe Harold's Pilgrimage."

Percy BYSSHE **Shelley** also appears, and the answer for Shelley is usually his middle name. Several of his poems, namely, "Ozymandias," "Queen Mab," "Ode to the West Wind," and "To a Skylark," have been clues for his name, as has "The Cenci," a play. The American poet William Cullen **Bryant**, abolitionist, critic, and editor-in-chief of the *New York Evening Post* (founded by Alexander Hamilton), might be clued by "Thanatopsis," "To a Fringed Gentian," or "To a Waterfowl."

If John **Keats** is in a clue, the answer is usually ODE, based on his "Ode on a Grecian Urn." ODE is the most frequent poetic entry in puzzles, and the strange word, ODIST, for poet, has appeared several times. URN appears, too, probably because of Keats's poem. He has also been clued by his poem titled "The Eve of St. Agnes," but there are many others, such as "Endymion," "On First Looking into Chapman's Homer," "To Autumn," and "Ode to a Nightingale." Heinrich **Heine** is nearly always clued by "Die Lorelei," now a famous German folksong, but "Don't Send a Gentleman to London" has also been a clue.

Moving to those born in the 19th century, clues for Henry Wadsworth **Longfellow** usually relate to "The Children's Hour," "The Village Blacksmith," "Tales of a Wayside Inn," "Evangeline," "The Ballad of San Blas," or "The Song of Hiawatha." John GREENLEAF **Whittier**, known for his poems of New England, such as "Snow-Bound," also wrote poems that reflected his opposition to slavery, such as "Voices of Freedom." Puzzles usually need his middle name.

The title of a poem such as "Annabel Lee," "To Helen," "Ulalume," "Berenice," "Eldorado," "The Bells," or "The Raven" (the last with its reference with Lenore) is a clue for Edgar ALLAN **Poe** (either his middle or last name). Alfred, Lord **Tennyson** is in clues with two outcomes: the first is one of his heroines, ENID ("the fair"), and the second is IDYLL, for his poem, "Idylls of the King." (An idyll (or idyl) is a pastoral poem, and has been clued as such.) Other poems are "Crossing the Bar," "The Charge of the Light Brigade," and "Enoch Arden." Elizabeth Barrett **Browning** and her husband, Robert **Browning**, sometimes appear in puzzles, usually linked to her "Sonnets from the Portuguese," which include, in Sonnet XLIII, "How Do I Love Thee? Let Me Count the Ways . . ." and to his "My Last Duchess."

"The Good Gray Poet," WALT **Whitman**, is nearly always clued by "Leaves of Grass," an epic poem using unconventional meter and rhyme, on which he spent much of his life rewriting and supplementing. It includes his poem, "Song of Myself." Another poem used as a clue is "Crossing Brooklyn Ferry." No poet has celebrated the greatness of America as he has.

Although Matthew **Arnold** is known for his critical essays, it is his poetry that one finds in crosswords; examples are "Dover Beach," "Merope: A Tragedy," and "Isolation: To Marguerite." Dante Gabriel **Rossetti**, who was also an artist and a founder of the pre-Raphaelite Brotherhood, is usually clued by his poem titled "The Blessed Damozel."

The author of at least 1,775 poems on nature, love, and death, EMILY **Dickinson** is sometimes clued by her hometown of Amherst, Massachusetts, where she lived the life of a recluse. Some of her poems begin with the words "Because I could not stop for Death . . . ," "I never saw a Moor . . . ," and "How happy is the little Stone . . . ." James Whitcomb **Riley** is typically clued as the "Hoosier poet" or "children's poet." He used speech patterns typical of Indiana, and two of his most popular works are "Little Orphant [sic] Annie" and "The Raggedy Man." The English classical scholar and poet A.E. (Alfred Edward) **Housman** is nearly always clued by "A Shropshire Lad." The Irish poet and playwright, William Butler **Yeats** (Nobel, 1923), might be clued by his play, "The Countess Cathleen," or by such poems as "Byzantium," "Easter 1916," "Leda and the Swan," or "On Being Asked for a War Poem." A poetry colllection, *The Winding Stair*, has also been a clue, as has his being a cofounder of the Abbey Theatre.

The American poet, Robert **Frost**, is usually clued in one of two ways: (1) as the author of one of his poems, such as "Mending Wall," "Stopping by Woods on a Snowy Evening," or "The Road Not Taken" or (2) as having read one of his poems at the inauguration of President John F. Kennedy. He received Pulitzers in 1924, 1931, 1937, and 1943. Rainer Maria **Rilke**, born in Prague, is known for both his poetry and prose; his volume of poetry, *Sonnets to Orpheus*, has been a clue to his name, and other collections are *The Book of Hours* and the *Duino Elegies*.

As the "laureate of industrial America," Carl **Sandburg** received two Pulitzers for his poetry (for "Corn Huskers" in 1919 and for *Collected Poems* in 1951). He is known not only for his poems, such as "Fog" and "Chicago," but also for his several biographies of Abraham Lincoln. One of these was *Abraham Lincoln: The War Years*, for which he received another Pulitzer in 1940.

SARA **Teasdale** is by far the most popular female poet in crosswords, but she is clued so unimaginatively: by her last name. EZRA **Pound**'s name is used ambiguously in clues (but just his last name, since it is both a noun and a verb). When his first name is to be an answer, it is sometimes clued by his "Cantos." MARIANNE **Moore** (Pulitzer, 1951), editor of *The Dial* from 1925 to 1929, is known for her wit and irony, and the four vowels in her name help, too. Two clues that have been in crosswords: (1) she was asked to submit names for the car that became the Edsel and (2) she threw the first pitch for the 1968 season at Yankee stadium.

Dame Edith **Sitwell**'s poetry includes "Still Falls the Rain" and the collection, *Clowns' Houses*. ELINOR **Wylie**, both a poet and novelist, is probably best known for her collections of poems, *Angels and Earthly Creatures* and *Nets to Catch the Wind*, as well as her novel, *Jennifer Lorn*. She was the second wife of the American poet and novelist William Rose **Benét**, who might be clued by *The Dust Which Is God: A Novel in Verse*, which won a Pulitzer in 1942. He was also well known for *The Reader's Encyclopedia*, which covers world literature, as well as *Benét's Reader's Encyclopedia of American Literature*. (See his younger brother, Stephen Vincent, below.)

The poet (Alfred) Joyce **Kilmer** is always clued by his most famous poem, "Trees." He was killed in the Second Battle of the Marne in World War I. RUPERT **Brooke** is known for his collection of five sonnets, "1914 and Other Poems." He, too, died during World War I, on his way to Gallipoli. The male poet's name having the greatest frequency in crosswords is T.S. (Thomas Stearns) **Eliot** (Nobel, 1948); his monogram "TSE" is also popular in puzzles. A tip-off for Eliot is "Cats" in a clue (from *Old Possum's Book of Practical Cats*), although "The Waste Land," "The Hollow Men," "Four Quartets," and "The Love Song of J. Alfred Prufrock" are used, too.

Conrad **Aiken**, a lifelong friend of Eliot's, was not only a poet, but also a novelist and critic. He won a Pulitzer in 1930 for *Selected Poems* and a National Book Award in 1954 for *Collected Poems*, as well as many other prizes. In 1950 he was appointed Poetry Consultant to the Library of Congress. Some of his poems are "Chance Meetings," "The Dance of Life," and "Morning Song of Senlin." Edna Saint Vincent **Millay**, who won a Pulitzer in 1923 for "The Harp Weaver and Other Poems," appears in puzzles, as does Wilfred **OWEN**, an English poet killed in World War I; he wrote poems reflecting his experiences of that war.

Federico GARCIA **Lorca**, Spain's leading modern poet and dramatist, has been clued by both his poems and plays. The former have included

"Happy Ballads" and "Poet in New York" and the latter "The House of Bernarda Alba" and "Blood Wedding." He was executed by fascists in the Spanish civil war.

Stephen Vincent **Benét** is best known for his long Civil War poem, "John Brown's Body," for which he received a Pulitzer in 1929. His short stories include "The Devil and Daniel Webster" and "By the Waters of Babylon." A posthumous Pulitzer was awarded for an unfinished epic poem, "Western Star." The short-lived HART **Crane**, like Whitman, celebrated America. He is usually clued by "The Bridge," inspired by the Brooklyn Bridge, or "At Melville's Tomb."

Moving on to those poets born in the 20th century, Langston **Hughes** is important for his contributions to the Harlem Renaissance through poetry ("Weary Blues"), prose ("The Ways of White Folks"), and drama ("Simply Heavenly," "Black Nativity," and "Little Ham"). His poem, "I, Too," has appeared several times as an entry (ITOO). Ogden **Nash** is especially popular for his light verse and limericks, as is the Englishman, Edward **Lear** (born 90 years earlier), for his nonsense verse, also in limerick form. Examples of Nash's verse are "Candy is dandy but liquor is quicker" and "Happiness is having a scratch for every itch." It has been helpful to know that Nash was born in RYE, New York.

The Chilean poet and diplomat Pablo **Neruda** (Nobel, 1971) has appeared only a few times, in spite of the three vowels in his name. He has been clued by his homeland, by his poem, "Ode to Common Things," and also by his Nobel Prize. He chose his pen name, which became his legal name, after the Czech poet, Jan Neruda. One of his collections to appear in puzzles is *Twenty Love Poems and a Song of Despair*.

Robert **Penn Warren**, not only a poet, but also a critic and novelist, won a Pulitzer in 1947 for *All the King's Men* and two Pulitzers for poetry, in 1958 and 1979. He was named the first poet laureate of the U.S. in 1985. The poems of the British-born American author W.H. (Wynstan Hugh) **Auden** are in collections such as *The Double Man*. He is the author of "The Dance of Death," a play in verse and prose. He also wrote a long poem in six parts, which won a Pulitzer in 1948: "The Age of Anxiety: A Baroque Eclogue." One of his poetry collections is *Promises: Poems*.

The American poet and critic John **Ciardi** is probably best known for his translation of "The Divine Comedy." Like Frost before her, MAYA **Angelou** also spoke at an inauguration, that of President Clinton in 1993; she recited "On the Pulse of Morning." And like Penn Warren, she is also a novelist. Her first autobiography (of six) is *I Know Why the Caged Bird Sings*. The British poet laureate from 1984 until his death in 1998, TED **Hughes** won several prizes for *Birthday Letters*, a sequence of poems about his relationship with his late wife, the American writer, Sylvia **Plath**, author of poems as well as her only novel, *The Bell Jar*. One of her poetry collections to appear in a crossword was *The Colossus and Other Poems*.

The usual instances relating to poetry, however, are (1) contractions and (2) poetic or archaic words. Some of the contractions are EEN (e'en) for "even," "evening," "night," or "twilight"; EER (e'er) for "ever" or "always" and NEER (ne'er) for "never"; NEATH ('neath) for "beneath" or "under"; OER (o'er) for "over," "beyond," "atop," "across," or "above"; OFT for "often"; OPE for "open," "unlock," "unseal," or "unfold"; THO for "although," "however," "even if," or "nevertheless"; THRO for "through"; TIS ('tis) for "it is"; and TWIXT (betwixt) for "between."

Examples of poetic or archaic words are AFORE for "before" or "earlier than"; AMAIN for "suddenly"; ANEAR and ANIGH for "close by"; ANON for "at another time," "later," "shortly," "in a while," "by and by," or "soon"; APACE for "rapidly"; ART for "are"; CLIME for "weather" or "region"; DREAR for "bleak" or "gloomy"; EBON for "dark" or "black"; ENORM for "large" or "vast"; ENOW for "enough," "plenty," or "sufficient"; ERE for "before"; ERST for "once" or "formerly"; ETERN or ETERNE for "endless," "everlasting," or "eternal"; ETHER for "sky" or "heavens"; EVENTIDE for "sunset" or "nightfall"; FAIN for "gladly"; and HAP for "chance."

Some others are HIE for "hasten" or "hurry"; HITHER and THITHER for "here and there"; MORN for "dawn" or "morning"; NIGH for "nearby" or "soon"; ORB for "globe" or "sphere" or "eye"; PERFORCE for "of necessity"; PHOEBE for "moon" or "planet"; PHOEBUS for "sun"; SCORE for "twenty"; THRICE for "three times"; TRICE for "instant"; TROW for "think" or "believe"; LEARNT for "learned"; and WERT for "were." The clues for these are often introduced as "___, to Byron" (or to Poe or Tennyson or another poet), or "___, poetically," or "___, to the bard."

With respect to words such as "art" and "wert" above, readers familiar with Shakespeare or the King James version of the Bible (1611) will have no problem with these or other archaic terms. Clues for language of this period sometimes contain the word "friends," as in Quakers, who may use such terms as "thee," "thou," and "thine." A clue might be "___,

Biblical style." A rather common poetic construction is to put an "a" before a word, as in "anear" and "afar"; these appear in crosswords with poetic clues.

Be on the lookout for poetic clues relating to a foot or to feet, since IAMB, TROCHEE, and ANAPEST are each a type of metrical foot. (In one puzzle, the Latin IAMBUS was the answer.) A metrical analysis of poetry is known as SCANSION and a CAESURA is a pause in verse. Three rhyming lines are known as a TERCET, and when the first, third, and seventh lines of a poem are identical, you have a RONDELET. OCTET has occurred as an entry many times, with the clue being "Sonnet stanza," and the last six lines of a sonnet as well: SESTET (It.). From the above, it is obvious that there are 14 lines in a sonnet.

Does anyone know the word EPOS? This is when we need our dictionary: "a number of poems, not formally united, that treat an epic theme." Clues for this solution have been "Body of heroic poetry" and "Poetry of tradition." Also found in puzzles have been EPODE (a lyric poem or a classical poem, as well as other definitions) and EPOPEE (a long, narrative, epic poem, once clued as "Lofty verse"). A word from Old English appears, too: SCOP refers to an Old English bard. And a RONDEAU is a type of French lyrical poem. Few puzzles have these words, but they would not be here if they had not appeared in at least one.

A bit of trivia, but both have appeared in crosswords: APR (April) is national poetry month and ORIANA is the poetic nickname for Queen Elizabeth I.

Classical Music

The subject of music includes many words for puzzles: songs, singers, composers, instrumentalists, and all those Italian words. Two very common words in this category are ARIA and Verdi's opera, AIDA, which had its debut on Christmas Eve in 1871 at the opera house in Cairo; these three facts have been clues for "Aida." Others are "Ethiopian princess" and "slave girl." One of her arias has also been in puzzles: "O patria MIA."

Related to "aria," but of lesser occurrence, is DIVA. And of all the arias in all the operas, the same one keeps appearing: ERITU ("Eri tu"), for the tenor, from Verdi's "Un Ballo in Maschera." Perhaps second in frequency is Puccini's "Vissi d'arte," from TOSCA, with the name of the opera the answer. Third seems to be "Pari siamo," from Verdi's

RIGOLETTO, and fourth is probably "Nessun DORMA," from Puccini's "Turandot."

The four general choral voices are sometimes used, especially the second: SOPRANO, ALTO, TENOR, and BASS (or BASSO). An individual singer can also be a CONTRALTO or a BARITONE or, less frequently, a COUNTERTENOR. On occasion, an answer will precede or follow a clue word that is a note of the musical scale: do, re, mi, fa, sol, la, and ti. (Remember the song from "The Sound of Music"?) Sometimes these notes are referred to by their number on the scale; unless it is a plural, it is usually "Musical fifth," or SOL, since that is the only one having three letters. One indicator of a musical clue is the construction "___, on a score."

The lines that notes are positioned on, the STAFF (or STAVE), and its designation, called a CLEF, appear now and then. In this regard, be aware that "staff" in a clue often refers to the *musical* staff, not to the staff of an organization, but there are exceptions. For example, "Staff member" as a clue usually yields NOTE as an answer. But contrarily, "Note *for* a staff" would typically result in MEMO.

Concerning clefs, on a musical score for piano, the left-hand symbol is the FCLEF (bass) and the right-hand symbol the GCLEF (treble). Believe it or not, the word NEUME (also neum) was once an entry; it is a notational sign used in Gregorian chant. Speaking of Gregorian chant, MELISMA has also appeared in a puzzle; it is a group of notes sung on one syllable.

Another term used in both clue and answer is "key," with its adjectives MAJOR and MINOR. The clue "Having one sharp, in music" means that the key is ING (in G). When you see a clue like this, a major key is generally assumed if the entry is three squares. (The related key of E minor also has one sharp.) Two other related keys are D major and B minor. If you should ever need the related minor, simply look for the key on the piano that is three half-tones below.

For other "Having ___ sharps" clues, the entries would be as follows:

2 sharps = IND (in D)
3 sharps = INA (in A)
4 sharps = INE (in E)
5 sharps = INB (in B)

The keys in six and seven sharps are F sharp and C sharp, but would not fit three squares. If a clue is "Having one flat," the entry would be INF (in F). The keys having more flats would probably not appear in a puzzle, at least if three cells were to be filled.

Speaking of sharps and flats, sometimes a clue will be something like "C neighbor." The entry for five cells is either CFLAT or DFLAT. If six squares are to be filled, the answer is CSHARP. On occasion, a clue will be something like "Key to the left" or "Key to the right"; the entries for these are FLAT and SHARP, respectively. "Enharmonic" means that the same pitch can be expressed in a different key, such as C sharp and D flat. You can easily figure out all the others.

When constructors reach the end of their ropes, perhaps after they have already used the word "enharmonic," they ask us for the keys that pieces are written in, as if anyone could remember. For evidence of this, in the year 2006, puzzles needed the keys of Mendelssohn's Symphony No. 3, which happens to be in AMINOR, Brahms's Piano Trio No. 1, which is in BMAJOR, and Beethoven's Symphony No. 3, which is in EFLAT (a major key is assumed here).

If a key is not sharp or flat (as discussed above), then it will be either major or minor, at least in a puzzle. (A key like F sharp (F#) minor would likely not be in a puzzle.) So in a six-letter answer, you can write in the second, fifth, and sixth letters, M and OR (which apply to both "major" and "minor"), and let a crossing word determine the first. Sometimes these are abbreviated, though, as in AMAJ and EMIN; you can tell when the abbreviated form is needed, since the entry is so short.

For puzzles needing the "flat" or "sharp" entries instead of the "major" or "minor" entries, as in the Beethoven above, with the letter of the major key in front, the number of squares will determine whether it is FLAT or SHARP; a crossing letter provides the key. Then there was Chopin's EMINORETUDE (E-minor Étude) in 2007. You just have to stick with it when puzzle makers have a bad day.

A popular constructor expected the solver to know the answer to the clue, "Written in a major key, in music." The answer is DUR, German for major key (and MOLL is German for minor key). It was a Saturday puzzle, which is when a clue-answer of this sort can be expected. Both these terms are familiar to musicians. Much easier in puzzles is TRA for the clue, "Chorus syllable"; this is a frequent entry.

TRIAD was an answer on several occasions, the clue being "Common chord," and the musical interval, TRITONE, or augmented fourth, has also been an answer. CODA appears rather frequently, the clue being "Musical ending"; not all compositions have a coda, but some do. A CADENZA is a solo near the end of a concerto, where the artist can either show off his or her virtuosity at improvisation or play a cadenza composed by someone else.

A tricky one was the clue "Fine, in music," which is Italian for END. Then there was SEGNO, Italian for "sign," as in "Dal Segno," or "from the sign"; the clue is "Dal ___." Another Italian term is "Da Capo," or "from the beginning," literally, "from the head." Easy for a musician (as all these are), but hard for anyone else is the clue "___ breve," the entry being ALLA; it means that the half-note, or MINIM (Brit.), should be regarded as the unit of time rather than the customary quarter-note, or CROTCHET. And that vertical line attached to a note is simply a STEM.

A frequent music clue including the word "silence" usually results in REST, and a break or interruption in music is a CAESURA, just as it is in poetry. A FERMATA indicates the prolongation of a note, chord, or rest beyond its indicated time value and the Latin word TACET in a score indicates that an instrument (or a voice) does not sound, usually for a long period. The term SLUR means to glide over a series of notes without a break; a slur is indicated by an ARC. And "una corda" is Italian for "one string," which in piano means to depress the left pedal. "Corda" is usually the clue and UNA the entry, a bit unfair, perhaps, for those who do not play the piano. An easy one is TEMA, Italian for theme or motif.

Some other musical terms are SONATA and one of its three movements (usually, that is), the RONDO or the MINUET (MENUET in French and MENUETTO in Italian), as well as various TEMPOS or TEMPI. To return to the previous tempo in a piece of music, composers use ATEMPO (a tempo). Some of these basic tempos are (generally, and depending on the piece, its composer, and its period of composition) as follows:

    GRAVE (heavy, serious, very slow)
    LARGO (broad, stately, with dignity)
    LENTO (slow)
    ADAGIO (leisurely, slow)
    ANDANTE (medium tempo, even, moving along)
    MODERATO (moderate speed)
    ALLEGRO (bright, brisk, cheerful)

VIVACE (lively)
PRESTO (very fast)
PRESTISSIMO (as fast as possible)

The term ASSAI, which means "quite," "very," or "extremely," is used to modify tempos; it is a little stronger than MOLTO, which also means "very." And POCO means "a little" or "somewhat." In Italian, "più" means more and "meno" means less; these terms help to modify tempos. The terms AGITATO and STACCATO, which are self-explanatory, have also appeared, as well as the latter's opposite, LEGATO. A close overlapping of fugue voices is called STRETTO. Some other terms you might come across are CONBRIO (con brio) (spirited) and GRAZIOSO (gracefully or elegantly). ARIOSO (or ARIOSE) means "airy" or "melodious" in music and CANTABILE means lyrical, or songlike.

On occasion, tempo indications will be in German rather than Italian, especially in compositions from German-speaking composers. Two of these tempos are LANGSAM (which the author actually came across in a puzzle once), meaning slow, and SCHNELL, which means fast. And the Italian dynamics markings have occurred, too, although rarely: the two in crosswords are PPP and FFF, which in musical notation are always lower-case (very soft and very loud, respectively). The letter "p" stands for the Italian adverb "piano," or "softly," and "f" for "forte," or "loud."

RUBATO means a slight variation in the strict value of notes; many of Chopin's piano compositions provide examples of rubato. And "ritardando" means SLOWER, (actually, gradually slowing). On a score, it is often abbreviated to "rit," and thus in puzzles, RIT.

Two other terms are CANTATA and CONCERTO. The former is a sung composition, usually with instrumental accompaniment; the most prolific composer of cantatas (over 200 of them) was J.S. BACH, who is often clued by "fugue," "oratorio," "partita," or "counterpoint," especially his "Art of Fugue," "Elijah," and "Christmas Oratorio." He has also been clued by the six Brandenburg concerti, the "Mass in B minor," the chorale preludes, the "Goldberg Variations," and even by the fact that he had 20 children. (However, only 10 lived to adulthood.) And he himself has been the clue for his primary instrument, the ORGAN.

The CONCERTO, at least in modern times, is usually a large-scale composition in several (most commonly, three) movements between a solo instrument and orchestra or between smaller and larger groups of instruments. Then there is the OVERTURE, which can be either (1) an independent composition, such as Tchaikovsky's "1812 Overture" or (2) the introduction to a larger work, such as an opera. A CAVATINA has popped up in a puzzle, too. It is an air or a short solo, but the term can also apply to song-like instrumental pieces. And a CABALETTA is a short, rhythmic aria.

Some other terms are LIED, a German art song (plural is LIEDER), MOTET, a short vocal composition for liturgical use, usually with accompaniment, and DESCANT, a decorative part added above a given melody, for example, a hymn tune. A GRACE note is one of many musical ornaments. The Latin word OPUS is a term given to a composer's works of music that have been classified or catalogued chronologically by publication date; for example, Beethoven's Fifth Symphony is known as his Opus 67.

Groups of singers or instrumentalists appear rather frequently, such as DUO, TRIO, QUARTET, QUINTET, SESTET or SEXTET, SEPTET, OCTET, and even NONET (or ENNEAD when a puzzle is to be difficult). "Nonet" and "ennead" have even been clued by the Supreme Court. On many occasions, "together" and "in unison" were in musical clues; the solution is their Italian equivalent, ADUE (a due). Similar, but for larger groups of singers or instrumentalists, is TUTTI, or all (all together).

ARCO, which means "bowed," is also encountered. Related to this is the English word "arc"; musical ties are indicated by an ARC (they look like eyebrows on a sheet of music). The opposite of "arco" is PIZZICATO, which has also been in a puzzle. GLISSANDO means to slide rapidly through a scale-like passage. The term "bel canto," or "beautiful singing," has been in clues, the answer sometimes being NORMA, an opera by Bellini. Many operas by Bellini or Donizetti would fit the bill. From "Norma," the most memorable aria has been "Casta diva." Norma was a Druidic priestess, the clue in another puzzle. The heroine of Bellini's "La Sonnambula" also appears; her name is AMINA.

Clues that elicit a "musical" answer often contain the word "Met" (Metropolitan Opera) or "La Scala" (Teatro alla Scala), the opera house in Milan, which opened in 1778. Speaking of opera, ELSA is known as the "Lohengrin lady" or "Lohengrin bride," from Wagner's eponymous opera. And MIMI, from Puccini's "La Bohème," and Floria TOSCA, from his opera, "Tosca," also appear, as well as Tosca's nemesis and ultimately her victim, SCARPIA. By the way, Tosca premiered at the Teatro Costanzi in Rome in 1900, sometimes a clue.

From Verdi's opera, "Otello," you will come across EMILIA, Iago's wife and Desdemona's maid. Beethoven's only opera, FIDELIO, will usually need its protagonist, LEONORE, with all her vowels, and the jailer, ROCCO, has also been in puzzles. From Verdi's "Il Trovatore," there is LEONORA, who is a countess, and from "La Traviata," VIOLETTA appears. There are also the lovers ERIC and SENTA in Wagner's "The Flying Dutchman" and OLGA in Tchaikovsky's "Eugene Onegin." Two other characters it is helpful to remember are Aida's lover, RADAMES, and her father, AMONASRO. Another is the heroine of Bizet's "The Pearl Fishers," who is the priestess LEILA. And especially in a puzzle on New Year's Eve or New Year's Day, you might encounter ADELE, the maid in Johann Strauss the younger's "Die Fledermaus." One of the three words of the title of Mozart's "Così Fan Tutte" is sometimes needed; it is invariably COSI.

The most popular opera singer in crosswords is the former soprano, ALMA Gluck, an American born in Romania; her husband was the famous violinist, Efrem Zimbalist (their son Efrem Jr. is a well-known actor). Some other sopranos for whom the *last* name was provided as a clue were the following: ERNA Berger, MARIA Callas ("La Divina"), EMMA Calvé, EILEEN Farrell, RENEE Fleming, KIRI Te Kanawa (whose clue might include "Maori"), LOTTE Lehmann, JENNY Lind (the "Swedish nightingale"), EVA Marton, LEONA Mitchell, LILY Pons, ROSA Ponselle, LEONTYNE Price, ELLEN Shade, and LUISA Tetrazzini (for whom the dish was named).

Several times the *first* name of a soprano was the clue, with the last name being the answer. Some of these were as follows: Lucine AMARA, Emma EAMES, Dame Nellie MELBA (for whom the dessert, "Peach Melba," was named and who has also been clued by her autobiography, *Melodies and Memories* . . .), Anna MOFFO, Roberta PETERS, Sarah REESE, Sylvia SASS, Renata SCOTTO, Beverly SILLS, and Renata TEBALDI. The coloraturas Joan Sutherland and Kathleen Battle have both been in clues.

The only mezzo-sopranos in puzzles were Dame Janet BAKER, TERESA Berganza, Marilyn HORNE, ISOLA Jones, LOTTE Lenya, NAN Merriman, ELENA Obraztsova, and TATIANA Troyanos; the only contraltos were MARIAN Anderson and ELENA Nikolaidi. Some tenors were Roberto ALAGNA, ANDREA Bocelli, JOSE Carreras, ENRICO Caruso, FRANCO Corelli, PLACIDO Domingo, LUCIANO Pavarotti, TITO Schipa, and JON Vickers. Baritones were TITO Gobbi and Sherrill Milnes; bass-baritones were Simon ESTES, ITALO Tajor, and

Bryn TERFEL; and bassos were ARA Berberian, ENZO Dara, Simon ESTES, EZIO Flagello, EZIO Pinza, and Cesare SIEPI.

Of composers, Richard Strauss has been encountered, where the names of two of his operas were needed; these were SALOME and ELEKTRA. Sometimes a clue contains Chopin's name, and the answer is usually ETUDE, although PRELUDE, MAZURKA, NOCTURNE, and POLONAISE have also occurred. A modern composer now found in puzzles is the Estonian, ARVO Pärt.

Franz Josef Haydn is affectionately referred to as PAPA, and his oratorio, "The Creation," has been a clue. Beethoven has been in clues several times, where the answers were his third, or EROICA, symphony, originally dedicated to Napoleon and first performed in Vienna in 1805 (three clues); the sixth, or PASTORAL, symphony; and the ninth, or CHORAL, symphony. On many occasions it helped to know that one of Beethoven's most popular works was dedicated to ELISE ("Für Elise"); it was once disguised in a clue as "Bagatelle in A minor." One puzzle required the number of Anton Dvořák's last symphony, his NINTH: "From the New World." Sometimes the number of symphonies for composers is a clue, such as 4 for Brahms, 9 each for Beethoven and Bruckner, 10 for Mahler, 41 for Mozart, and 104 for Haydn.

Many other composers are found in crosswords. One of the most popular is the Englishman, Thomas ARNE, a near contemporary of HANDEL. He composed "Comus" (a masque), "Judith" (an oratorio), and the operas "Alfred" and "Rosamond," as well as "Rule, Britannia!" If a "composer" answer of four letters is ever needed, you just might try Arne, especially if the clue relates to England.

Even earlier than Handel was Henry PURCELL, whose clue usually relates to "Dido and Aeneas" or to his being a composer of baroque music. Earlier still was Johann Pachelbel, whose entry is nearly always his CANON (in D). Domenico SCARLATTI is also sometimes clued by the baroque (he was a friend of Handel, and born in the same year, 1785). And can you believe that J.S. Bach was born that year, too? Speaking of Bach, he is one of the "three Bs," along with Beethoven and Brahms.

Some other composers found in puzzles are listed in alphabetical order below (some followed by typical crossword references):

Isaac Albéniz (Spain), "Iberia"
Anton Arensky (Russia)

Samuel Barber (U.S.) (it has helped to know that the niece in his opera "Vanessa" is ERIKA; the name of the opera itself has also been an answer)
Béla Bartók (Hungary, but he lived in the U.S. the last five or so years of his life)
Alban Berg (Austria), "Wozzeck"
Leonard Bernstein (U.S.)
Georges Bizet (France), "Carmen" and "L'Arlesienne"
Ernest Bloch (Switzerland)
Luigi Boccherini (Italy)
Arrigo Boito (Italy), "Mefistofele"
Aleksandr Borodin (Russia), "Prince IGOR," an opera
Anton Bruckner (Austria)
Aaron Copland (U.S.)
César Cui (Russia)
Claude Debussy (France), "La Mer"
Léo Delibes (France)
Ernö (or Ernst) Doknányi (Hungary)
Manuel de Falla (Spain)
Sir Edward Elgar (England), "Pomp and Circumstance" marches and "Enigma Variations"
Georges Enesco (Romania), "Romanian Rhapsodies"
Gabriel Fauré (France)
Lukas Foss (U.S., but born in Germany)
César Franck (France, but born in Belgium)
George Gershwin (U.S.)
Christoph Willibald Gluck (Germany)
Charles Gounod (France), "Faust"
Edvard Grieg (Norway), "Peer Gynt Suite"
Ferde Grofé (U.S.), "Grand Canyon Suite"
Roy Harris (U.S.)
Gustav Holst (England), "The Planets"
Jacques Ibert (France)
Charles Ives (U.S.), "Concord Sonata"
Leos Janácek (Czech Republic)
Aram Khachaturian (Russia)
Zoltán Kodály (Hungary)
Erich Korngold (Austria)

Edouard Lalo (France)
Franz Lehár (Hungary), "The Merry Widow"
Gustav Mahler (Austria, but born in Bohemia), whose "Das Lied von der Erde" has been both clue and answer
Pietro Mascagni (Italy)
Jules Massenet (France)
Gian Carlo Menotti (U.S., but born in Italy), whose opera "AMAHL and the Night Visitors" has been both clue and answer, as well as "The Consul" and its heroine, MAGDA
Modest Mussorgsky (Russia)
Otto Nicolai (Germany, but born in Russia)
Carl Nielsen (Denmark)
Ivor Novello (Wales, UK)
Carl Orff (Germany), "Carmina Burana"
Sergei Prokofiev (Russia)
Sergei Rachmaninoff (born in Russia, died a U.S.citizen)
Joachim Raff (Switzerland)
Jean-Philippe Rameau (France)
Maurice Ravel (France)
Ned Rorem (U.S.), "Santa Fe Songs" and "Air Music"
Gioacchino Rossini (Italy)
Nino Rota (Italy), especially his association with Federico Fellini
Camille Saint-Saëns (France)
Antonio Salieri (Austria, but born in Venice)
Erik Satie (France)
Lalo Schifrin (Argentina)
Arnold Schönberg (Austria), atonal composition
Franz Schubert (Austria), Lieder (songs)
Robert Schumann (Germany)
Dmitri Shostakovich (Russia)
Jean Sibelius (Finland)
Bedřick Smetana (Czech Republic)
Richard Strauss (Austria), tone poems
Igor Stravinsky (U.S., but born in Russia)
Karol Szymanowski (Poland)
Peter Ilich Tchaikovsky (Russia), "The Nutcracker" and its heroine, CLARA
Carl Maria von Weber (Germany), "Der Freischutz"
Ralph Vaughan Williams (England)

A brief glance at the names in the above list illustrates the fact that puzzle makers usually prefer composers having at least one rather short name for a composer rather than, for example, Englebert Humperdinck, composer of "Hänsel und Gretel" (although he has been in clues). But Nicolai Rimsky-Korsakov has appeared in puzzles more than once with "Le Coq d'Or," or "The Golden Cockerel." The clue is "Le Coq ___" and the answer is DOR.

Several conductors ("maestros" usually in puzzles) have appeared, and are listed below.

Ernest Ansermet
Daniel Barenboim
Plácido Domingo
Antal Dorati
Lukas Foss
Herbert von Karajan
Eri Klas
Otto Klemperer
André Kostelanetz
Erich Leinsdorf
Kurt Masur
Eduardo Mata
Zubin Mehta
Dmitri Mitropoulis
Riccardo Muti
Daniel Oren
Eugene Ormandy
Seiji Ozawa (white turtleneck a clue)
André Previn
Erno Rapee
Fritz Reiner
Esa-Pekka Salonen
Sir Georg Solti
George Szell
Jeffrey Tate
Arturo Toscanini
Edo de Waart
Bruno Walter

A very special musician of the 20th century was NADIA Boulanger, who helped to further the careers of many of the performers listed below. Although she composed, she also conducted such orchestras as the New York Philharmonic, the Boston Symphony Orchestra, and the Philadelphia Orchestra. But she will be remembered especially as a teacher.

It is safe to say that you need to know few instrumental performance artists for crosswords, as the only ones who have appeared to the author are (1) the pianists Claudio ARRAU, Alfred BRENDEL, EMIL Gilels, Glenn GOULD, Dame Myra HESS, ALICIA Keys, OSCAR Levant, JON Nakamatsu, ARTUR Rubinstein, ARTUR Schnabel, and Rudolf and his son Peter SERKIN, (2) the violinists Leopold AUER (a teacher of Heifetz), OLE Bull, Mischa ELMAN, HILARY Hahn, Jascha HEIFETZ, ANI Kavafian, Yehudi MENUHIN, MIDORI, NATHAN Milstein, NICCOLO (also NICOLO) Paganini, Itzhak PERLMAN, ISAAC Stern, OTO Ughi, and EFREM Zimbalist, Sr., (3) the cellists Leonard ROSE, and YoYo (YOYO) Ma, (4) the English classical guitarist Julian BREAM, and (5) the sitarist RAVI Shankar.

The most common musical instrument in crosswords is a double-reed woodwind, the OBOE (sometimes HAUTBOIE or HAUTBOY), which is used in orchestra tuning (this fact occurs in puzzles more than you would think). It has also helped to know that the oboe represents the duck in Prokofiev's "Peter and the Wolf." And sometimes a string instrument, the CELLO (its characteristic F-hole has been in puzzles), and a brass instrument, the TUBA, appear.

When you come across the word "string," "wind," "reed," or "brass" in a clue, a musical instrument might be the answer. As for strings, CREMONA was an important city. The earliest violin-maker (or luthier) there was Andrea AMATI, followed by his sons, Antonio and Girolamo. One of the latter's sons, Niccolò (also Nicolò), was the most famous in the family. ANTONIO Stradivari followed in the Amati tradition, but his relation to the Amati family is unknown, in spite of clues to the contrary. The third family of violin-makers in Cremona was that of the Guarneris, especially one member, Giuseppi Guarneri del GESU.

To close this section, it might be appropriate to mention that St. CECILIA, with her four vowels, is the patron saint of musicians.

Roman Numerals

Roman numerals in crosswords are clued in five typical ways. The first is a "date" clue like "Early 2nd century date," resulting in an entry beginning with C. This numeral will be followed by one or more others, depending on the crossing entries; one of these is usually an I. In the second case, a clue will be something like "Twice XX" (or twice 20), the entry being XL (or 40). In the third case, the clue will be an Arabic number with a modifier, such as "1900 on a building" (or cornerstone) or "1800, Roman style" or "2013, to Caesar." In the fourth case, the clue will refer to a clock or sundial, thus, I through XII. In the fifth case, if a Latin word is in the clue, a Roman numeral might be the answer. For example, assume the clue is "Weeks per annum"; its entry would be LII (52).

Quite common in crosswords are the Super Bowls, which are identified using Roman numerals; for example, Super Bowl XLVII was played in 2013. Another popular use is in the Olympics; examples are the winter Olympiad XXI, held in 2010, and the summer Olympiad XXX, held in 2012.

For those unfamiliar with Roman numerals, they are quite easy to learn. Instead of our nine digits plus zero for creating numbers, there are only seven Roman numerals (which are actually letters), namely, I (1), V (5), X (10), L (50), C (100), D (500), and M (1,000). (One puzzle maker managed to create an entry with all seven numerals.) To make a number *larger*, add numerals to the right, and to make it *smaller*, subtract numerals on the left. The examples given below should help:

A. For *reducing* a numeral (or *subtracting* from it): Since V is 5, placing an I on the left (to subtract) results in IV. (The Arabic 4 is typically expressed as Roman IV, although IIII is also found occasionally, especially on clock faces.) Examples of subtraction using the other five numerals: IX = 9, XL = 40, XC = 90, CD = 400, XD = 490, and CM = 900. Not to complicate the issue, but there are certain conventions concerning what numerals the smaller ones, such as I and V, can be subtracted from. For example, I can precede only V and X, but it is doubtful this issue will ever arise in a puzzle.

B. *Increasing* one of the seven numerals (or *adding* to it) is just as easy: VI = 6, VIII = 8, XII = 12, XV = 15, LV = 55, LVI = 56, CL = 150, CLX = 160, DCC = 700, DCCL = 750, MMXIII = 2013.

C. Here are three examples of combining addition and subtraction to create a number: (a) XLVI = 46; use the largest numeral—in this case, L—as a base, and subtract the numeral on the left (X) and add those on the right (VI). (b) XCV = 95; subtract the X and add the V. That is, simply take the largest numeral as a base, subtract what is to the left of it, and add what is to the right, repeating this instruction each time. (c) MCMLX = 1960. There is nothing to the left of the first M, so the number is at least 1,000. The next largest numeral is another M, but there is a C to the left of it, so the combination of these two numerals is 900; thus, 1,900 so far. The next largest numeral, L, is 50; thus, 1,950. Adding the remaining X, or 10, results in 1960.

It is a testament to the ancient Romans that we still use their cumbersome number system today in various contexts, such as for outlines (I. and i., II. and ii., for example), on clock dials, with family names such as John Doe III, with the names of kings, queens, and popes, and as the numbering system for the Super Bowls, Olympics, "Star Wars" episodes, Apollo flights, and other events. Fortunately, we do not use them for calculating. If it makes you feel any better, even the Romans had trouble with Roman numerals.

Sports

Sports references can be to players, to games such as baseball, or to teams, their cities, arenas or stadiums, or leagues and conferences. SHEA (razed in 2009) and Arthur ASHE stadiums are the most popular, whose clues sometimes include their location, in Queens. (In puzzles, the N.Y. Mets Citi Field has not yet replaced Shea Stadium in popularity.) To use the Orioles as an example for references, Baltimore is their city, Oriole Park at Camden Yards is the name of their home stadium, and they are in the American League (AL in clues). Fenway Park, in Boston, is the oldest major league baseball (MLB) stadium still in use; it opened in 1912.

In baseball, it is helpful to know which teams are in the American League and which are in the National League, as these are often clues. Incidentally, ALER (American League player) and NLER (National League player) appear from time to time; the clue is simply a player's name. If you do not know which league they play(ed) in, just write in the last three letters. And subdivisions of leagues are encountered in crosswords, such as ALE (for America League East). Other examples for leagues are ALEAST and NLWEST. So be aware of all the possibilities that might fit the number of squares, especially if you know the answer.

If words like "Eagles," "Pirates," "Rangers," "Ravens," "Lions," "Tigers," and "Bears" (or any other word that could possibly be the name of a team) appear in clues, look for a sports-related answer. Those who solve puzzles know that New York-based teams are the most popular, so New Yorkers have an edge there. And it helps to know which football team won a Super Bowl or which baseball team won a World Series, as well as when, since these are clues to the name of a team.

The Olympics appear in puzzles, and usually require one to remember the year and/or the city, since these are clues for the winning country or medal-winning contestant. Such information is available in various almanacs, as are winners of Super Bowls and World Series. A clue containing "Colorado Springs" often leads to USOC, as the U.S. Olympic Committee is based there. And the IOC, or International Olympic Committee, is sometimes clued by its headquarters in Lausanne.

The most common sports answers are ARENA, RAH, PRO, REF, and UMP. For five squares, you might have to write ZEBRA instead of UMP, and a clue for REF is sometimes "Striped shirt." References are not limited to professional teams, so a knowledge of NCAA (National Collegiate Athletic Association) teams is also helpful; for example, the TERPS (Terrapins) refers to the University of Maryland; the Bruins are a UCLA team in the PAC-10, the Cavaliers are at UVA (University of Virginia), and the Fighting Tigers are at LSU (Louisiana State University). If you should come across the College World Series, it is played in OMAHA.

Speaking of the NCAA, it is headquartered in Indianapolis and has been linked to its Scholarship Award (two clues). In basketball clues, it has been referred to as the "Final Four" organization as well as sponsor of "March Madness." Leading up to the "Final Four" are the "Sweet Sixteen" and "Elite Eight." And "Final Four" has also led to SEMI (for "semifinals").

Some terms are general to more than one sport, such as ALL for "tied" or "even," UPSET, EDGE, PENALTY, ROOKIE, ROSTER, PRO for a major leaguer, SEMIPRO, and PLAYOFFS; also, a sports clue containing "last" sometimes means "in the CELLAR" in sports parlance. "First-stringers" and "starters" are the ATEAM (A-team) and "second-stringers" the BTEAM (B-team). MVP (most valuable player) is typically in a clue, but has also occurred as an entry. Then there are ONTHEDL (on the disabled list), ESPY, the cable TV sports award, and ESPN, the cable sports channel.

Baseball. Just as French is the most popular foreign language and Ireland the most popular country in crosswords, baseball is the most popular sport. Also, it has a long and well-documented history as America's pastime. The clues are sometimes metaphoric (diamond, nine, and home). Other terms eliciting the game are Cooperstown, ball, base or bag, box, plate, strike, hit, first, second, third, etc. The answers are often abbreviations, such as DBL (double), RBI (runs batted in), ERA (a pitcher's earned run average), and SLO pitch.

The puzzle solver will encounter other short expressions as either clues or entries. Some of three to six letters are listed below, and if two words make up an expression, they have been separated; for example, "no hit" is with the five-letter terms (five squares to fill). Some of these are: bat, fly, out, peg, pop, lob, tag, run, hit, balk, bunt, drag, foul, loft, safe, mitt, shag, snag, walk, at bat, drive, error, homer, one on, no-hit, mound, pop-up, slide, steal, swing, tag-up, whiff (swing and a miss of the pitch charged as the third), assist, lineup, call up (promote from the minors), closer, dinger (a home run), fanner (a strike-throwing pitcher), on base, on deck, one-hop (a type of grounder), opener (first game of the season), pop fly, put-out (a tag), slider, squeeze (a run-scoring bunt), smoker (a fast ball), heater (also a fast ball), sac fly, single, double, triple, and others. If a pitcher is right-handed, a ball that goes to the left is a HOOK, and if to the right, a SLICE.

There have been longer entries, too, from seven to 12 letters, and these are listed below. Some of these are: lineout (a hard, low ball that is caught), shutout (when a pitcher allows no runs in a complete game), bean ball, reliever, wild pitch, set-up man, no-hitter, check swing (a batter's change of mind), go the route (to pitch nine innings), four-bagger (or homer), high heater (a hard-to-hit fastball), strike zone, perfect game (a rare feat performed by pitcher Randy Johnson, of the Arizona Diamondbacks, against the Atlanta Braves in the 2004 season), squeeze play, season opener, and switch-hitter.

But beware of "Pitcher" in a clue, as it could refer to MOLLY Pitcher or simply EWER. It has helped to know that OCT is the month of the World Series, that an extra inning is the TENTH, that homers are TATERS, that Yankee uniforms are PINSTRIPED (New York again), that a baseball has 108 double stitches, and that TOPPS and FLEER are big names in baseball cards. The longest baseball entry to appear was SHOESTRINGCATCH.

Baseball players are frequently answers. Those who have appeared in puzzles are listed below, with whichever of their names (first or last) is more common as an entry appearing in capital letters. If you should come across others, there is plenty of space to write them in on the page. For players who became managers and are mentioned in puzzles in that capacity, they are listed in the last paragraph of this section.

Hank AARON
CAL (Abie) Abrams
Tommie AGEE
Grover Cleveland Alexander (Old PETE)
Roberto ALOMAR
ALOU family (see following paragraph)
Rubén AMARO
CAP Anson
Jeff BAGWELL
SAL Bando
Ernie BANKS (Mr. Cub)
LEN(NY) Barker
ERIK Bédard
James BELL (Cool Papa)
ARMANDO Benítez
YOGI Berra
BERT Blyleven
WADE Boggs
Barry BONDS
CLETE Boyer
Ralph BRANCA
RYAN Braun
LOU Brock
RICO Brogna
KEVIN Brown
LEW Burdette
ROY Campanella
Bernie CARBO
Rod CAREW
Steve CARLTON
Orlando CEPEDA
Ron CEY (the Penguin)
Roger (ROG) CLEMENS (the Rocket)
ROBERTO Clemente

Ty COBB (the Georgia Peach)
NATE Colbert
EARLE Combs
STAN Coveleski
RON Darling
Dizzy DEAN
Bucky DENT
DOM DiMaggio (the Little Professor)
"Joltin' JOE" DiMaggio
Bobby DOERR
ABNER Doubleday
Don DRYSDALE
LEO (the Lip) Durocher
Howard ELSTON
John ELWAY (also football)
Shawn ESTES
Nick ETTEN
Buck EWING
Ferris FAIN
ROBERT (Bob) Feller
ROLLIE Fingers
Carlton FISK
Whitey FORD
Nelson (NELLIE) Fox
Andres GALARRAGA
NOMAR Garciaparra
Ralph GARR
LOU Gehrig (the Iron Horse)
Dwight (DOC) Gooden (Dr. K)
HANK Greenberg
MIKE Greenwell
PEDRO Guerrero
RON Guidry
TONY Gwynn (Mr. Padre, Captain Video)
"Smilin' STAN" Hack
ROY Halladay
COLE Hamels
RICKEY Henderson
ORLANDO Hernández (El Duque)

OREL Hershiser (also a baseball analyst)
GIL Hodges
NAT Holma
ELSTON Howard
WAITE Hoyt
OMAR Infante
Hideki IRABU
Reggie JACKSON (Mr. October)
DEREK Jeter
RANDY Johnson (the Big Unit)
WALTER Johnson (the Big Train)
CLEON Jones
ADDIE Joss (the Human Hairpin)
George KELL
Ralph KINER
SANDY Koufax
TONY Kubek
CHET Lemon
TIM Lincecum
Billy LOES
"Steady Eddie" LOPAT
Sparky LYLE
GREG Maddux
SAL Maglie
Mickey MANTLE
Roger MARIS
Billy MARTIN
EDGAR Martinez
PEDRO Martinez
TINO Martinez
Hideki MATSUI
Willie MAYS (the Say Hey Kid)
Bill Mazeroski (MAZ)
WILLIE McGee
MARK McGwire
DENNY McLain
MINNIE Miñoso (Mr. White Sox)
MOLINA brothers (see following paragraph)
Melvin MORA

JACK Morris
Manny MOTA (also a coach)
Jamie MOYER
Stan MUSIAL (Stan the Man)
Earle "Greasy" NEALE (also football)
Robb NEN
Phil NEVIN
Hideo NOMO (the Tornado)
Irv NOREN
Johnny Lee ODOM (Blue Moon)
Tony OLIVA
REY Ordóñez
Jesse OROSCO
David ORTIZ (Big Papi)
Mel OTT (Master Melvin)
Leroy "Satchel" PAIGE
MILT Pappas
Alejandro PENA
Tony PENA
LOU Piniella
OMAR Quintanilla
VIC Raschi
JON Rauch (tallest MLB player (at 6 ft., 11 in.)
Jimmie REESE
PEEWEE (Pee Wee) Reese (the Little Colonel)
ALLIE Reynolds
CAL Ripken, Jr.
EPPA Rixie
Phil Rizzuto (SCOOTER)
Brooks ROBINSON
Jackie ROBINSON
ALEX Rodriguez (usually AROD in puzzles)
Pete ROSE
Al ROSEN
EDD Roush
BABE Ruth (the Bambino, the Sultan of Swat)
NOLAN Ryan (and his Ryan Express)
CC (for Carsten Charles) SABATHIA
BRET Saberhagen

Chris SABO
REY Sánchez
RYNE Sandberg
DEION Sanders (also football)
BENITO Santiago
TOM Seaver (the Franchise)
ENOS Slaughter
OZZIE Smith (the Wizard of Oz)
DUKE Snider
Alfonso SORIANO
"Slammin' Sammy" SOSA
WARREN Spahn
TRIS Speaker
RUSTY Staub
Dave STIEB
DARRYL Strawberry
ICHIRO Suzuki
Mark Teixeira (TEX)
LUIS Tiant
Frank TORRE
PAUL Toth
ALAN Trammell
Dizzy TROUT (father of Steve)
Steve TROUT (son of Dizzy)
Chase UTLEY
ANDY Van Slyke
OMAR Vizquel
HONUS Wagner (the Flying Dutchman)
Lloyd WANER (Little Poison), brother of
Paul WANER (Big Poison)
EARL Webb
HOYT Wilhelm
TED Williams
MIKE Witt
EARLY (Gus) Wynn
Carl (YAZ) Yastremski
Eddie YOST (Walking Man)
Cy YOUNG

Then there is the family of Felipe, Jesus, Matty, and Moises ALOU (and it helps to know that Felipe Alou was once manager of the San Francisco Giants). Another baseball family are the MOLINA brothers: Bengie (or Benjie, for "Benjamin"), Jose, and Jadier.

Baseball clues and answers have *not* included the following players in puzzles the author has solved: Lefty Gomez, Al Kaline, Jim Palmer, Andy Pettitte, Jorge Posada, or Frank Robinson. Perhaps the reader will encounter them. *Note*: In sports-related puzzles, the names of players will, of course, be more frequent than they are in, say, the puzzles of daily newspapers and other general media.

On occasion, baseball general managers (GMs in clues) have appeared in puzzles: these include Walter ALSTON, LEO (the Lip) Durocher, GIL Hodges, Tommy LASORDA, Connie MACK (Cooperstown's "Tall Tactician"), JOE McCarthy, JOHN McGraw, OMAR Minaya, Tony PENA, CASEY Stengel, Joe TORRE and NED Yost. Some managers who seem not to have made it into puzzles are Sparky Anderson, Bobby Cox, Bucky Harris, and Tony La Russa. In several cases you were expected to know the number on a player's shirt (the clue): Phil Rizzuto's 10, Willie Mays's 24, and Jackie Robinson's 42. And Bud SELIG has appeared as MLB commissioner, starting in 1992. Baseball-Reference.com is a helpful source.

Football. If "eleven" or "11" is in a clue, something related to football or soccer is likely the answer. Some of the abbreviations in clues for the former are QB for quarterback, TD for touchdown, FG for field goal, and OT for overtime. Two other terms that appear are "pass" and "end," sometimes as clues, since they are ambiguous. And punt, snag, clip (an infraction), yards and yardage, guard, carry, huddle, end run (also sweep), end zone, lateral, quarter, dropkick, screen pass, T-formation, linebacker, first string, flying wedge, and interference have been answers.

It has helped to know that a COINTOSS (coin toss) starts a pro football game, that quarterbacks call HUT, that a reserve group is a TAXISQUAD, that the ref throws down a FLAG, that OTS (overtimes) are NFL tie-breakers, that six-pointers are TDS (touchdowns), that running backs are RBS, that ARENA football has eight players on a team, that the area between the goal line and the 20-yard line is the RED zone, and that a surprise punt is a QUICKKICK. The various linemen also appear, most of them as plurals: CENTER, LGS and RGS (for left and right guards), and LTS and RTS (for left and right tackles).

Puzzle makers assume that solvers know that NFL stands for "National Football League," in which there are 32 teams in two conferences, 16 in each, called the American Football Conference, or AFC, and the National Football Conference, or NFC. Each of these is further divided into North, East, South, and West. If you come across CFL in a clue, it stands for the "Canadian Football League" and has been referred to as the Grey Cup sports group.

The author has come across the names of the following football players in puzzles of the major newspapers. Presented in the same format as baseball players above, the capitalized name is the one typically required in puzzles.

TROY Aikman
David AKERS
Flipper ANDERSON
OTIS Armstrong
Sammy BAUGH
FRED Biletnikoff
MEL Blount
DRE Bly
BRET Boone
NEAL Colzie
RANDALL Cunningham
LEN Dawson
ERIC Dickerson
Trent DILFER
John ELWAY (also baseball)
BOOMER Esiason
Brett FAVRE
DOUG Flutie
LEN Ford
RUSS Francis
George GIPP
OTTO Graham
ROSEY Grier
BOB Griese
STEVE Grogan
LOU Groza

George "Papa Bear" HALAS
ARNIE Herber
SAM Huff
Michael IRVIN
Bo JACKSON
SETH Joyner
Tommy LASORDA
Howie LONG
Ronnie LOTT
SID Luckman
ELI Manning
PEYTON Manning
GINO Marchetti
DAN Marino
RON Mix
"Broadway Joe" NAMATH
Earle "Greasy" NEALE (also baseball)
Merlin OLSEN
ALAN Page
Walter PAYTON
Rodney PEETE
AHMAD Rashad
KNUTE Rockne
Barry SANDERS
DEION Sanders (also baseball)
GALE Sayers
Phil SIMMS (also a TV sportscaster)
Bart STARR
Lynn SWANN
FRAN Tarkenton
VINNY Testaverde
JIM Thorpe (Wa-Tho-Huk his Indian name)
Y.A. TITTLE
AMANI Toomer
Johnny UNITAS
DOAK Walker
ARNIE Weinmeister

Coaches are also included, such as Mike DITKA, WEEB Ewbank (the only coach to win both NFL and AFL championships), TOM Landry, ARA Parseghian, and Don SHULA (the "winningest coach"), as well as his sons Dave and Mike. The sportscasters BOB Costas, IRV Cross, and DAN Dierdorf appear, too, and even the NFL commissioner, PETE Rozelle. Another name that comes up in puzzles is AMOS Alonzo Stagg, head football coach at the University of Chicago; he is credited as an innovator of the huddle and of numbers on uniforms, among other advances.

But for a sport as popular as football, it is not that well represented in crosswords. In puzzles the author has solved, he has not come across the names of Joe Montana or Roger Staubach, both of whom are well remembered and who have a suitable number of vowels in their names. If you should come across the Vince Lombardi Trophy in a clue, it is awarded to the winning team of the Super Bowl. (See "Roman Numerals" above for Super Bowl numbering.)

Soccer. Little related to soccer appears, but one can expect to encounter its most famous player, PELE (Ed(i)son Arantes do Nascimento), with the clue usually relating to his home, Brazil. If the FIFA World Cup is in a clue, it often refers to him. And MIA Hamm and Alexi LALAS, of the U.S., have appeared several times, as has Brandi Chastain. The only soccer clues encountered for the game itself were "Certain forward," with the entry being OUTSIDEMAN, and "Area around goal," with the clue being CREASE.

Basketball. If "NBA," "hoops," "five," or "5" is in a clue, the answer may relate to basketball. Even the date the National Basketball Association was organized has been a clue: June 6, 1946. The NBA, which includes 30 teams, 15 each in the Eastern Conference and the Western Conference, has also been referred to as the All-Star Game organization. If you should come across the Larry O'Brien Championship Trophy, it is awarded to the winning team of the NBA Finals. As in other professional sports, knowledge of teams, cities, and conferences is helpful.

The only answers for the game itself that the author has come across are ring (with its net), save, sink, dunk, trey (a long shot from beyond the three-point line), press, pivot, spike, tap-in (an easy basket), layup, tip-in, assist, points, screen (also known as a pick), dribble, slam dunk, one-on-one, swish-shot, air ball, and BBALL ("hoops" and "cagers' game" were the clues for the last term). "Court" in a clue can refer to either basketball or tennis. The various positions appear now and then, usually as clues: center (often the tallest player), forward, and guard. The answer for Michael Jordan's nickname is AIR, and if "Magic" is in a clue, one can be rather confident that it refers to Magic JOHNSON. If a player's name is the clue, the answer could be simply NBAER (NBAer).

Other players' (or hoopsters' or cagers') names are listed below like those of baseball and football players, with the more typical crossword answer in capitalized letters.

    Danny AINGE
    Carmelo (MELO) Anthony
    NATE "Tiny" Archibald
    ELGIN Baylor
    Larry BIRD
    Manute BOL (7 ft., 7 in. tall)
    ELTON Brand
    KOBE Bryant
    WILT Chamberlain (the Stilt)
    Derrick COLEMAN
    CLYDE Drexler
    Craig EHLO
    Mario ELIE
    Wayne EMBRY
    Julius "Dr. J." ERVING
    Patrick EWING
    WALT Frazier
    PAU Gasol
    ARTIS Gilmore
    ELVIN Hayes
    NAT Holman (Mr. Basketball)
    Dan ISSEL
    ALLEN Iverson (the Answer)
    Jerry LUCAS
    JASON Kidd
    TONI Kukoc
    KARL Malone
    MOSES Malone
    RON Manute

DICK McGuire
KEVIN McHale
YAO Ming
EARL Monroe
ALONZO Mourning
Chris MULLEN
Lamar ODOM
HAKEEM Olajuwon
LOUIS Orr
ARIEL Ortega
BOB Pettit
PAUL Pierce
OSCAR Robertson
NATE Robinson
Cazzie RUSSELL
John SALLEY
Ralph SAMPSON
ISIAH (ZEKE) Thomas
NATE Thurmond
RUDY Tomjanovich
WES Unseld
Nick Van EXEL
Jerry WEST (his silhouette is on the NBA logo)

Notable for their *absence* from puzzles the author has solved were Bill Bradley and George Gervin (the Iceman). Several coaches have appeared: Hank IBA, BOB Knight (the General), Ray MEYER, Rick PITINO, PAT Riley, and Adolph RUPP. Basketball commentators MARV Albert, LEN Elmore, and Dick VITALE (Dickie V.) have also been encountered.

The most frequent answer related to a person, however, is SHAQ, for the center, Shaquille O'Neal, also known as "Big Aristotle" and "the Attacker"; with the Phoenix Suns, he is the "Big Cactus." The L.A. Lakers' Kareem Abdul-Jabbar (né Lew Alcindor) has been mentioned in both clues and answers. His name has been the clue for his alma mater, UCLA, and on another occasion, one needed to know that "noble" or "exalted" in Arabic means KAREEM. It has also helped to know that a basketball brand is VOIT.

Ice Hockey. If "NHL," "six," "6," "rink," "puckster," or "stick" is in a clue, the answer may relate to ice hockey; in fact, the clue "Hockey team" once resulted in SEXTET. There are 30 teams in the National Hockey League, divided into an Eastern Conference and a Western Conference. The only terms for the game itself have been deke (for a feint or deceptive maneuver), slap (and slap shot), check, assist, crease, dangle, one-timer, spin-o-rama (a 360° maneuver), and yellow card.

Perhaps because the game of ice hockey originated in Canada, most players mentioned are Canadian. Wayne Gretsky, great as he is, does not have a very useful name for crossword answers. One hockey player's name seen many times in puzzles was Bobby ORR, who played for the Bruins; he makes up for the rest of the players, as he is in lots of puzzles. Other players found are as follows:

MARCEL Dionne
Phil (ESPO) Esposito
STU Grimson
Gordie HOWE
IAN Laperrière
MARIO Lemieux
Stan MIKITA
Andy MOOG
CAM Neely
DENIS Potvin
LUC Robitaille
Patrick ROY
Terry SAWCHUK
BRAD Shaw
PETR Sykora
ESA Tikkanen
BRYAN Trottier
Oleh (OLEG) Tverdovsky

Where are Brett Hull and Mark Messier? Perhaps you will find them in a puzzle.

There are many awards in this game: the Stanley Cup is awarded annually to a winning team; other awards are the Art Ross Trophy for the highest scorer at the end of the season; the Hart Trophy for the MVP, selected by the Professional Hockey Writers' Association; the CONN Smythe Trophy for the MVP in the Stanley Cup Playoffs; the James Norris Memorial Trophy for the best defenseman; the Vezina Trophy for the best goalkeeper; the Ted Lindsay Award (formerly the Lester B. Pearson Award) for the most outstanding player; the Maurice Richard Trophy for the leading goal scorer; and the Calder Memorial Trophy for rookie of the year.

Of these, the Stanley Cup appears most frequently in clues, while CONN, used as an entry, is typically clued by its two following words (Smythe Trophy). The Jack ADAMS Award is a trophy for the NHL's coach of the year. These awards are listed because, when in a clue, they signify the game of ice hockey, thus narrowing the search for a player.

Golf. Answers to golf clues are usually short words, such as ACE (for ace in the hole or hole-in-one), BIRDIE (one under par), EAGLE (two under par), PAR (what is expected), and BOGEY (or BOGIE) (one over par). Other answers are CUP, TEE, LIE (location or position), PIN (target), CHIP (and CHIPSHOT), FORE, GRIP, PUTT, GREEN, ROUGH, SLICE, TEEUP, LIPOUT (lip-out), BADLIE (bad lie), DOGLEG, DUFFER, TEETIME, and MEDALPLAY (scoring system based on total strikes). Then there are the competitions: PGA, PROAM, OPEN (which can stand for either the British Open or the U.S. Open), USOPEN (which ends in SEPT), DAVISCUP, RYDER, and AUGUSTA National, site of the Masters Golf Tournament).

Clues are often plays on the terms "18," "trap," "iron," "wood," "links," "drive" and "driver," "swing," "wedge," "green," "rough," "mashie" (an old name for a 5-iron) and "spade mashie" (an old name for a six-iron), and "at deuce." The term "3-wood" has been a clue for SPOON, which is the antique golf club that most resembles today's 3-woods. "Tiger" and "Woods" (for Tiger Woods, of course) are quite common in puzzles, especially as the first word in clues, where they are capitalized, and thus ambiguous.

Some golfer's names in puzzles are listed below, with the more typical entry in capital letters.

AMY Alcott
ISAO Aoki (the Tower)
PAUL Azinger
SEVE (Severiano) Ballesteros
Frank BEARD
RACHEL Connor
Beth DANIEL
John DALY

OLIN Dutra
LEE Elder
Ernie ELS (the Big Easy)
Nick FALDO
JIM Furyk
TAMMIE Green
Irwin HALE
Ben HOGAN
JULI Inkster
ANA Ivanovic
Bernhard LANGER
"Champagne Tony" LEMA
NANCY Lopez
Davis LOVE III
Sandy LYLE
Roscoe MEDIATE
PHIL Mickelson
Larry MIZE
JACK Nicklaus
Greg NORMAN
Lorena OCHOA
Jeff OGILVY
Mark OMEARA (O'Meara)
Se Ri PAK
Arnold PALMER
Jerry PATE
Stewart PAYNE
Calvin PEETE
GARY Player
BETSY Rawls
RORY Sabatini
MARAT Safin
GENE Sarazen
Vijay (or sometimes Veejay or even VJ) SINGH
"Slammin' SAM" Snead
ANNIKA Sorenstam
Curtis STRANGE
Louise SUGGS

HAL Sutton
Sherri TURNER
Bob TWAY
KEN Venturi
Mike WEIR
Michelle WIE
IAN Woosnam (the Wee Welshman)

In addition to these, ELY Callaway has also appeared, where the clue was "Golf innovator." The Callaway brand is very popular in this sport. On one occasion, it helped to know that a piece of the fairway flying in the air is a DIVOT, and on several others that golf skirts are ALINES (A-lines), which might be worn by members of the LPGA, the Ladies Professional Golf Association. Marlene HAGGE, a founder of the association, has also been in puzzles, as has the LPGA's founding date, 1950.

The VARDON Trophy, named for Harry Vardon, will also be found in puzzles; it is awarded to the golfer with the lowest adjusted scoring average over a minimum of 60 rounds, but with no withdrawals. Vardon, along with James Braid and John Henry Taylor, were members of the "Great Triumvirate" in Great Britain.

Tennis. Entries are NET, LET (when the ball hits the net cord), ACE (for an unreturnable serve) and ACER (for perfect server), and CHOP (for a certain tennis stroke). Others are LOB, LOVE, SEED (ranking), DINK (a shot that falls just over the net), ADIN (ad in, or server's advantage and score after deuce), ADOUT (ad out, a score for the receiver), COURT, DEUCE (a tie), SMASH, SLICE, SERVE, MISHIT (mis-hit, to hit the ball incorrectly with the racquet), and SETPOINT. One or more words in the sequence of (1) game, (2) set, and (3) match are sometimes used to elicit one of the others as an answer.

OPENERA (open era) has also appeared; it dates to 1968, a clue. The tennis court surface HAR-TRU has been in puzzles, with one-half the term the clue and the other half the entry. More common in puzzles, however, are some of its outstanding players, such as the 1975 Wimbledon champion, Arthur ASHE; a stadium in Queens is named after him, which is sometimes a clue, as is his alma mater, UCLA, and his autobiography, *Off the Court*. Another of his memoirs was *Days of Grace*, also a clue. ANDRE Agassi has also been clued by a book: *Open: An Autobiography*.

Others encountered are listed below.

BORIS Becker
Bjorn BORG
OMAR Camporese
EVONNE Goolagong Cawley
Michael CHANG
Jimmy CONNORS
Albert COSTA
STEFAN Edberg
Chris EVERT
ROGER Federer
NEALE Fraser
ALTHEA Gibson
Steffi GRAF
TIM Henman
Lew HOAD
GORAN Ivanisevic
ANA Ivanovic
RENE Lacoste
Rodney (ROD) Laver
IVAN Lendl
Chris EVERT Lloyd
HANA Mandlikova
John MCENROE (McEnroe)
ANABEL Medina Garrigues
Carlos MOYA
ILIE Nastase
JANA Novotna
Alejandro ("Alex") OLMEDO
RENEE Richards
Bobby RIGGS
MARC Rosset
GREG Rusedsky
MARAT Safin
PETE Sampras (his autobiography *A Champion's Mind*)
Monica SELES
MARIA Sharapova
PAM Shriver

STAN Smith
Michael STICH
Fred STOLLE
HAL Sutton
Bill TILDEN
TONY Trabert
Guillermo VILAS
MATS Wilander
SERENA and VENUS Williams
NOAH Yannick
VERA Zvonareva

Then there is the Sánchez Vicario family from Spain, with "Arantxa" Isabel Maria and her brother, Emilio Angel. *Absent* from puzzles the author has solved were Billie Jean King and Martina Navratilova. Players belong to the USTA (U.S. Tennis Association).

Volleyball. The only clue-answer combination was "smash" and SPIKE. The answer LET, from the "Tennis" section above, also applies to volleyball. It was once the answer for the clue "Action between bump and spike."

Boxing. The following have occurred: TKO, JAB (a set-up punch), DECK, DIVE (an intentional loss), KAYO, RING, SPAR, MATCH, REACH, ROPES, ROUND, ONETWO, ERASER (a knockout punch), WEIGHIN, UPPERCUT, and ONETWOPUNCH (one-two punch). The sport is governed by the WBA, or World Boxing Association.

A popular answer is Muhammad ALI (né Cassius Clay), as might be expected, and other appellations for him have been "The Greatest" and "Sting Like a Bee." The first name of his trainer, ANGELO Dundee, has also been required. On one occasion, it helped to know that he was born in KENTUCKY, and on another, that he converted in 1964, and on yet another that his daughter, LAILA, is a professional boxer.

The following boxers have also appeared in puzzles as answers, with the more common name capitalized.

ABE Attell
Max BAER (but not his boxer brother, Buddy)
Riddick BOWE
JAMES J. Braddock (the Cinderella Man)
PRIMO Carnera (the Ambling Alp)
Rubin "Hurricane" CARTER

Billy CONN (the Pittsburgh Kid)
Jack DEMPSEY (the Manassa Masher and the first athlete to appear on the cover of *Time*)
Roberto DURAN (Hands of Stone)
Joe GANS (Old Master)
EMILE Griffith
Marvin HAGLER
PETE ("Kid") Herman
EVANDER Holyfield
SUGARRAY (Sugar Ray) Leonard
Joe LOUIS (the Brown Bomber)
Rocky MARCIANO
TAMI Maurillo
KEN Norton
FLOYD Patterson
Pete RADEMACHER
LEON Spinks
GENE Tunney
"Iron Mike" TYSON
JESS Willard

Notable for their *absence* in puzzles the author has solved were the following: George Foreman, Joe Frazier, Rocky Graziano, Ingemar Johansson, Sonny Liston, Sugar Ray Robinson, Max Schmeling, John L. Sullivan, and "Jersey Joe" Walcott.

Just because the word "boxer" is in a clue, however, does not mean the solution relates to boxing. Sometimes it refers to BARBARA Boxer, U.S. senator from California, and sometimes to the breed of dog. The longest boxing-related word in a puzzle was ROUNDHOUSERIGHT (round-house right).

Note: On occasion, the name of a person who has performed a notable athletic feat in a category other than one of those listed above appears in a crossword. Perhaps the most frequent of these is Gertrude EDERLE, the first woman to swim the English Channel, in 1926. Second most frequent is probably Jesse OWENS, the championship U.S. runner in the 1936 Berlin Olympics, who won four gold medals.

Then there is the gymnast OLGA Korbut, in the 1972 and 1976 Olympics, with four gold medals and two silver medals. Another is the gymnast NADIA Comaneci in the 1976 and 1980 Olympics, with five gold medals, three silver, and one bronze; also notable was her perfect score (10) in the uneven bars event at the 1976 Olympics in Montreal. The Japanese figure skater Midori ITO was the 1989 world champion and a silver medalist in the 1992 Olympics and Carol HEISS was the 1960 Olympics figure skating champion in ladies singles. The runner Sebastian COE also appears; he won two gold medals and two silver medals at the 1980 and 1984 Olympics.

If a clue relates to auto racing, it may lead to someone in the UNSER family. A sport not mentioned above, but very popular in crosswords, is jai alai. The clue is usually "Jai" and the entry ALAI. The jai alai ball is called a PELOTA, the handball basket that catches and propels the ball is a CESTA, and the arena is a FRONTON. All are found in crosswords.

Entertainment

The subject of entertainment encompasses so many forms: the stage, including drama, dance, comedy, and the musical; classical music, including solo, choral, and instrumental works, as well as combinations thereof, such as opera (see "Classical Music" above); and the comics, movies, television, and popular music. Gambling also appears in puzzles, most notably in the answers RENO, KENO, and LOTTO, but some other answers are RED (or ROUGE), BLACK (or NOIR), ODD, and EVEN, as in roulette.

Clues and answers from all these topics appear in crosswords. Characters from the comics who have made their way into movies and TV are, as a rule, mentioned only in the "Comics" section below, but *actors* who have taken the parts of such characters, for example, Superman, will be found in the "Movies" section. And keep in mind, too, that movies have made their way into TV series, such as "M*A*S*H." And vice-versa: for example, "Star Trek," a TV series, had film spinoffs. In this book, you will find "M*A*S*H and Star Trek" in the "Television" section. The old superheroes of the comics such as Batman, Superman, and Wonder Woman have acquired new characteristics and new foes over the years

Comics

A familiarity with comic strips is helpful for crosswords, and there are quite a few common clues and answers. Before introducing them, it is helpful to know that a cartoon still, or animation frame, is called a CEL (from the word "celluloid"), that Japanese cartoon art is ANIME, and that an abbreviation of "cartoon" is TOON. The cartoonist's award is the REUBEN. A popular interjection in cartoons, especially those involving animals, is EEK. One of the oldest strips is "ETTA Kett"; the clue is usually the teenager's last name, the answer her first. The strip's creator, Paul Robinson, has been in a clue, as has Bud Fisher, creator of the strip "Mutt and Jeff."

The characters in the old comic strip "Bringing Up Father" have been needed; these were MAGGIE and JIGGS; another puzzle required their daughter NORA. ANNIE, of "Little Orphan Annie," is sometimes clued as "Daddy Warbucks' ward," and one of Warbucks' henchmen is the ASP. From the "Nancy" comic strip you may come across ROLLO (the rich kid), Aunt FRITZI, Nancy's friend IRMA, SLUGGO (her lazy boyfriend), POOCHIE (her dog), TEDDY (her bear), as well as the cartoonist, ERNIE Bushmiller.

Then there are ANDY Gump, his wife, MIN, and the maid, TILDA; Broom HILDA; ARLO and JANIS; Krazy KAT and his antagonist, Ignatz Mouse; the Katzenjammer KIDS; Barney Google and Snuffy Smith, with Barney's horse named SPARKPLUG; TOM and Jerry; Fritz the CAT; and HAZEL, the bossy maid. "The Little King" usually needs its cartoonist, OTTO Soglow.

Another comic strip is "Blondie," dating to 1930, in which Dagwood Bumstead and his wife Blondie (née Boopadoop), interact with various characters: their son ALEXANDER, daughter COOKIE, and dog DAISY; next-door neighbor and coworker HERB Woodley and his wife, TOOTSIE; the five-year-old ELMO Tuttle; Dagwood's boss, Mr. (Julius C.) DITHERS, and his wife CORA; Mr. BEASLEY, the postman; and LOU, the counterman. The creator of "Blondie" is also in puzzles: Murat Bernard "CHIC" Young (the cartoon is now done by his son, Dean, whose father died in 1973). Even after over 80 years, "Blondie" is read by about 250 million people in over 2,000 newspapers in 55 countries and in over 30 languages.

Beginning in 1934, "Terry and the Pirates," by Milton Caniff, featured a young Terry LEE and an older PAT Ryan. Clues about Prince Valiant need his bride's name, which is ALETA (she is also clued as "comic-strip queen" or as "Queen of the Misty Isles"), as well as his son's name, which is Prince ARN (and Arn's bride is MAEVE). And everyone over a certain age knows that ARCHIE Andrews, who wears an

"R" on his sweater, is a redhead who goes to Riverdale High and that he, Veronica, Moose (or Big Moose), and Jughead are TEENS. Moose was once clued as a poor student. This strip was created by Don DeCarlo and began in 1941, two clues for its title.

Perhaps harder to recall is that the swamp critter (or 'possum) POGO's friend Howland is an OWL and that the alligator's name is ALBERT; the cartoonist, Walt Kelly, has also been in puzzles. Dick Tracy and TESS Truehart appear, as do POPEYE the sailor, Olive OYL (who wears large shoes), SWEE-Pea, and Popeye's nemesis, BLUTO. Olive Oyl has an older brother, CASTOR. It has helped to know that Popeye's tattoo is an ANCHOR, that he has MUSKLES (muscles), and that his favorite food is SPINACH. One of Popeye's sayings is "Iyam what Iyam." The clues are such that the entry is IYAM. Popeye's creator, Elzie SEGAR, has also been needed as an entry.

Very common are the "Superman" characters Clark Kent (both his first and last names are used as clues and answers) and the reporter Lois Lane (again, both names), of the *Daily Planet* (this strip began on April 18, 1938). Perry WHITE was the editor and Jimmy OLSEN a reporter and photojournalist for that newspaper. It has helped to know that Clark Kent changes his clothes in a PHONEBOOTH to become the Man of Steel, that he was ADOPTED, and that he shaves with heat vision. His mother is LARA, his birth name is KALEL (Kal-El), and one of his foes is LEX (at least, in the movie version). His pet dog, KRYPTO, has also turned up in puzzles. A clue to this strip is the mention of Metropolis, where the action takes place. (A villainess in the film "Superman II" was URSA; other Kryptonian villains were ZOD and NON.)

Speaking of supermen, Batman (the Caped Crusader) and Robin are known as the "dynamic duo" in clues, and one puzzle required the name of Batman's creator, Bob KANE. Also helpful to know is the butler's name, ALFRED, Batman's alter ego, Bruce WAYNE, and Robin's alter ego, Dick GRAYSON. Even the sound effect, BAM, has been an entry. Several of Batman's enemies are the Joker, the Penguin, the Riddler, Two-Face, Mr. Freeze, and Poison Ivy. Batman and Robin live at Wayne Manor, a clue for this strip; another clue is the locale, Gotham.

Knowing Captain Marvel's magic word, SHAZAM, is helpful, but Billy Batson has yet to appear. Two of Captain Marvel's nemeses are Mr. ATOM and Mr. MIND. The Green Hornet is yet another outsize hero, whose sidekick, KATO, is a good entry for puzzles; the Green Hornet's real name is Britt REID, publisher of the *Daily Sentinel*. And Flash

Gordon has appeared, requiring as an answer one of his villains, MING. Not to be outdone is Wonder Woman; she usually needs the name of her long-time arch-nemesis, whose name is ARES.

Dogpatch characters from Al Capp's "L'il Abner" make an appearance, especially Daisy MAE; his mother's name, Pansy YOKUM, has also been needed. Pappy's full name is Lucifer Ornamental Yokum. Usually his parents are simply MAMMY and PAPPY Yokum. A SHMOO has also appeared, but you have to be over a certain age to remember what shmoos were. Another character is Joe BTFSPLK, who can be easily identified, as he always has a cloud over his head. (Do not confuse Al Capp, the creator of "L'il Abner," with ANDY Capp, a comics figure who hangs out in a PUB, whose wife is FLO (short for Florrie), and addressed by Andy as LUV.)

At Camp Swampy, Mort Walker's Pvt. Beetle Bailey reports to SARGE Snorkle, whose bulldog is named OTTO (very popular in crosswords); other characters in this strip are General HALFTRACK (AMOS to his wife, MARTHA), Lt. FUZZ, Lt. FLAP, Lt. COSMO (the chaplain), Sgt. Louise LUGG (Sarge's friend), Pvt. ZERO, Pvt. ROCKY, GIZMO (the general's "techie"), JULIUS (the general's driver), KILLER, Miss BUXLEY, COOKIE the cook, and others. Beetle can often be found ONKP (on KP, or kitchen patrol).

Garfield is the fat and lazy orange cat whose "victim" is the yellow-furred beagle ODIE (even more popular than Otto, above), who drools, sometimes a clue. JON Arbuckle is the human in the strip, created by Jim Davis. (The cat's name is taken from Davis's grandfather, President James Abram Garfield.) It has also helped to know that Garfield's vet is LIZ, that his favorite food is LASAGNA, and that he also likes COFFEE. A waitress in the strip is IRMA. Felix the cat's nephew is INKY; and Little Orphan Annie's dog is SANDY, his clue sometimes being "Arf!"

Charlie Brown, of "Peanuts" fame, has quite a few friends: the philosophical LINUS van Pelt; the pianist SCHROEDER, who plays Beethoven; VIOLET; PIGPEN; the tomboy PEPPERMINTPATTY and her friend, MARCIE; his sister SALLY; and his beagle SNOOPY, who wears a flier's helmet. (In a song and album, as well as a video game and an animated movie, Snoopy's nemesis is the RED Baron.) His sister LUCY is Charlie's tormentor. His expletive, RATS, occurs in puzzles, as well as GOODGRIEF (Good Grief!). It has also helped to know that the design on his shirt is a ZIGZAG. Charles Schulz produced 17,897 strips of "Peanuts" with no assistants; begun in 1950, it is read in about 2,600 newspapers in 21 languages in 75 countries, and is the most widely syndicated cartoon in the world.

In another strip, DENNIS Mitchell is his neighbor Mr. Wilson's "menace," his girlfriend is GINA or MARGARET, depending on how he feels at the time, his friend is JOEY, his dog is RUFF, and his parents are HENRY and ALICE; the cartoonist is Hank Ketcham. A short entry for Dennis is IMP. If "Viking" is in a clue, the answer may relate to a character in "Hägar the Horrible," such as Hägar's wife HELGA, their daughter HONI, their son HAMLET, his girlfriend HERNIA, their dog SNERT, Dr. ZOOK, Lucky EDDIE, or Fast FREDDIE; the characters live in the NORWAY of 1,000 years ago. The cartoon was created by Dik Browne and has been continued by his son, Chris.

Also encountered in puzzles were Brenda STARR; Betty BOOP, Reporter; Fearless FOSDICK; Alley OOP (a caveman from MOO who rides on Dinny the Dinosaur and who was once on a 33-cent postage stamp, the clue) and his girlfriend OOOLA; LUANN, who has been clued as a blonde; Little JOE and brother ADAM; DILBERT and the curly-haired ALICE, as well as ASOK, who is the company IT intern, and Wally and Carol.

Others are Hi and LOIS and their four children (Chip, Dot, Ditto, and Trixie); HAROLD; SMITTY; Smilin' JACK; JOE Palooka; Major Hoople (whose first name is AMOS) and his exclamation, EGAD; DONDI, a large-eyed war orphan; CALVIN and Hobbes (Calvin does not like TAPIOCA); Rose Is Rose and the selfish family cousin, CLEM; CASPAR Milquetoast in "The Timid Soul"; Abbie an' SLATS; and the superhero group, the XMEN. The X-men and Spider-Man are properties of Marvel Entertainment; an enemy of the X-men is MAGNETO; two Spider-Man enemies are ELECTRO and Dr. OTTO Octavius.

This section would not be complete without some mention of the Disney characters, even though they are not often found in puzzles. Besides Donald and Daisy Duck and Mickey and Minnie Mouse, one might also encounter Donald's three nephews, who are Huey, Dewey, and Louie. Then there are Bugs Bunny, Elmer Fudd, Porky and Petunia Pig, Doc (who has been clued as wearing glasses and who is prone to Spoonerisms), Dopey (the only beardless dwarf), Goofy, Pluto, Grumpy, and Daffy Duck. (It has helped to know that Daffy lisps.) Three others are Pepé le Pew, an amorous, malodorous, Parisian skunk, Wile E. Coyote, and Penelope Pussycat. The "Looney Tunes" animator who created Bugs Bunny, Porky Pig, and Daffy Duck has also been an answer: Tex AVERY. Another animator who has appeared is FRIZ Freleng. And "Merrie Melodies" is sometimes a clue for a Disney character.

The cartoonist of "The Family Circus," BIL Keane, has been an answer, and another Bil with only one "l" who appears in crosswords was the puppet-maker, BIL Baird. You may also come across MELL Lazarus, creator of both "Miss Peach" and "Momma." And last is ZIGGY, clued by its creator, Tom Wilson.

Movies

An entry related to the movies is the OSCAR award, and on more than one occasion, the year of the first awards, 1947, has been in the clue. Other entries are (1) NOIR, a film genre, (2) OATER, synonym for a Western (or horse opera), (3) EPIC, such as a film directed by Cecil B. de Mille, and (4) INDIE, often used for an art film. If you should come across "Bollywood" in a clue, the term refers to the film industry in Mumbai, more formally, Hindi cinema.

Two foreign synonyms for movies are also common: CINE and CINEMA. The Cannes film festival is cited, as well as its award, the Palme d'Or, usually clued as "Palme ___," with the entry being DOR. The French film award has also appeared; it is the CÉSAR, first given in 1975. Some actors subsequently became directors or screenwriters, and some, such as Stu Erwin, went into TV. In this handbook, those who were in both the movies and TV are included in both sections, when appropriate.

With respect to movies themselves, the most popular character and her plantation home come from the 1939 film based on Margaret Mitchell's novel, *Gone With the Wind* (sometimes simply "GWTW" in clues); these are Scarlett OHARA (played by Vivien Leigh) and TARA, respectively. RHETT Butler (played by Clark Gable) also shows up on occasion. Both MYDEAR and DAMN have been answers, from his famous statement, "Frankly, my dear, I don't give a damn." Another of his quotes appearing in various forms in puzzles is "And you, miss, are no lady." Ashley Wilkes's neighboring plantation of TWELVEOAKS has also been an answer. It is helpful to remember that Melanie Hamilton was played by Olivia de Havilland, Ashley Wilkes by Leslie Howard, Mammy by Hattie McDaniel, and Prissy by Butterfly McQueen. Even the name of Scarlett's mother has been needed: ELLEN.

Another film frequently cited is "The Wizard of Oz," also from 1939, based on a story by L. Frank BAUM. Many of its characters find their way into puzzles: the heroine DOROTHY, played by Judy Garland; her Auntie Em, whose family name was GALE, played by CLARA Blandick; her dog TOTO, who bothered Miss GULCH and who escaped in a bicycle basket (yes, that clue was in a puzzle); the tin man, who needed a HEART (as well as OIL), played by Jack Haley; the scarecrow, who needed a BRAIN, played by Ray Bolger; the cowardly lion, who needed COURAGE, played by Bert Lahr (he also played ZEKE, a farmhand); the wizard, played by Frank Morgan; GLINDA, the good fairy, played by Billie Burke; and the dual roles of Miss Gulch and the Wicked Witch of the West, played by Margaret Hamilton. Dorothy and her friends were on their way to the Emerald City. It helps to know that Dorothy and Auntie Em are from KANSAS.

Yet another popular source for crosswords is Dashiell Hammett's "The Thin Man" series, five mystery movies from 1934 to 1947, starring William POWELL as Nick Charles and Myrna LOY as Nora Charles. Hammett is used as both clue and answer, as are the characters and their players. But they are upstaged in puzzles by ASTA, sometimes clued as "Hammett hound." (The original dog in the novel, *The Thin Man*, was a schnauzer, and puzzles may use either that breed or wire fox terrier as a clue.)

The film "Casablanca," from 1942, starred Humphrey Bogart as RICK Blaine, the proprietor of Café Americain (also known as Rick's gin joint), and Ingrid Bergman, who played ILSA Lund, a popular name in puzzles. Other actors were Paul Henreid as Victor Laszlo, Claude Rains as Capt. Louis Renault, Peter Lorre as Ugarté, and Sydney Greenstreet as Ferrari. Every now and then you will also come across SAM Wilson, the pianist in the café, who played the theme song, "As Time Goes By," a clue to his name. And there is also the line from the movie, "We'll always have PARIS." Another movie is "Sunset Boulevard," of 1950; the heroine, NORMA Desmond, was played by Gloria Swanson and the down-and-out writer was played by William Holden.

The "Star Wars" movies, by George LUCAS, appear, and the most popular entry is Princess LEIA. Others are LUKE Skywalker and his father ANAKIN (sometimes ANI), who became Darth VADER, and YODA, a Jedi master. Both ALEC Guinness and EWAN McGregor have played the role of OBI-Wan Kenobi and Harrison FORD appeared in the role of Han SOLO, who has been clued as a hero. The JEDI order represents the good, or light, side of the Force and the SITH order represents the dark side of the Force.

As for *screenwriters*, the most popular are NORA Ephron, James AGEE, and William INGE. The most frequent *directors* in entries seem to be INGMAR Bergman, Joel and Ethan COEN, WES Craven, CECIL B. de Mille, Federico FELLINI, ABEL Gance, ALFRED Hitchcock, RON Howard, ELIA Kazan, AKIRA Kurosawa, Fritz LANG, David LEAN, Norman LEAR, ANG Lee, Spike LEE, Sergio LEONE, BARRY Levinson, Frank LLOYD, ERNST Lubitsch, George LUCAS, Sidney LUMET, DAVID Lynch, Louis MALLE, ROMAN Polanski, CARLO Ponti, OTTO Preminger, Rob REINER, MARTIN Scorsese, Oliver STONE, Jacques TATI, François TRUFFAUT, and GUS Van Sant.

Some other directors you may come across, in either clues or entries, are Woody Allen, Robert Altman, Wes Anderson, Hal Ashby, Frank Capra, John Cleese, Vittorio de Sica, Atom Egoyan, Francis Ford Coppola, Howard Hawks, John Huston (son of actor Walter Huston), Stanley Kubrick, Brian de Palma, Sam Raimi, Jean Renoir, Eli Roth, Stephen Spielberg, George Stevens, Quentin Tarantino, Orson Welles, Lina Wertmuller, and Billy Wilder. And *critics* are not to be left out: Pauline KAEL and Rex REED make rather frequent appearances, too.

Some of the earliest actors appeared in the genre of horror movies. Among them were Peter LORRE and LON Chaney, Jr. (he played the Wolf Man). A common crossword answer is IGOR, Dr. Frankenstein's assistant in the movies adapted from Mary Shelley's novel, *Frankenstein*. In the 1931 classic, Boris Karloff played the monster, and in the second Frankenstein film, in 1935, Elsa Lanchester played the bride in "The Bride of Frankenstein."

Speaking of early actors, the first two lists below include those whose birth dates occurred before 1901. They may be especially helpful for clues that mention "silver screen," "silent screen," or "old-time" actors. Some stars, such as Joan Crawford, successfully made the move to the "talkies," which began in 1927, but most could not do so. The modern generation could lose sight of them, but they can be seen in reruns on the TCM (Turner Classic Movies) channel.

The lists below are organized by the decade of an actor's birth date, further classified by women, then men. If your favorite leading man or leading lady is not in any of the lists below, the reason is that he or she has not been found by the author in a puzzle.

Women by last name (born through 1900):

Renée Adorée
Theda Bara (the Vamp)
Ethel Barrymore (sister of Lionel and John)
Enid Bennett
Edna Best
Billie Burke
Mae Busch
Ilka Chase
Ina Claire
Lotta Crabtree
Irene Dunne
Helen Gahagan (wife of Melvyn Douglas)
Dorothy Gish
Lillian Gish ("first lady of the silent screen")
Helen Hayes
Lotte Lenya
Hattie McDaniel
Agnes Moorehead
Nita Naldi
Pola Negri
Mabel Normand
Edna May Oliver
ZaSu Pitts
Edna Purviance
Irene Rich
Ruth Roland
Norma Shearer
Alison Skipworth
Gloria Swanson
Ethel Waters
Mae West
Peggy Wood

Men by last name (born through 1900):

Bud Abbott (movie partner of Lou Costello)
Fred Astaire

John Barrymore (brother of Lionel and Ethel)
Lionel Barrymore (brother of John and Ethel)
Wallace Beery (uncle of Noah, Jr.)
Eric Blore
Humphrey Bogart
William Boyd (Hopalong Cassidy)
Charles Boyer
Nigel Bruce
James Cagney
Harry Carey, Sr.
Lon Chaney, Sr.
Sir Charles Spencer (Charlie) Chaplin
Ronald Coleman
William Farnum
W.C. Fields
Sydney Greenstreet
Edmund Gwenn
Sir Cedric Hardwicke
Oliver Hardy (movie partner of Stan Laurel)
George (Gabby) Hayes
Leslie Howard
Moe Howard (the middle of the three stooges)
Shemp Howard (the eldest of the three stooges)
Emil Jannings
Boris Karloff
Buster Keaton
Bert Lahr
Stan Laurel (movie partner of Oliver Hardy)
Harold Lloyd
Peter Lorre
Béla Lugosi
Fredric March
Arthur Marx (Harpo)
Julius Marx (Groucho)
Leonard Marx (Chico)
Milton Marx (Gummo)
Raymond Massey
Adolphe Menjou
Tom Mix

Paul Muni
J. Carrol Naish
Conrad Nigel
Ivor Novello
Pat O'Brien
Charles Ogle
Warner Oland (as Charlie Chan)
Walter Pidgeon
Claude Rains
Basil Rathbone
John Reid
Edward G. Robinson
Cesar Romero
Akim Tamiroff
Spencer Tracy
Rudolph Valentino
Ed Wynn (father of Keenan)

Women by last name (born 1901-1910):

Mary Astor
Josephine Baker
Bea Benaderet
Joan Blondell
Clara Bow (the "It" girl of the '20s)
Joan Crawford
Bebe Daniels
Bette Davis
Dolores del Rio
Marlene Dietrich
Glenda Farrell
Greta Garbo
Greer Garson
Janet Gaynor
Katharine Hepburn
Elsa Lanchester
Lila Lee
Myrna Loy (especially as Nora in "The Thin Man")
Jeanette MacDonald

Anna Magnani
Ilona Massey
Una Merkel
Thelma Ritter
Ann Sothern
Barbara Stanwyck
Anna Sten
Jessica Tandy
Thelma Todd
Claire Trevor
Fay Wray

Men by last name (born 1901-1910):

Brian Aherne
Philip Ahn
Eddie Albert
Don Ameche
Leon Ames
Dana Andrews
Gene Autry
Lew Ayres
Lon Chaney, Jr.
Gary Cooper
Lou Costello (movie partner of Bud Abbott)
Joseph Cotton
Buster Crabbe (played Tarzan, Flash Gordon, and Buck Rogers)
Robert Donat
Melvyn Douglas (husband of Helen Gahagan)
Dan Duryea
Buddy Ebsen
Stuart (Stu) Erwin
Tom Ewell
Errol Flynn
Henry Fonda (father of Peter and Jane)
Clark Gable
John Gielgud
Rex Harrison
Paul Henreid

John Houseman
Jerome "Curly" Howard (replaced Shemp as one of the three stooges)
Burl Ives
Peter Lorre
Fred MacMurray
Herbert Marx (Zeppo)
James Mason
Joel McCrea
David Niven
Dennis O'Keefe
Sir Laurence Olivier
Sir Michael Redgrave (father of Vanessa and Lynn)
Eric Rhodes
Robert Ryan
James Stewart
Lyle Talbot
Jacques Tati
John Wayne
Johnny Weissmuller (Olympic gold medalist in swimming who played Tarzan)
Emlyn Williams

Women by last name (born 1911-1920):

Lucille Ball
Ingrid Bergman (mother of Isabella Rossellini)
Laraine Day
Olivia de Havilland
Ann Doran
Dale Evans (wife of Roy Rogers)
Nanette Fabray
Joan Fontaine
Magda Gabor (sister of Eva and Zsa Zsa)
Zsa Zsa Gabor (sister of Eva and Magda)
Uta Hagen
Jean Harlow
June Havoc
Susan Hayward
Rita Hayworth

Eileen Heckart
Sonja Henie
Celeste Holm
Ruth Hussey
Lila Kedrova
Hedy Lamarr
Vivian Leigh
Ida Lupino
Mary Martin
Osa Masson
Virginia Mayo
Butterfly McQueen
Noel Neill
Merle Oberon
Maureen O'Hara
Maureen O'Sullivan
Lilli Palmer
Ginger Rogers
Esther Rolle
Ann Sheridan
Ilse Steppat
Gene Tierney
Lana Turner
Loretta Young

Men by last name (born 1911-1920):

Robert Alda (father of Alan and Antony)
Pedro Armendáriz, Sr.
Lex Barker
Noah Beery (nephew of Wallace)
Turhan Bey
Ernest Borgnine
Rossano Brazzi
Lloyd Bridges (father of Beau and Jeff)
Yul Brynner
Raymond Burr
Art Carney
Montgomery Clift

Lee J. Cobb
Hans Conried
Jeff Corey
Wendell Corey
Hume Cronyn
Ossie Davis (husband of Ruby Dee)
Kirk Douglas (father of Michael)
Jack Elam
Larry Fine (one of the three stooges)
Glenn Ford
Gert Fröbe
Lorne Greene
Alec Guinness
Lom Herbert
William Holden
Tim Holt
Danny Kaye
Gene Kelly
Alan Ladd
Fernando Lamas (husband of Arlene Dahl and father of Lorenzo Lamas)
Burt Lancaster
Lash LaRue
Karl Malden
Dean Martin
Victor Mature
Robert Mitchum
Clayton Moore (the Lone Ranger)
Harry Morgan
Zero Mostel
Edmund O'Brien
Gregory Peck
Tyrone Power
Vincent Price
Anthony Quinn
Tony Randall
Ronald Reagan
Fernando Rey
Roy Rogers (King of the Cowboys and husband of Dale Evans)
Mickey Rooney

Jay Silverheels (Tonto)
Frank Sinatra
Emil Sitka
Raf Vallone
Eli Wallach
Orson Welles
Joseph Wiseman
Keenan Wynn (son of Ed)

Women by last name (born 1921-1930):

Edie Adams
Bea Arthur
Lauren Bacall
Diana Barrymore (daughter of John)
Eva Bartok
Anne Baxter
Amanda Blake
Ann Blyth
Cyd Charisse
Phyllis Coates
Arlene Dahl (wife of Fernando Lamas and mother of Lorenzo Lamas)
Denise Darcel
Linda Darnell
Doris Day
Yvonne DeCarlo
Ruby Dee (wife of Ossie Davis)
Gloria DeHaven
Joanne Dru
Deanna Durbin
Rhonda Fleming
Nina Foch
Mona Freeman
Eva Gabor (sister of Magda and Zsa Zsa)
Ava Gardner
Judy Garland
Mitzi Gaynor
Lee Grant

Kathryn Grayson
Julie Harris
June Haver
Tippi Hedren
Audrey Hepburn
Kim Hunter
Betty Hutton
Grace Kelly
Deborah Kerr
Veronica Lake
Angela Lansbury
Janet Leigh
Gina Lollobrigida
Anne Meara (wife of Jerry Stiller and mother of Ben Stiller)
Dina Merrill
Vera Miles
Ann Miller
Marilyn Monroe (née Norma Jean Baker)
Patricia Neal
Hildegarde Neff (née Knef)
Nancy Olson
Geraldine Page
Irene Page
Irene Papas
Estelle Parsons
Charlotte Rae
Ella Raines
Gena Rowlands
Simone Signoret
Maureen Stapleton
Shirley Temple
Sada Thompson
Marta Tore
Lana Turner
Gwen Verdon
Elena Verdugo
Dana Wynter

Men by last name (born 1921-1930):

Claude Akins
James Arness
Ed Asner
Theodore Bikel
Marlon Brando
Mel Brooks
Rory Calhoun
Harry Carey, Jr.
Sir Sean Connery
Tony Curtis
Richard Crenna
Vic Damone
William Daniels
Sammy Davis, Jr.
John Derek (husband of Bo Derek)
Clint Eastwood
Richard Egan
Peter Falk
Fred Gwynne
Charlton Heston
Hal Holbrook
Rock Hudson
Lash LaRue
Jack Lemmon
Jerry Lewis
Lee Marvin
Alec McCowen
Darren McGavin
Steve McQueen
Yves Montand
Sir Roger Moore
Pat Morita
Leslie Nielsen
Paul Newman (husband of Joanne Woodward)
Milo O'Shea
Fess Parker
Christopher Plummer

Sidney Poitier
Aldo Ray
Alejandro Rey
Jason Robards
Sabu (last name Dastagir), the elephant boy
Telly Savalas
George C. Scott
George Segal
Peter Sellers
Rod Steiger
Jerry Stiller (husband of Anne Meara and father of Ben Stiller)
Sir Peter Ustinov
Abe Vigoda
Max von Sydow
Oskar Werner
Adam West (especially as Batman in 1966 film)

Women by last name (born 1931-1940):

Anouk Aimée
Bibi Andersson
Ursula Andress
Julie Andrews
Ina Balin
Anne Bancroft
Brigitte Bardot
Karen Black
Claire Bloom
Eileen Brennan
Ellen Burstyn
Dyan Cannon
Leslie Caron
Irina Demich (also Demick)
Dame Judith (Judi) Dench
Angie Dickinson
Samantha Eggar
Anita Ekberg
Jane Fonda (daughter of Henry and sister of Peter)
Eileen Fulton

Mitzi Gaynor
Glenda Jackson
Lainie Kazan
Diane Ladd (mother of Laura Dern)
Mildred Landon
Sophia Loren
Tina Louise
Ali MacGraw
Shirley MacLaine (sister of Warren Beatty)
Yvette Mimieux
Rita Moreno
Kim Novak
Debra Paget
Jo Ann Pflug
Laurie Piper
Mala Powers
Paula Prentiss
Vanessa Redgrave (daughter of Michael and sister of Lynn)
Lee Remick
Madlyn Rhue
Janice Rule
Gia Scala
Romy Schneider
Elke Sommer
Inger Stevens
Inga Swenson
Sylvia Syms
Dame Elizabeth Taylor
Tina Turner
Cicely Tyson
Liv Ullmann
Joanne Woodward (wife of Paul Newman)

Men by last name (born 1931-1940):

Alan Alda (son of Robert and brother of Antony)
Woody Allen
Alan Arkin (father of Adam)
John Drew Barrymore (son of John and father of Drew)

Alan Bates
Ned Beatty
Warren Beatty (brother of Shirley MacLaine)
Jeremy Brett
Horst Buchholz
James Caan
James Cain
Sir Michael Caine
Len Cariou
Ronny Cox
Alain Delon
Bruce Dern (father of Laura)
Keir Dullea
Ron Ely
Marty Feldman
Albert Finney
Peter Fonda (son of Henry, sister of Jane, and father of Bridget)
James Fox
Morgan Freeman
Gene Hackman
Darryl Hickman (brother of Dwayne)
Dwayne Hickman (brother of Darryl)
Dustin Hoffman
Sir Ian Holm
Sir Anthony Hopkins
Tab Hunter
John Hurt
Sir Derek Jacobi
Raúl Juliá
Harvey Keitel
Alan Ladd
Frank Langella
Bruce Lee
Christopher Lloyd
Sir Ian McKellen
Sal Mineo
Sir Dudley Moore
Nick Nolte
Sir Peter O'Toole

Al Pacino
Tony Perkins
Richard Pryor
Robert Redford
Burt Reynolds
Omar Sharif
William Shatner
Martin Sheen
Paul Sorvino
Donald Sutherland
George Takei
Russ Tamblyn
Rip Torn
Gene Wilder

Women by last name (born 1941-1950):

Francesca Annis
Sonia Braga
Cher
Julie Christie
Jill Clayburgh
Tyne Daly
Sandra Dee (daughter of Ruby Dee)
Patty Duke
Faye Dunaway
Mia Farrow (daughter of Maureen O'Sullivan)
Sally Field
Teri Garr
Whoopi Goldberg
Ilene Graff
Tess Harper
Goldie Hawn
Madeline Kahn
Diane Keaton
Jessica Lange
Sondra Locke
Shelley Long
Sue Lyon

Hayley Mills
Gilda Radnor
Lynn Redgrave (daughter of Michael and sister of Vanessa)
Susan Sarandon
Talia Shire
Cissy Spacek
Alana Stewart
Meryl Streep
Barbra Streisand
Cheryl Tiegs
Rita Tushingham
Trish Van Devere
Dianne Wiest

Men by last name (born 1941-1950):

Armand Assante
John Belushi (brother of James)
Beau Bridges (son of Lloyd and brother of Jeff)
Jeff Bridges (son of Lloyd and brother of Beau)
John Candy
Ian Charleson
Chevy Chase
Tom Conti
Ben Cross
Ted Danson
Robert De Niro
Danny DeVito
Harrison Ford
Richard Gere
Ed Harris
Jeremy Irons
Stacy Keach
Harvey Keitel
Sir Ben Kingsley
David Ladd (son of Alan)
Steve Martin
Ian McShane
Sam Neill

Craig T. Nelson
Ryan O'Neal (father of Tatum)
Franco Nero
Edward James Olmos
Michael Palin
Joe Pesci
Harold Ramis
Stephen Rea
Roger Rees
Alan Rickman
Ron Silver
Brent Spiner
Sylvester (Sly) Stallone
Jim Varney
Ben Vereen
Oleg Vidov
James Woods

Women by last name (born 1951-1960):

Carol Alt
Alicia Ana
Ellen Barkin
Kim Basinger
Amanda Bearse
Irene Cara
Lynda Carter (Wonder Woman)
Geena Davis
Rebecca DeMornay
Bo Derek (wife of John)
Jennifer Grey
Glenne Headly
Marilu Henner
Holly Hunter
Amy Irving
Cheryl Ladd
Lorna Luft (daughter of Judy Garland and half-sister of Liza Minelli)
Andie MacDowell
Edie McClurg

Kate Mulgrew
Kate Nelligan
Lena Olin
Amanda Plummer
Annie Potts
Tanya Roberts
Mimi Rogers
Isabella Rossellini (daughter of Ingrid Bergman)
Mercedes Ruehl
Rene Russo
Lori Singer
Imelda Stanton
Sharon Stone
Tilda Swinton
Lauren Tewes
Emma Thompson
Sela Ward
JoBeth Williams
Debra Winger

Men by last name (born 1951-1960):

Antony Alda (son of Robert and brother of Alan)
Tim Allen
Adam Arkin (son of Alan)
Rowan Atkinson
Dan Aykroyd
Alec Baldwin
Roberto Benigni
James Belushi (brother of John)
Sir Kenneth Branagh
Pierce Brosnan
Kevin Costner
Tom Cruise
Willem Dafoe
Mel Gibson
Tom Hanks
Tom Hulce
Chris Isaac

Val Kilmer
Lorenzo Lamas (son of Fernando Lamas and Arlene Dahl)
Mark Lester
Liam Neeson
Mandy Patinkin
Sean Penn
Oliver Platt
Dennis Quaid
Aidan Quinn
Christopher Reeve (especially as Superman)
Ving Rhames
Eric Roberts (brother of Julia)
Jeffrey Rush
Ron Silver
Kevin Spacey
Patrick Swayze
John Travolta
Jean-Claude van Damme (the "Muscles from Brussels")
Denzel Washington
Adrian Zmed

Women by last name (born 1961-1970):

Paula Abdul
Jennifer Aniston
Halle Berry
Juliette Binoche
Cate Blanchett
Lara Flynn Boyle
Sandra Bullock
Tia Carrere
Helena Bonham Carter
Rae Dawn Chong
Laura Dern (daughter of Bruce and of Diane Ladd)
Amanda Donohoe
Jodie Foster
Anna Gasteyer
Salma Hayek
Anne Heche

Helen Hunt
Moira Kelly
Téa Leoni
Bai Ling
Jennifer Long
Nia Long
Jennifer Lopez
Jena Malone
Debra Messing
Ari Meyers
Demi Moore
Tatum O'Neal (daughter of Ryan)
Sarah Jessica Parker
Nia Peeples
Teri Polo
Julia Roberts (sister of Eric)
Meg Ryan
Mia Sara
Kyra Sedgwick
Elizabeth Shue
Ione Skye
Mira Sorvino
Lili Anne Taylor
Charlize Theron
Uma Thurman
Marisa Tomei
Nia Vardalos
Naomi Watts
Yvette Wilson
Pia Zadora
Renée Zellweger
Catherine Zeta-Jones

Men by last name (born 1961-1970):

Eric Bana
Jack Black
Nicolas Cage
Jim Carrey

Tom Cruise
John Cusack
Matt Damon
Johnny Depp
Cary Elwes
Will Farrell
Jamie Foxx
Zach Galifianakis
Paul Giamatti
Ethan Hawke
Philip Seymour Hoffman
Brandon Lee (son of Bruce)
Rob Lowe
Esai Morales
Eddie Murphy
Denis O'Hare
Brad Pitt
Keanu Reeves
Chris Rock
Adam Sandler
Charlie Sheen
Christian Slater
Wesley Snipes
Ben Stiller (son of Anne Meara and Jerry Stiller)
Will Smith (father of Jaden)
Owen Wilson

Women by last name (born 1971 or later):

Amy Adams
Jessica Alba
Gemma Atkinson
Drew Barrymore (daughter of John Drew Barrymore)
Jessica Biel
Kirsten Dunst
Erica Durance
Dakota Fanning
Eva Green
Katie Holmes

Mila Kunis
Jena Malone
Alyssa Milano
Gwyneth Paltrow
Anna Paquin
Elsa Pataki
Amanda Peet
Natalie Portman
Tara Reid
Zoe Saldana
Leelee Sobieski
Emma Stone
Mena Suvari
Hilary Swank
Aimee Teegarten
Tia Texada
Liv Tyler
Emma Watson
Kate Winslet
Reese Witherspoon
Evan Rachel Wood

Men by last name (born 1971 or later):

Ben Affleck
Sean Astin
Christian Bale
Ewen Bremmer
Adrien Brody
Scott Caan (son of James Caan)
Hayden Christensen
Macauley Culkin
Leonardo DiCaprio
Seth Green
Lukas Haas
Neil Patrick Harris
Jonah Hill
Emil Hirsch
Cuoco Kaley

Ashton Kutcher
Shia LaBoeuf
Joey Lawrence
Samm Levine
Jared Leto
Ewen McGregor
Trevor Morgan
Eli Roth
Jason Segel
Jaden Smith (son of Will)
Wil Wheaton

As in the comics, dogs in movies have a place in crosswords, too, such as Dorothy's dog TOTO and Nick and Nora Charles's schnauzer (or wire fox terrier, depending on the source) ASTA, also known as Skippy (Toto and Asta are mentioned earlier, with their movies), the collie LASSIE from the eponymous movies (and also TV series), and NANA, the dog in "Peter Pan." Beethoven and Benji were DOGs, as was RINTINTIN (RinTin Tin), who has been clued as a barker. (Be aware, though, that the clue "Dog star" can also refer to the constellation SIRIUS.) NEMO is the name of the fish in "Finding Nemo," a Pixar film.

Other animals one encounters are ELSA the lioness, from "Born Free"; NALA the lioness cub and her mate, SIMBA, from "The Lion King," as well as Simba's father, MUFASA, and the villain, SCAR; FELIX the cat; Bambi's aunt ENA, who was her mother's sister; and the horse, FLICKA, from "My Friend Flicka." And the star of "Ben" was a RAT. The 1998 Dreamworks computer-animated adventure movie, ANTZ, has also been in puzzles.

The Lone Ranger's horse, SILVER, appears (tricky when in a clue), but TONTO's horse, SCOUT, is more popular. (Clayton Moore played the Lone Ranger and Jay Silverheels played Tonto.) HIYO has been in a puzzle, as in "Hiyo, Silver, away!" Tonto's appellation for the Lone Ranger, Kemo Sabe, has been both clue and answer. Speaking of those on horseback, puzzles have needed the actual name of Roy Rogers, which was Leonard SLYE, as well as the name of his horse, Trigger (and Dale Evans's palomino was named Buttermilk). Hopalong Cassidy's name was William Boyd, and his horse was named Topper. Gene Autry's horse was named Champion.

The films based on Edgar Rice Burroughs' *Tarzan* feature (in addition to Tarzan and Jane) CHEETAH the chimp and Tarzan's adopted five-year old son, Boy, who has been cleverly and ambiguously used as the first word in a clue. (The names CHEETAH, CHEETA, and CHETA all appear in crosswords.) The first sound version, *Tarzan the Ape Man*, was made in 1932, starring Johnny Weissmuller and Maureen O'Sullivan.

The combination of Bob Hope and Bing Crosby together in a movie, along with Dorothy Lamour, invariably results in one of the "Road to ___" movies they made, with "Road to RIO," "Road to UTOPIA," and "Road to BALI" perhaps being the most popular in crosswords. The first was "Road to Singapore" and others were "Road to Zanzibar," "Road to Morocco," and "Road to Hong Kong." Even a *voice* was needed several times for an answer: Eddie MURPHY's in "Shrek" and Mel BLANC's for several Disney characters. And Walt DISNEY has also been a voice.

This section would not be complete without the reminder that HAL 9000 was the computer, sometimes clued as a villain, in Stanley Kubrick's 1968 classic, "2001: A Space Odyssey."

Television

If a clue contains the word "tube," the answer may well relate to TV (or it could be a sock or a worm or the London subway or something else). Another such clue word is "anchor." Not only are the evening news anchors on the major networks in puzzles, but also the personalities on the morning shows. A clue containing the word "soap" (for soap opera) will usually refer to TV. Similar to the Oscars for movies, there is the EMMY for excellence in TV, which is also a statuette, and sometimes Emmy winners are answers, such as Ed ASNER, for "Roots." The CLIO award also appears, for creative ads.

Hosts of "The Tonight Show," which debuted in 1954, long before Jay LENO, were Steve ALLEN (the first host), Jack PAAR, and Johnny CARSON, and most early TV viewers also watched the "Texaco Star Theater," with Milton BERLE ("Uncle Miltie" and also "Mr. Television"), as well as "Your Show of Shows," with SID Caesar and Imogene COCA.

Among the five Marx brothers (listed in the "Movies" section) were Groucho and Harpo. The former is sometimes used in clues, where one of the props in his quiz show, "You Bet Your Life," such as his CIGAR, or the DUCK, is the answer. HARPO, with his red wig, has appeared with a taxi horn as his prop (the clue).

It is helpful to remember the puppet program, "Kukla, Fran, and Ollie" (the last a dragon), where one or two of the three is usually the clue and the other the entry. "Fran" is Fran Allison, the only human of the three. Another program was "Howdy Doody," who was a puppet; live characters were Buffalo BOB and CLARABELL the clown, who tooted a HORN.

If the word "Friday" is in a clue, the reference might be to Sergeant Joe Friday of the LAPD (in real life, Jack WEBB), of the very successful "Dragnet" police series (which began on radio); the answer is usually SGT. On one occasion, it helped to know that he always wanted FACTS ("Just the facts, ma'am"), and on another there was the clue "714," which was his badge number. And speaking of sergeants, Sgt. BILKO, of the "Phil Silvers Show," has also appeared.

"The Honeymooners" characters, RALPH and ALICE Kramden (played by Jackie Gleason and Audrey Meadows), and their upstairs pals, Ed and TRIXIE Norton (played by Art Carney and Joyce Randolph), have entertained puzzle solvers, as have the real-life Lucille Ball and her husband, DESI Arnaz (the latter sometimes referred to in clues by his Cuban origin or the character name "Ricky Ricardo"), along with their friends and landlords on "I Love Lucy," FRED and ETHEL Mertz, played by William Frawley and Vivian Vance.

Then there were Buddy EBSEN and Irene RYAN of "The Beverly Hillbillies," who played the widower JED Clampett and his mother-in-law, DAISY "Granny" Moses. Other characters were Jed's only daughter, Elly MAY (played by Donna Douglas), and cousin JETHRO Bodine (played by Max Baer, Jr.). If a clue should refer to the autobiography titled *The Other Side of Oz*, it was written by Buddy Ebsen.

"All in the Family" characters appear, too: ARCHIE Bunker (played by Carroll O'Connor), a BIGOT, and his wife EDITH (played by Jean Stapleton) and called DINGBAT on occasion by Archie, as well as daughter GLORIA (played by Sally Struthers) and her husband, MIKE Stivic (played by Rob Reiner), called MEATHEAD by Archie.

One character's name that crops up frequently from "The Andy Griffith Show" is OPIE, referred to in clues as the "Mayberry boy" or "Aunt Bee's great-nephew" or "Sheriff Andy Taylor's kid." Opie was played by Ron(ny) Howard and the widowed sheriff, ANDY Taylor, was played by Andy Griffith. Others were Don Knotts as the deputy Barney FIFE and Frances Bavier as Aunt BEE. Another character from the show is OTIS, usually clued as a drunk. From the "Dick Van Dyke Show," it is helpful to remember, "Oh, ROB!" This was an exclamation of Laura Petrie (Mary Tyler Moore) to her husband, Rob (Dick Van Dyke).

The Munsters' pet bat IGOR flies into puzzles from time to time, but also important to remember is that Yvonne DeCarlo played LILI, whose maiden name was Dracula. The only child of Lili and Herman Munster is EDDIE, a normal boy, except for being a werewolf and sleeping in a chest of drawers. Characters from "The Addams Family," though, are more popular: these are MORTICIA (sometimes shortened to TISH) and husband GOMEZ, cousin ITT, Uncle FESTER Frump, and LURCH.

"Star Trek" began as a TV series in 1966, became a movie, and had several spinoffs; puzzles use any of these. The most popular answers are Captain KIRK, played by William SHATNER, Hikaru SULU (Mr. Sulu), the helmsman, played by George TAKEI, Jean-LUC Picard, played by Michael Stewart, and Mr. SPOCK, played by Leonard NIMOY. You might also come across Lt. UHURA, played by Michelle Nichols; the constable or security chief ODO, played by René Auberjonois; Ensign (or ENS) Ro Laren, played by Michelle Forbes; Dr. Leonard (BONES) McCoy, a surgeon, played by DeForest Kelly; Deanna TROI, played by Marina Sirtis; their starship, the U.S.S. ENTERPRISE; and the enemy KLINGONS. BEAMUP (beam up) has occurred several times, usually linked to Mr. Montgomery Scott (or "Scotty"), who was played by James Doohan.

BEA (Beatrice) Arthur, of MAUDE, has been both clue and answer. Still popular in reruns, the "Seinfeld" characters appear: JERRY Seinfeld, ELAINE Benes, GEORGE Costanza, and COSMO Kramer; Jerry's Uncle LEO and the "soup NAZI" show up from time to time, too. Larry DAVID went on to write "Curb Your Enthusiasm."

Among the popular shows in crosswords is "Frasier," which aired from 1993 to 2004. Dr. Frasier Crane was played by Kelsey Grammer. The character ROZ was played by PERI Gilpin (the word "peri," by the way, means Persian fairy, and has been in puzzles itself). Other characters are Frasier's brother NILES (David Hyde Pierce), his dad MARTIN (John Mahoney), RONEE (Wendy Malick), DAPHNE (Jane Leeves), and the dog, EDDIE.

An animated show is "The Simpsons," which debuted on "The Tracey Ullman Show," a clue. Marge and Homer's 10-year-old kid is BART (sometimes clued as a brat), Bart's younger sister is LISA, and there is an even younger sister, MAGGIE, who still uses a pacifier. Homer's father's name is ABE, and his mother's is MONA. Marge has two older twin sisters, Selma and Patty, called the "Gruesome Twosome." A neighbor of the Simpsons is NED Flanders, who owns the Leftorium, a store for those who are left-handed; the bartender is MOE (his tavern is MOES, in Springfield), and he says "Oh, geez."

Homer hangs out with APU, his Indian friend and Kwik-E-Mart convenience store owner (or shopkeeper, or clerk, or doughnut supplier, depending on the puzzle), who sells Squishees. Other characters are LOU the cop, Disco STU, who has been clued by his platform shoes, Sideshow BOB Terwilliger, and Bart's teacher, EDNA Krabapple (or Mrs. K.). It has helped to know that Homer says DOH (d'oh!), that his middle name is JAY, that Bart says "Ay Caramba!" and that Bart and Lisa's school bus driver is OTTO, who is employed by Springfield Elementary School. Puzzles have required the names of Hank AZARIA, a voice man, and MATT Groening, creator of the show.

Another program is "Friends," actually the second show of that name. Some of the friends are MONICA (Courteney Cox) and CHANDLER (Matthew Perry), RACHEL (Jennifer Aniston) and ROSS (David Schwimmer), PHOEBE (Lisa Kudrow) and her identical twin sister, URSULA (also Lisa Kudrow), and JOEY (Matt LeBlanc). The family name of Monica and Ross is GELLAR. The coffee shop in the show is Central Park and clues to the program have been "Oh-my-God" and "Going commando."

"M*A*S*H" was first a movie, then a TV series two years later, in 1972. The usual "M*A*S*H" clues and answers are Alan Alda's first and last names, as he played the character Captain "Hawkeye" Pierce. Perhaps the third most frequent answer after ALAN and ALDA is CPL, for Corporal Maxwell KLINGER. RADAR O'Reilly, another corporal, also appears frequently, and once even his hometown of OTTUMWA, Iowa, was required. He has also been clued as Colonel Potter's sidekick; Colonel Potter is the commanding officer of the 4077th. MAJOR Burns has also appeared, as has the locale of the action, KOREA. It helps to know that Radar drinks NEHI (or GRAPENEHI) soda and that his radio contact is SPARKY. Another clue for NEHI is that it has been around since 1924.

In addition to shows going from movies to TV or vice versa, there are also "spinoffs," which are sometimes in clues. Some of these are the following:

"Frasier" from "Cheers," "The Simpsons" from "The Tracey Ullman Show," "The Jeffersons" from "All in the Family," "Laverne and Shirley" from "Happy Days," "A Different World" from "The Cosby Show," "Rhoda" from "The Mary Tyler Moore Show," "The Colbys" from "Dynasty," "Knots Landing" from "Dallas," "Enos" from "The Dukes of Hazzard," and "Melrose Place" from "Beverly Hills 90210."

A few miscellaneous clues and answers from various television shows are listed alphabetically below by the name of the program. They are all found in current crosswords, so the present tense is used, even though a show might no longer be aired.

"All My Children": Susan LUCCI as Erica Kane
"Armageddon": LIV Tyler as Grace Stamper
"The Avengers": DIANA Rigg as Mrs. EMMA Peel
"Barnaby Jones": Buddy EBSEN as Barnaby
"Barney Miller": HAL Linden as Capt. Miller and ABE Vigoda as Sgt. Fish
"Baywatch": TRACI Bingham as Jordan Tate and ERIKA Eleniak as Shauni McClain
"Benson": INGA Swenson as Gretchen Krause
"Beulah": Ethel Waters as BEULAH
"Beverly Hills Cop": Eddie Murphy as AXEL Foley
"Bonanza": LORNE Greene as Ben Cartwright, Dan Blocker as his son HOSS, Pernell Roberts as his eldest son ADAM, and Michael LANDON as his son Little Joe
"The Brady Bunch": Robert REED as Mike Brady, Eve Plumb as JAN Brady, Maureen McCormick as MARCIA, and Barry Williams as GREG
"Burke's Law": Gene Barry as AMOS Burke
"Cagney & Lacey": Sharon GLESS as Christine Cagney and TYNE Daly as Mary Beth Lacey
"Charlie's Angels": KATE Jackson as Sabrina Duncan and Farrah Fawcett (and then Cheryl Ladd) as Jill MONROE
"Cheers": RHEA Perlman as Carla the waitress; DAN Hedaya as her first husband, Nick Tortelli; Ted DANSON as SAM Malone,

the owner-bartender; Nicholas Colasanto as ERNIE "Coach" Pantusso; Woody BOYD as assistant bartender; Roger REES as Robin Colcord; and Shelly LONG as Diane Chambers, a waitress

"Chicago Hope": ADAM Arkin as Dr. Shutt and Christine LAHTI as Dr. Austin

"CHiPs": ERIK Estrada as Ponch and RANDI Oakes as Bonnie

"Columbo": Peter FALK as Lt. Columbo of the LAPD

"The Cosby Show": Lisa BONET as Denise Huxtable and Malcolm-Jamal Warner as THEO

"Dallas": Larry Hagman as J.R. EWING, Linda GRAY as J.R.'s wife, Sue Ellen, Barbara BEL Geddes as the matriarch, Miss Ellie, Patrick DUFFY as son Bobby Ewing, and Victoria Principal as Bobby's wife, PAMELA

"Desperate Housewives": EVA Longoria as Gabrielle Solis, TERI Hatcher as Susan Delfino, and Marcia Gross as BREE Hodge

"Dr. Kildare": Richard Chamberlain as Dr. KILDARE

"Dukes of Hazzard": Sonny Shroyer as ENOS Strata

"Dynasty": Joan Collins as ALEXIS, the first wife, and John Forsythe as BLAKE Carrington; Linda Evans as his new wife, KRYSTLE

"ER": George Clooney as Dr. Doug ROSS, NOAH Wylie as Dr. John Carter, LAURA Innis as Dr. Kerry Weaver, Paul McCrane as Dr. Robert ROMANO, and ERIQ La Salle as Dr. Peter Benton

"Everybody Loves Raymond": Ray ROMANO as Ray BARONE and Doris Roberts as his mother, MARIE

"Fantasy Island": Hervé Villachaize as TATTOO

"Father Knows Best": Robert YOUNG as Jim Anderson and Jane Wyatt as his wife, Margaret; children are Betty, Bud, and Kathy

"The Fugitive": DAVID Janssen as Dr. Richard Kimble

"Full House": John STAMOS as Adam Cochran and LORI Laughlin as Rebecca Donaldson

"Get Shorty": Danny DEVITO as Shorty

"Gilligan's Island": BOB Denver as Gilligan and TINA Louise as Ginger Grant

"Growing Pains": ALAN Thicke as Dr. Jason Seaver and JOANNA Kerns as Maggie Seaver

"Gunsmoke": AMANDA Blake as Miss Kitty Russell, James ARNESS as Marshal MATT Dillon, and Dennis Weaver as Chester B. GOODE, the deputy who is LAME

"Happy Days": Henry Winkler as Arthur Fonzarelli (FONZIE or the FONZ), ANSON Williams as Potsie Weber, Don MOST as Ralph Malph, ERIN Moran as Joanie Cunningham, and RON Howard as Richie Cunningham

"Hercules": Lucy Lawless as XENA and RENEE O'Connor as Gabrielle

"Hill Street Blues": Veronica HAMEL as Joyce Davenport, Joe SPANO as detective Lt. Henry Goldblume, and Michael WARREN as the officer Robert (Bobby) HILL

"Hogan's Heroes": Bob CRANE as Col. Hogan and WERNER Klemperer as the bumbling Col. Wilhelm Klink; the setting is a P.O.W. camp (STALAG in one puzzle)

"House" or "House M.D.": OMAR Epps as Dr. Eric Foreman, Hugh LAURIE as Dr. Gregory House, Jesse Spencer as Dr. Robert CHASE, Lisa Edelstein as Dr. Lisa CUDDY, and Jennifer Morrison as Dr. Allison CAMERON

"I Dream of Jeannie": Barbara EDEN as Jeannie

"Jericho": ESAI Morales as Major Beck

"Judging Amy": TYNE Daly as Maxine Gray

"Kate and Allie": Susan Saint James as KATE McArdle, ARI Meyers as Emma Jane McArdle, and Jane Curtin as ALLIE Lowell

"Knots Landing": Kathleen NOONE as Kate's mother, Claudia Whittaker, TERI Austin as Jill Bennett, and Stacy GALINA as Kate Whittaker

"L.A. Law": Susan DEY as Grace Van Owen, Corbin Bernsen as ARNIE Becker, and Jimmy SMITS as a lawyer

"Laugh-In": ARTE Johnson, LILY Tomlin, ART Carney, Judy CARNE, and Goldie HAWN as themselves

"Laverne and Shirley": Penny Marshall as LAVERNE De Fazio and Cindy Williams as Shirley FEENEY

"Leave It to Beaver": Tony DOW as brother Wally Cleaver, HUGH Beaumont as father Ward Cleaver, Barbara Billingsley as mother JUNE Cleaver, and Jerry Mathers as BEAVER

"Lois & Clark: The New Adventures . . .": TERI Hatcher as Lois Lane and Dean CAIN as Superman/Clark Kent

"MacGyver": Richard Dean Anderson as ANGUS Webb

"Marcus Welby": Robert YOUNG as Marcus Welby and Margie McGurney as HEATHER Menzies

"Married with Children": Ed ONEILL as Al Bundy and Katey SAGAL as Peggy Bundy

"Maverick": James Garner as BRET Maverick and Jack Kelly as his brother BART

"Melrose Place": Andrew SHUE as Billy Campbell, the shrink, Rob ESTES as Kyle McBride, and Heather Locklear as AMANDA Woodward

"The Mod Squad": Michael COLE as Pete Cochran, Clarence Williams III as LINC Hayes, Peggy LIPTON as Julie Barnes, and TIGE Andrews as police captain Adam Greer

"Mork and Mindy": Robin Williams as the alien MORK and PAM Dawber as Mindy; the planet is ORK

"My Three Sons": Don GRADY as Robbie Douglas

"Night Court": Richard MOLL as bailiff Bull Shannon

"NYPD Blue": ESAI Morales as Tony Rodriguez

"The Office": Steve CARELL as Michael Scott, RAINN Wilson as Dwight Shrute, and John Krasinski as JIM Halpert

"Once and Again": SELA Ward as Lilly Manning

"One Life to Live": ERICA Slezak as Victoria Lord Carpenter

"Our Miss Brooks": Eve ARDEN as Miss Brooks and Richard Crenna as student Walter DENTON

"Parks and Recreation": AMY Poehler as Leslie Knope, Nick Offerman as RON Swanson, and Aubrey Plaza as APRIL Ludgate

"The Partridge Family": Susan DEY as Laurie

"Peyton Place": Ryan ONEAL as Rodney Harrington

"Rhoda": Valerie HARPER as Rhoda Morgenstern, Julie Kavner as her sister BRENDA, and David Groh as JOE Gerard

'"St. Elsewhere": William DANIELS as Dr. Mark Craig

"Sanford and Son": REDD Foxx as Fred Sanford and Demond Wilson as his son LAMONT

"77 Sunset Strip": EDD Byrnes as Gerald Lloyd "Kookie" Kookson III and ROGER Smith as Jeff Spencer

"Sin in the City": Sarah Jessica Parker as CARRIE Bradshaw

"Sisters": SELA Ward as Teddy Reed

"The Sopranos": James Gandolfini as TONY, EDIE Falco as his wife CARMELA, Robert ILER as son A.J. Soprano, Jamie-Lynn Sigler as daughter MEADOW, Drea deMatteo as GINA, Lorraine Bracco as psychiatrist Dr. Jennifer MELFI, and Nancy

Marchand as Tony's mother, LIVIA; the chef, Artie BUCCO, is played by John Ventimiglia

"South Park": Chef's voice is that of ISAAC Hayes; kids are STAN, KYLE, KENNY, and ERIC (better known as CARTMAN); the setting is COLORADO

"Spenser: for Hire": AVERY Brooks as Hawk and Robert URICH as Spenser

"Starsky and Hutch": Paul Michael GLASER as David Starsky and David SOUL as Ken "Hutch" Hutchinson

"Thirtysomething": Ken OLIN as Michael Steadman

"Twin Peaks": JOAN Chen as Josie Packard and Piper LAURIE as Catherine Marell

"The Waltons": a daughter is ERIN (played by Mary Beth Mc Donough) and ZEB (played by Will Geer) is Grandpa to John-Boy (played by Richard Thomas); the general store is IKES (Ike's)

"The West Wing": Alan ALDA as Senator Arnold Vinick, Martin SHEEN as President Josiah (JED) Bartlet, Stockard Channing as First Lady ABIGAIL Bartlet, and Rob LOWE as Sam Seaborn

"Will and Grace": MEGAN Mullally as Karen Walker, ERIC McCormack as Will, DEBRA Messing as Grace, SEAN Hayes as Jack McFarland, and Shelley Morrison as ROSARIO Salazar, the maid

The game shows such as "Wheel of Fortune," "Who Wants to Be a Millionaire?" and "Jeopardy!" are also grist for crosswords, where ART Fleming, REGIS Philbin, ALEX Trebek, Kathie LEE, MERV Griffin, VANNA White, and PAT Sajak come on stage. Every now and then a clue will be "Wheel of Fortune purchase." Since you purchase a letter, and since an entry must be at least three letters long, the answer will be the indefinite article "an" plus a letter, as in the construction, AN_, where the blank will be an A, E, F, H, I, L, M, N, O, R, S, or X. The old TV show called "What's My Line?" is still in puzzles, and its most popular panelist is ARLENE Francis.

OPRAH has been an answer, with her book club as a clue. ALF is clued as a TV terrestrial and, as mentioned above, XENA, played by Lucy Lawless, is known as TV's warrior princess. On occasion, it has helped to know that the "TV handyman" is Bob VILA. The Jetson's dog ASTRO has made an appearance, as have two horses: FLICKA, from "My Friend Flicka," and MRED (Mr. Ed), who has been clued as a palomino and whose owner is Wilbur Post.

Those familiar with TV programming have an advantage in that shows (clues) are often related to the networks they appear on (answers), such as ABC, CBS (the logo an EYE), or NBC. The last is sometimes clued by "Rainbow network," or "Peacock logo," as well as by SNL, or "Saturday Night Live," which debuted in 1975, as well as NBC's musical notes G, E, and C. Others are CNN and HBO. PBS, which began in 1970, has been clued as "Masterpiece Theater" channel, "Mystery" channel, "Sesame Street" channel, and "Antiques Roadshow" channel. The former hosts of "Masterpiece Theater," Alistair Cooke and Russell Baker, continue to be in puzzles.

Speaking of "Sesame Street," its success led to "The Muppet Show," with the host, Jim HENSON. Among his muppets are Miss Piggy (who says "MOI?") and the bald scientist, Dr. BUNSEN Honeydew. Characters from "Sesame Street" who have appeared in puzzles are BERT, his best friend ERNIE, who is orange and plays the SAX, GROVER, and KERMIT the frog. Others are Big BIRD and OSCAR the Grouch. Then there is the finger puppet ELMO, who has been clued as red, as furry, as a giggler, and as a baby monster. Nickelodeon's "DORA the Explorer," who is seven years old, has also been found in puzzles.

TNT can refer to a channel or the explosive; it is often an answer for the latter. And QVC is a shopping channel. The four- and five-letter channels are somewhat easier to guess, as there are fewer of them, for example, ESPN for sports, CSPAN for government proceedings and public affairs programming, and MSNBC, the last sometimes clued by "Morning Joe."

Popular Music

There are so many pop music clues and entries in crosswords today that it is nearly impossible to keep up with the trends and performers and their music. In addition, genres have merged, so that in rock music alone you will find subcategories like rockabilly, folk rock, country rock, blues rock, gospel rock, punk rock, and others.

The performers listed below are seldom limited to one genre, but for purposes of classification, they are included under the genres (printed in italics) for which they seem to be best known, with other genres listed after their names, where applicable. If one of your favorites cannot be found in this section, it may be because constructors seem to prefer short names and/or those with a suitable number of vowels (see paragraph immediately below for such examples).

The earliest genre is *folk music*, originating from the people and passed down orally. A very popular "folk" answer in crosswords is ARLO Guthrie (also folk rock, blues, and country), son of Woody Guthrie. Others are Joan BAEZ (also folk rock and country), Bob DYLAN (also rock, blues, country, and gospel), Emmylou HARRIS (also country, rock, and pop), Phil OCHS (also folk rock), ODETTA (also blues), Danny O'Keefe (OKEEFE), PETE Seeger, and Charlie WEAVER. One of the earliest folk singers and instrumentalists was Huddie W. Ledbetter (also blues), born in 1888. He was known as "LEAD Belly" (his preference) or "Leadbelly." Three folk groups that appear are (1) Paul SIMON and ART Garfunkel, (2) Peter, PAUL, and Mary, and (3) the Kingston TRIO.

Blues evolved from southern African-American secular songs. ETTA James (also R&B, jazz, soul, gospel, and R&R) and Eartha KITT are very popular in puzzles. Ms. Kitt portrayed blues singer Billie Holliday in the musical "Lady Day at Emerson's Bar and Grill," which has been a clue for her name; she also played the role of Catwoman in the "Batman" TV series, another clue. Other singers are B.B. KING (also jazz, R&B, and soul), Jonny LANG (also gospel and rock), Bonnie RAITT (also country, folk rock, and pop), OTIS Taylor, JOSH White (also gospel and pop), and ETHEL Waters (also jazz, gospel, and pop). One of the earliest artists to appear in this genre is Muddy WATERS, the father of "modern Chicago blues."

Ragtime (or *rag*) or honky-tonk is a music genre characterized by its syncopation; Scott JOPLIN is ragtime's most famous composer; the two others in the ragtime "triumvirate" are Joseph LAMB and James SCOTT. Others are EUBIE Blake, a ragtime pianist (also jazz), Ernest HOGAN, and Jelly-Roll MORTON (also Dixieland and swing). Morton was also very important in the development of jazz, as the first arranger and the first important jazz composer.

Jazz is also native to the U.S., and even more structured than blues. The most popular jazz-related clue and answer are ELLA Fitzgerald and her specialty, SCAT. Also known for scat was the bandleader, singer, and songwriter CAB Calloway (also blues); he is sometimes clued by the Cotton Club in Harlem and by "Hi De Ho," a song as well as a short film.

Others are Herb ALPERT and the Tijuana Brass (also R&B and pop), LOUIS Armstrong ("Satchmo"), Count BASIE, BIX Biederbecke, DAVE Brubeck, NAT King Cole (also pop), Chick COREA, ALANA Davis, and MILES Davis, one of the most influential musicians of the last century. He was a bandleader, instrumentalist, and composer, not only in jazz, but also bop and rap.

Still others are DUKE Ellington, GIL Evans, PETE Fountain, Errol Garner, DIZZY Gillespie (also bop), EARL (Fatha) Hines, LENA Horne, WALTER Jackson (also soul and R&B), ETTA Jones (also pop and R&B), NORAH Jones (daughter of Ravi Shankar), STAN Kenton, CLEO Laine, JONI Mitchell (also folk and pop), WES Montgomery (jazz guitarist and bandleader who influenced many later artists), ANITA O'Day (also bop), TITO Peunte (also salsa), DELLA Reese (also gospel, R&B, and pop), SADE (also soul, R&B, and pop), NINA Simone (also blues, R&B, folk, and gospel), ART Tatum, SARAH Vaughan (also bop), FATS Waller, and KAI Winding.

Bop (or *bebop* or *be-bop*) is a postwar style of jazz, which has even more complexity than jazz. Dizzy Gillespie is sometimes a clue for BOP. Bebop has been a clue for Thelonius MONK, and SARAH Vaughan (above) is known especially for her complex bebop phrasing.

Rhythm and blues (or *R&B*) combines blues and jazz; several names that appear are ANITA Baker (also soul and jazz), BEYONCE, TONI Braxton, RON Bryson, RAY Charles (also jazz, C&W, gospel, and pop), Des'Ree (one part of the name the clue and one part entry), Marvin GAYE, a singer-songwriter associated with Motown (also soul), KOOL and the Gang, TEENA Marie, and RIHANNA (also hip hop, reggae, and pop).

SMOKEY Robinson is usually clued by Motown, as he was one of its founders. Also linked to Motown was one of its star singers, TAMMI Terrel (also soul and pop), who made recordings with the singer Marvin Gaye (above), who also recorded with Motown. FATS (Antoine) Domino, R&B pianist, singer, and songwriter, was one of the first to perform what would become R&B. A very popular singer in several genres is Mary J. BLIGE (also gospel). STACY Lattisaw began her career in R&B, but since the 1990s has focused on contemporary gospel music.

DIANA Ross, a singer very popular in several genres, such as soul, jazz, and pop music, became lead singer of the Supremes. After leaving the Supremes, she went solo. In addition, she performed in the movie, "Lady Sings the Blues," loosely based on the autobiography of Billie Holiday. Another R&B singer was AMY Winehouse (also soul and jazz).

Doo wop is one style of R&B that was popular in the 1950s, and two doo wop syllables, DUM and SHA, have been in puzzles ("dum" is also a syllable in scat). Sometimes its early exponents, the Ink Spots, a quartet, will be found in puzzles as a clue for DOOWOP. A later group was the Five Satins.

Soul music was developed by African-Americans, and has elements of gospel and R&B. The "queen of soul," ARETHA Franklin, was the theme of a puzzle in March 2012. Known also for rock 'n' roll, she was the first woman inducted into the Rock and Roll Hall of Fame in Cleveland. Some others noted for soul music are JAMES Brown (or J.B., who has been referred to as the "godfather of soul) (also R&B), RAY Charles (also R&B, gospel, pop, and country), SAM Cooke (also R&B, country, rock, and pop), Al GREEN (also R&B), ISAAC Hayes (also blues, jazz, and pop), CURTIS Mayfield (also R&B), LOU Rawls (also gospel, R&B, jazz, and blues), OTIS Redding (also R&B and pop), LIONEL Richie (also R&B, country, rock, and pop), and STEVIE Wonder (also R&B, jazz, and pop).

Gospel singers who have appeared in puzzles are OLETA Adams (also soul, jazz and pop), MAHALIA Jackson, ERMA Franklin (also R&B), and CeCe (CECE) Winans (also R&B). This might be the place to mention the DOVE Award, presented by the Gospel Music Association.

Country or *country and western* (usually C&W in clues) is popular music based on the style of the south or cowboys of the west. REBA McIntyre is popular in this genre and others are ROY Acuff, EDDY Arnold, Bill BOYD, GARTH Brooks, Johnny CASH, the DIXIE Chicks, ROY Clark, the EBERLY Brothers (also R&B), NANCI Griffith, MERLE Haggard, ALAH Jackson, RONNIE Millsap, John PRINE, LEANN Rimes (also pop), Hank SNOW, and Lee ANN Womack.

You may also come across CLINT Black, David Allan COE, TERRI Gibbs, TRACY Lawrence, LORETTA Lynn, K.T. OSLIN, TEX Owens, Dolly PARTON, JIMMIE Rodgers, MEL Tillis, PAM Tillis, MERLE Travis, RANDY Travis, TRAVIS Tritt, TANYA Tucker, DOTTIE West, and TAMMY Wynette. If you should come across "CMA" in a clue, it refers to the Country Music Association, a Nashville-based organization.

Rock 'n' roll, which became popular in the 1950s, comes from several styles, especially R&B, country, and gospel; it is characterized by being heavily accented and amplified. The most popular "rocker" in puzzles is the British composer and producer Brian ENO, an ambient music pioneer; he is associated with Roxy Music, often the clue. The term "rock pop" can also be applied to him. Perhaps second and third are the bands named AC/DC and ELO; the latter stands for Electric Light Orchestra. Then there are RATT, a glam metal quintet, and REM (R.E.M.), an alternative American rock band with Michael STIPE.

Some early rock groups were the MONKEES (the term bubblegum rock has been applied to them), the VELVET Underground (managed by Andy Warhol), the Beach Boys, Bill HALEY and His Comets, and the Mamas and the Papas, who were known especially for their folk rock. An early solo rock performer was DION DiMucci (also doo-wop, blues, R&B, and pop). The CARS is an American rock band that originated from "New Wave" music; its lead guitarist is RIC Ocacek. Speaking of "New Wave," the former band called OINGO Boingo has been in puzzles.

Another rocker's name in puzzles is that of the short-lived JIMI Hendrix, and another who did not live very long was Buddy HOLLY. TINA Turner (also pop, soul, and R&B) is known as the "queen of rock and roll." Elvis ("The King") Presley usually needs his middle name in crosswords: ARON. Then there is Fleetwood MAC. Jerry LEE Lewis (the Killer) mixed country and R&R.

The Fab Four, or the BEATLES, sometimes appear, but hardly in relation to their popularity. For the record, here are their names: John (Winston) Lennon, Sir (James) Paul McCartney, George Harrison, and Richard Starkey, Jr. (Ringo Starr). Lennon's widow, Yoko ONO, is very popular. Their manager, BRIAN Epstein, appears, as well as an early member of the Beatles, STUART Sutcliffe, who played bass.

Members of the Rolling Stones are Mick Jagger ("Sir Michael"), Keith Richards, Charlie Watts, and Ronnie Wood, who have released over 200 million albums. The WHO has been referred to as one of the three bands of the "trinity of British rock," along with the Beatles and the Rolling Stones.

Several other British bands are Jethro TULL (with its leader, IAN Anderson), known for its progressive rock, ASIA, with its progressive and hard rock, SLADE, GENESIS, DURAN Duran (sometimes described as English New Wave), the KINKS (also pop), PINK Floyd (and its guitarist-vocalist DAVE Gilmour, C.B.E.), and the SEX Pistols, a band that introduced punk rock in the U.K. A member of the Sex Pistols who appears in puzzles is SID Vicious.

An interesting name for crosswords is AXL Rose, lead singer of Guns n' Roses. Pearl JAM is an American alternative rock band with the vocalist Eddie VEDDER. Also found in crosswords is Iggy POP, who has performed in various rock genres, such as punk, as well as the RAMONES (also punk rock). EDIE Brickell is a singer and songwriter and Jimmy PAGE is the guitarist with the band, LED Zeppelin.

The British singer-songwriter, DAVID Bowie, appears, as well as the singer, AIMEE Mann. JOAN Jett is a singer and guitarist, and Jerry Garcia's band, the Grateful Dead, sometimes appears, with DEAD the entry. Others are the BYRDS (also country and pop), KURT Cobain (grunge), the FOO Fighters, the Four Seasons, with Frankie VALLI (also pop), Billy IDOL, NILS Lofgren, METALLICA (also jazz and New Age), TED Nugent, SUZI Quatro, TODD Rundgren, SANTANA, BOB Seger, Steely DAN, GWEN Stefani, and Three DOG Night.

Then there is the English singer-songwriter and instrumentalist STING (Gordon Sumner), who was lead singer of the rock group, the Police, one of the first new wave bands and the highest-earning in 2008. He performs in many genres besides rock, and was awarded the honor of Commander of the Order of the British Empire (C.B.E.) by the Queen in 2003. In addition, he has appeared in several movies.

There are many so-called EMO bands; one found in puzzles is Jimmy EAT World, whose lead vocalist is JIM Adkins. Emo has been defined as a confessional music genre. The highest-grossing rock bands, U2 and the Rolling Stones (the latter mentioned above), do not make it into crosswords very much except, perhaps, for U2's BONO, its head singer. Bruce Springsteen, the "Boss," appears in puzzles with the song, "Born in the USA."

Ska is popular music dating from the 1960s in Jamaica, with elements of R&B, jazz, and calypso, and having a fast tempo; SKA is nearly always an entry, not a clue. Speaking of calypso, Harry Belafonte has been called the King of Calypso. Another style of popular music from Jamaica is *reggae*, which has elements of calypso and R&B. A well-known singer-songwriter in this genre was BOB Marley.

Rap is African-American urban music, characterized by spoken or chanted rhyming lyrics; it is closely associated with the youth culture of hip-hop. The most popular "rapper" in puzzles is Dr. DRE (Andre Young), and if a hip-hop trio is needed, it could well be Salt-n-PEPA. Queen LATIFAH is an example of a hip-hop artist, as is ICET (Ice-T), whose real name is Tracy Marrow. EMINEM (Marshall Bruce Mathers III), the best-selling artist of the 2000s, was declared the "King of Hip Hop" by *Rolling Stone*.

Others (listed alphabetically by *first* names, are the Black Eyed PEAS (also R&B and pop music), FAT Joe, 50 CENT, FLO Rida, JAYZ (Jay-Z, who is married to Beyoncé), Kanye WEST, Li'l JON, Lil' KIM, Li'l WAYNE, Missy ELLIOTT, MOS Def (also an actor), NATE Dogg (also hip hop), Snoop LION (whose former name was Snoop DOGG, and who has moved from hip-hop to reggae), TUPAC Shakur, TYRESE Gibson (also R&B), and Vanilla ICE. There was also the rap duo KRIS Kross, with MAC Daddy (Chris Kelly) and Daddy MAC (Chris Smith).

Pop is simply popular music. A very common pop group in puzzles is the Swedish quartet, ABBA (named for its members), the clue usually their nationality or the term "Europop." They are also known as the "Mamma Mia group" in clues; that show was a successful Broadway musical. Although Michael Jackson (Jacko) was known as the "King of Pop," neither he nor other members of his family seem to appear in puzzles.

Several early singers were Paul ANKA, NAT King Cole, Frankie LAINE, Johnny MATHIS, PATTI Page, KAY Starr (also jazz), and RUDY Vallee (also a band leader). RAY Eberle sang with the big bands and an early group was the Bee Gees, a TRIO; the three Gibb brothers were Barry, Robin, and Maurice.

Céline DION sings in several genres, and is the best-selling Canadian artist; another Canadian is SARAH McLachlen. Then there are CHER, CASS Elliot (also known as Mama Cass), who was a member of the Mamas and the Papas (mentioned earlier), and CAROLE King (also soul and rock). The youngest pop singer in puzzles seems to be JUSTIN Bieber.

A very popular band no longer in existence is NSYNC, featuring JUSTIN Timberlake (its youngest member), which performed both pop and R&B. They were so successful that they sold over a million albums in one day. The top female recording artist is MADONNA. Known in many genres, such as pop, rock, and dance, she is also a songwriter, actress, producer, author, and fashion designer. Another very well-known singer is Lady GAGA. VAN Morrison O.B.E. (Van the Man) performs in many genres, such as soul, R&B, rock, folk, and jazz.

Some others are Ed AMES, David BOWIE, KAREN Carpenter (of the Carpenters), Taylor DAYNE (also rock, soul, and R&B), Kiki DEE, GLORIA Estefan, who has been clued as the "Queen of Latin pop," Brenda LEE (also country), HELEN Reddy, and Carly SIMON. Whitney HOUSTON was known in pop music as well as in R&B, soul, and gospel; she was one of the world's most successful music artists.

New Age originated in the 1980s, and is a popular genre in crosswords. It is characterized by being spiritual and holistic, dreamy and quiet, but is often acoustic, and includes such instruments as synthesizers. YANNI is one of its singers, and if you ever need an Irish New Age singer, it just might be ENYA, as she is very popular in puzzles.

Miscellaneous. The Big Band leaders such as Glenn Miller, Benny Goodman, and Tommy Dorsey are well known, but an earlier one, and the one who appears in puzzles the most is KAY Kyser, who has been clued by his "Kollege of Musical Knowledge," a radio program.

If "Rocket Man" is in a clue, it will no doubt be the song by ELTON John, who wrote the lyrics. If you ever come across the clue "___tú," the solution is ERES; this song was a 1974 pop hit with Spanish lyrics, but still appears in puzzles today. Some other miscellaneous entries are AMP (amplifier) and MOOG, named for Dr. Robert Moog, a pioneer of the synthesizer. Notice that many of the above answers are short, so even if you are not a rocker or a rapper, a crossing word or two might provide the answer.

Art and Architecture

On the subject of architecture, several practitioners are found in crosswords. Two of them are the Finns EERO Saarinen and his father ELIEL Gottlieb Saarinen, the former clued by his design of the TWA building at JFK airport, the Gateway to the West Arch in St. Louis, or by Dulles International Airport, which serves the Washington area. The father collaborated on some of his son's projects, but is also known for the railway station and the national museum in Helsinki, as well as the First Christian Church in Columbus, Indiana, and the Cranbrook Academy of Art in Bloomfield Hills, Michigan. Another Finn in puzzles is Alvar AALTO, known for international modernism in the 20th century; he is usually clued as a Finnish chair designer or as the architect of Finlandia Hall.

Three other architects are William Van ALEN, who designed the art deco Chrysler Building in New York City; Ludwig MIES van der Rohe, the clue sometimes being a part of his name, who designed the Seagram Building in New York City (with Philip Johnson) and the New National Gallery (Neue Nationalgalerie) in Berlin; and Frank Lloyd Wright, who designed the Guggenheim Museum in New York City and the 1923 Imperial Hotel in Tokyo.

Another was I.M. (IEOH MING) PEI, who designed the glass pyramids at the Louvre, the East Building of the National Gallery of Art in Washington, the Kennedy Library near Boston, the Bank of China in Hong Kong, and the Rock and Roll Hall of Fame in Cleveland. Norman FOSTER is known for his "high-tech" architecture, including the Great Court at the British Museum, London's Millenium Bridge, and the new German parliament, or Reichstag. The youngest architect in puzzles is MAYA Lin, who designed the Viet Nam Veterans Memorial in Washington, D.C., as well as the Civil Rights Memorial in Montgomery, Alabama, and the Storm King Wavefield at Storm King State Park in Mountainville, New York.

The Danish architect ARNE Jacobsen is typically clued by his furniture designs, but he also designed the SAS Royal Hotel in Copenhagen, St. Catherine's College at Oxford, and the Royal Danish Embassy in London. Going back a few centuries, Sir Christopher WREN is clued by St. Paul's Cathedral in London or the library at Trinity College, Cambridge. Even earlier was INIGO Jones, noted especially for his use of the Palladian classical style in England. The three vowels in his name make him a natural for crosswords.

On the subject of art, one of the most popular artists in puzzles seems to be the Swiss abstractionist, Paul KLEE (1879-1940); the clue is usually "Fish Magic artist" and the answer is always his last name; "Twittering Machine" and "Burning Giraffe" have also been clues. Second is probably the Spanish surrealist Salvador DALI (1904-1989), also always his last name, whose clues relate to his moustache or to a limp watch, a feature of one of his signature paintings, such as "Persistence of Memory" or "Sleep." But on several occasions, it helped to know that there is a museum dedicated to his work in St. Petersburg, Florida (and one in Figueres, Spain, too).

Perhaps third most popular is the Belgian surrealist, RENE Magritte (1898-1967), his last name the clue and his first name the entry; he has also been clued by "The Treasury of Images." And fourth is the American painter and sculptor Larry Rivers (1923-2002); he is in puzzles because of the obvious plays on his last name in clues.

Except for these and the artists listed below, the only frequent art-related answers in crosswords seem to be DADA, a short-lived artistic movement in Europe in the second and third decades of the 20th century; OPART (op art), or optical art, often associated with Victor Vasarely, the "father of op art," but in crosswords to Jean Arp (see below); MOMA, the

Museum of Modern Art in New York City; the TATE Gallery in London; and the Museo del PRADO in Madrid.

The list below hardly does justice to the history of art, but we are talking primarily about crosswords here, not art. The list is alphabetical by the most well-known name, and following each name is some brief information that could be used in clues, especially an artist's nationality. In some cases, either the first or last name is also a clue. All the artists listed below have been found in puzzles.

>Fra Angelico, 1387(?)-1455: Dominican friar at the convent of Cortona, painter of the Florentine school, "Madonna of the Linen Drapers Guild"
>Jean Arp (born Hans Arp), 1887-1966: French avant-garde abstract painter and sculptor, a founder of Dada, 3-D art, op art, biomorphic sculpture, and his "crumpled papers," "Mustache Hat"
>Rosa Bonheur, 1822-1899: French painter of animals, especially known for her monumental painting, "The Horse Fair"
>Pierre Bonnard, 1867-1947: French postimpressionist painter and printmaker, founding member of les Nabis, "The Bath"
>Heironymous Bosch, 1450-1516: Flemish painter of mainly religious allegories, "The Garden of Earthly Delights," "The Crowning of Thorns," "Ship of Fools"
>Sandro Botticelli, 1445-1510: Early Florentine Renaissance painter, "The Birth of Venus," "Primavera," "Adoration of the Magi," "Madonna of the Magnificat"
>François Boucher, 1703-1770: French artist whose works are representative of the rococo style, "Nude Lying on a Sofa"
>Marc Chagall, 1887-1985: Russian painter and illustrator resident in France, ballet designer, symbolism, power of love, Jewish life and folklore, "Flying over the Town," "I and the Village"
>John Constable, 1776-1837: British painter known for his landscapes, contemporary of Turner, "Salisbury Cathedral . . ."
>Jean Baptiste Camille Corot, 1796-1875: French landscape painter, the Barbizon school, "Pastorale," "Souvenir de Mortefontaine," "Bouquet de Fleurs," "Sens Cathedral"
>Salvador Dalí: (see fifth paragraph of this section)
>Honoré Daumier, 1808-1879: French caricaturist, painter, and sculptor, satirical lithographs

Jo(seph) Davidson, 1883-1952: American sculptor of portrait busts, including Franklin D. Roosevelt, Woodrow Wilson, Will Rogers, and Albert Einstein

Leonardo da Vinci, 1452-1519: Florentine, but also worked in Milan, artist and engineer, "La Giaconda" (or "Mona Lisa") in the Louvre, "The Last Supper" near Milan, "The Annunciation" in the Uffizi in Florence

Edgar Dégas, 1834-1917: French painter and sculptor, impressionism, pastel his favorite medium, ballet rehearsals and ballerinas, "The Ballet Class," "Women Ironing"

Andrea del Sarto, 1486-1530: Florentine high Renaissance painter, "Madonna of the Harpies," "Holy Family," "Birth of the Virgin," "John the Baptist" (a series of frescoes)

André Derain, 1880-1954: French painter and one of the original fauvists, but became more conservative, influenced by van Gogh, paintings of Collioure

Jim Dine, b. 1935: American pop artist, "Happening" artist, known especially for his hearts

Donatello, 1386-1466: Florentine sculptor, pioneer of the early Renaissance style, natural figures, "David" in the Bargello in Florence

Gustave Doré, 1832-1883: French artist, especially his illustrations for the Bible, the "Divine Comedy," "Paradise Lost," "Don Quixote"

Raoul Dufy, 1877-1953: French fauvist, bright colors, scenes of racing and the seaside

Albrecht Dürer, 1471-1528: German painter and engraver, his woodcuts unsurpassed, called the "Leonardo of the North," "St. Jerome in His Study"

Sir Jacob Epstein, 1880-1959: American-born British sculptor, massive and sometimes controversial works, religious and allegorical subjects, "Genesis," "Ecce Homo"

Max Ernst, 1891-1976: American born in Germany, originally a Dadaist, then surrealist painter, use of "frottage," collage artist, "Ubu Imperator"

Erté (Romain de Tertoff): 1892-1990: Russian-born French designer and illustrator, especially for *Harper's Bazaar*, leader in Art Deco movement, designer of costumes for "Ziegfeld Follies"

Paul Gauguin, 1848-1903: French painter, primitivism, Tahiti and the Marquesas are clues, "Spirit of the Dead Watching"

Francisco Goya, 1746-1828: Spanish painter and etcher, political and social themes, portraits of nobility, "The Third of May," "The Family of Charles IV," "The Dutchess of Alba," "The Naked Maja," "Los Caprichos"

El Greco (Doménicos Theotokópolos), 1541-1614: born in Crete, Spanish painter of religious works, elongated figures, deep shadows, "View of Toledo," "Assumption of the Virgin"

Juan Gris, 1887-1927: Spanish painter and sculptor in France, cubism pioneer, "Violin and Glass"

Franz Hals, 1580(?)-1666: Dutch painter of genre scenes and portraits, "The Laughing Cavalier," "Gypsy Girl," "The Jolly Toper," "Lucas de Clerq," "Shrovetide Revelers"

Jasper Johns, b. 1930: American painter, sculptor, and printmaker, neo-Dada, pop art, "flags" a clue

Frida Kahlo, 1907-1954: Mexican painter married to Diego Rivera, surrealist self-portraits, pain and suffering

Wassily Kandinsky, 1866-1944: Russian abstract painter, founder of the Blaue Reiter, a group of German abstract expressionists, Bauhaus teacher

Paul Klee: (see fifth paragraph of this section)

Fernand Léger, 1881-1955: French painter of urban life, posters, billboards, machine art, "The Cyclists"

Roy Lichtenstein, 1923-1997: American pop artist, artifacts of mass culture, comic-strip themes

Fra Filippo Lippi, 1406(?)-1469(?): Florentine Renaisssance painter, Carmelite monk, "Madonna Enthroned," "Adoration of the Magi"

Claude Lorrain, 1600-1682: French baroque painter known for his idealized landscapes and seascapes, "Embarkation of the Queen of Sheba," "Apollo and the Muses on Mount Helion"

René Magritte: (see sixth paragraph of this section)

Edouard Manet, 1832-1883: French painter, forerunner of impressionism, "Luncheon on the Grass," "Olympia," "The Fife Player"

Henri Matisse, 1869-1954: French painter, fauvism, pure color, simple shapes, cutouts, "The Dance," "Bathers by the River,"

"Woman with the Hat," "Le Bateau," "The Piano Lesson," "The Red Room"

Michelangelo Buonarotti, 1475-1564: Italian sculptor, painter, architect, and poet, ceiling of the Sistine Chapel, design of St. Peter's basilica, "Pietà," "Moses," "David"

Jean-François Millet, 1814-1875: French painter, especially of peasant farmers, a founder of the Barbizon school, "The Gleaners," "The Angelus," "Potato Planters," "Haymakers," "The Sower"

Joan Miró, 1893-1983: Spanish abstract art and surrealism, bright colors and bold forms, Catalan landscapes

Amedeo Modigliani, 1884-1920: Italian painter and sculptor who worked mostly in France, stylized bodies such as long necks, "Walking Man," "Reclining Nude"

Piet Mondrian, 1872-1944: Dutch abstract painter, perpendicular lines, planes of primary colors, abstract art, part of de Stijl movement, "Composition with Red, Yellow, and Blue"

Claude Monet, 1840-1926: French founder of impressionism, "Water Lilies," "Haystacks," "The Bridge at Argenteuil," "Gare St Lazare"

Elie Nadelman, 1882-1946: Polish-born American abstract modernist sculptor, influenced by folk art, "Dancer (High Kicker)"

Emile Nolde, 1867-1956: German painter and printmaker, expressionism, member of Die Brücke, "Christ and the Children," "Flower Garden"

Georgia O'Keeffe, 1887-1986: American painter known for her landscapes and close-up paintings of flowers, wife of Alfred Stieglitz, "Black Iris," "Blue and Green Music"

Claes Oldenburg, b. 1929: Swedish-born American painter and sculptor, oversize soft sculptures from stuffed vinyl and canvas, public pop sculpture such as "Lipsticks" in Picadilly Circus and "Typewriter Eraser" at the National Gallery of Art in Washington

Nam June Paik, 1932-2006: founder of video art, member of the Fluxus movement, "Video Fish," "TV Cello," "Something Pacific"

Pablo Picasso, 1881-1973: Spanish painter and sculptor who worked mostly in France, constant experimentation, cubism (especially with Braque), collage, portraits of Dora Maar, "Guernica," "Dove," "Head of a Woman," "The Old Guitarist"

Jackson Pollock, 1912-1956: American painter, drip paintings, leader of abstract expressionism, New York School, "Autumn Rhythm"

Raphael (Raffaello Sanzio da Urbino), 1483-1520: High Renaissance painter of portraits, religious subjects, and frescoes, "The School of Athens," "The Sistine Madonna," "The Transfiguration"

Man Ray, 1890-1976: American artist, Dada, the Rayograph, film, photography

Odilon Redon, 1840-1916: French artist who was a forerunner of surrealism; lithography and floral paintings

Rembrandt van Rijn, 1606-1669: Dutch painter and graphic artist, etching (not engraving), light and dark, contrast, shadow, "The Anatomy Lesson of Dr. Tulp," "The Night Watch," "Aristotle Contemplating the Bust of Homer"

Guido Reni, 1575-1642: Bolognese painter of the high baroque, "The Labors of Hercules," "Penitent Magdalene," the Aurora fresco

Pierre Auguste Renoir, 1841-1919: French impressionist, human figures, everyday life, realism, "Luncheon of the Boating Party," "Le Moulin de la Galette," "The Bathers," "Dance in the Country"

Joshua Reynolds, 1723-1792: British portrait painter, "The Age of Innocence," "Sarah Siddons," "Lord Heathfield"

Diego Rivera, 1886-1957: Mexican painter and husband of Frida Kahlo, murals in a style derived from folk art, frescoes, "The Fecund Earth"

Larry Rivers: (see sixth paragraph of this section)

François Auguste René Rodin, 1840-1917: prolific French sculptor whose works include "The Kiss," "The Thinker," "The Gates of Hell," "The Burghers of Calais," and "Bronze Age"

Dante Gabriel Rossetti, 1828-1882: English painter, illustrator, and poet who founded the Pre-Raphaelite Brotherhood, "Lady Lilith," "Found," "The Tune of the Seven Towers"

Henri Rousseau, 1844-1910: French painter of primitive and exotic works, "The Snake Charmer," "The Sleeping Gypsy"

Peter Paul Rubens, 1577-1640: Flemish baroque painter, religious and allegorical themes, Marie de Medici cycle, "Descent from the Cross," "Mystic Marriage of St. Catherine"

Egon Schiele, 1890-1918: Austrian expressionist painter, "Johann Harms," "Edith Seated," "Portrait of Gerti Schiele"

Georges Seurat, 1859-1891: French painter, a founder of neo-impressionism, pointillism ("dots" a clue), "Sunday Afternoon on the Island of La Grande Jatte," "Une Baignade"

Alfred Sisley, 1839-1899: British-born French impressionist landscape painter, "Footbridge at Argenteuil," "Boat During the Flood," "The Thames at Hampton Court"

John French Sloan, 1871-1951: American painter of urban life, especially Greenwich Village, member of the Ashcan school, "Sunday," "Women Drying Their Hair"

Jan Steen, 1626(?)-1679: Dutch genre painter, domestic life and revelry, "The Surprise," "The Feast of St. Nicholas"

Yves Tanguy, 1900-1955: French-born American painter, surrealism, "Rose of the Four Winds"

Giovanni Battista Tiepolo, 1696-1770: Italian painter, "The Martyrdom of Saint Agatha," "The Banquet of Cleopatra," "Adoration of the Magi"

Titian (Tiziano Vecelli), 1488(?)-1576: High Renaissance painter, introduced vigorous colors and the use of backgrounds to the Venetian school, "Venus of Urbino," "Venus and the Lute Players," "Assumption of the Virgin"

Henri de Toulouse-Lautrec, 1864-1901: French post-impressionist painter, printmaker, illustrator, and draftsman, posters of the Moulin Rouge, "La Goulue," "La Blanchisseuse," "La Toilette," "Jane Avril," "Aristide Bruant"

J.M.W. Turner, 1775-1851: English Romantic landscape painter known as "painter of light," "Battle of Trafalgar," "Snow Storm: Hannibal and His Army Crossing the Alps," "Eruption of Vesuvius"

Maurice Utrillo, 1883-1955: French painter, Paris street scenes, especially of Montmartre and Sacré-Coeur cathedral, "Le Lapin Agile"

Jan van Eyck, 1390(?)-1441: a founder of the Flemish school of painting, brilliant colors, realistic detail, early use of oil painting, "Arnolfini Wedding," "Adoration of the Lamb"

Vincent van Gogh, 1853-1890: Dutch post-impressionist painter, peasant life, sunflowers, "The Starry Night," "L'Arlésienne," "Arles," "Bedroom at Arles," his brother Theo, an art dealer, equally common in puzzles

Jan Vermeer, 1632-1675: Dutch painter of interior genre scenes, master of light and color, "Woman with a Water Jug," "Girl with a Pearl Earring"

Paolo Veronese, 1528-1588: Venetian school, devotional themes, pictures filled with people, "The Temptation of St. Anthony"

Andy Warhol, 1928-1987: American leader of pop art movement, silk-screen prints, commonplace images such as Campbell soup cans and Brillo boxes, his studio called the Factory, photographs of celebrities, his "Trash" film

Antoine Watteau, 1684-1721: French painter, "Embarkation for Cythera," "Pierrot" (or "Gilles")

James Abbott McNeill Whistler, 1834-1903: American painter influenced by Japanese art, "Arrangement in Grey and Black No. 1," known as "Whistler's Mother"

Grant Wood, 1891-1942: American painter known for his Midwest subjects, "American Gothic"

Geography

There is no limit as to what could be in a puzzle on this subject, but some places show up more than others. The island of Napoleon's exile, ELBA, is one of these (sometimes clued as situated in the Tyrrhenian Sea), as is Mt. ETNA (Mongibello in the local language), the highest volcano in Europe, in eastern Sicily, at 10,922 feet, southwest of Messina (all clues); its crater is named Bocca NUOVA. Others are ASTI, the Italian wine region (as well as its capital) southeast of Turin (sometimes clued by "Piedmont"); and the Arabian Sea's Gulf of ADEN. (Aden is also a port city in Yemen.)

Several others that appear are EDO, the former name of Tokyo, sometimes clued by "Shogun" or as once being a fishing village on Tokyo Bay ("Tokyo" itself means "eastern capital"); NARA, an ancient Japanese capital, which is less frequent; URI, one of the original cantons of Switzerland, sometimes clued by William Tell; IOS, in the Aegean Sea, said to be Homer's home; IONA, one of the Hebrides Islands off Scotland; OBAN, a Scottish seaport; ULM, the city of Einstein's birth; ESSEN, a German industrial city in the Ruhr valley, sometimes clued by "Krupp Works" or as a coal city or steel city or as being north of Bonn or Cologne; and the German region of the SAAR, a large coal basin.

Others are SAMOA (and its capital, APIA), clued as the site of Margaret Mead's sociological studies; RIO, usually clued by "Ipanema"; OSLO, clued as the skater Sonja Henie's birthplace or as the home of Edvard Grieg or of the Nobel Prize; ORAN, Algeria's second largest city and a seaport; OMAN, a sultanate on the Arabian Sea; two countries in Africa, namely, MALI and CHAD; ATTU, the largest of Alaska's Near Islands in the Aleutian chain in the Bering Sea, occupied by Japan for a short time during World War II, and sometimes clued as the "westernmost U.S. island." An island east of it, ADAK, has also been in puzzles, as has ATKA, even farther east. These three are sometimes clued by "Aleut" or "Aleutians." RAT Island, also in the Aleutian chain, is now free of rats after about 230 years.

Another popular subject is the Great Lakes, where ERIE is very common in puzzles; it borders four U.S. states. Sometimes cities on the lake are clues for Erie, such as Toledo, Cleveland, Sandusky, and Buffalo. Memorize the acronym "HOMES" to have the five Great Lakes at your fingertips: Huron, Ontario (the smallest), Michigan, Erie (the shallowest), and Superior (the largest). If a clue begins "Superior ___," the answer may well have something to do with the lake or a city on it. "Homes" itself is sometimes a clue, where a puzzle will ask for the lake represented by the fourth letter, for instance. By the way, the province of ONTARIO touches four of the Great Lakes. Erie is the name of a port in Pennsylvania as well as a canal, more frequent than any other canal in puzzles, but the KIEL Canal in Germany also appears; it links the North Sea with the Baltic.

Close to "Erie" in construction are the Gaelic EIRE and the poetic ERIN (for Ireland). Just as French is the most popular foreign language for crosswords and baseball the most popular sport, so is Ireland the most popular country. For example, in a puzzle in April 2004, there were five references to that country. In Ireland, the River ERNE flows into Donegal Bay; the name of this river has been used several times as an entry. Not to confuse, but ERNE is also the name of an Irish lake. (Usually, though, when puzzle makers want ERNE as an answer, the clue relates to the sea eagle having a white tail, also spelled ERN.)

The poetic ERIN is often referred to in clues as "Celtic land," "Fairie land," or "Leprechaun's land." The clue "Hibernia" (the Latin name for Ireland) needs EIRE as the answer, as do "Green land," "Emerald Isle," "Innisfail," "Highlands," and "Auld sod." An old name for Ireland is IERNE and if you ever need the symbol for Ireland, it is the HARP.

Another "E"-word is ERSE, the Goidelic language of both Scotland and Ireland. (It includes Irish and Scottish Gaelic as well as Manx.) Long before "Gone with the Wind," TARA was the capital and home of ancient Eire's high kings. The ARAN Islands are usually clued by their location in Galway Bay. The unusual word OGHAM (also OGAM) has appeared in a puzzle; it is an alphabet system of Old Irish. And the Irish phrase of allegiance, "Erin go bragh," has been found in puzzles, as has Ireland's coronation stone, Lia Fáil.

Mountains are common in crosswords; as mentioned above, the most popular is Mt. ETNA. Another is Mt. SINAI, once clued by its Arabic name of Jabal Musa; it is in the Sinai Peninsula of Egypt. Quite frequent are the URAL Mountains, which separate Europe and Asia; the ALAI in Kyrgyzstan (just west of the border with China), which have been clued as "Tien Shan range" as well as "Kirghiz range" (the Alai are a western branch of the Tien Shan, not to be confused with the ALTAI range in central Asia, also sometimes in puzzles); the ANDES in South America, as well as one of its peaks, El MISTI, in Peru; and the ATLAS in northwest Africa. The highest peak in the world is Mt. EVEREST, previously known as Peak XV (a clue), first scaled in 1953 by Sir Edmund Hillary and the Sherpa, Tenzing Norgay (two other clues).

If the highest peak in Turkey is ever needed, it is Mt. ARARAT, a peak near the Iranian border, upon which Noah's ark is said to have settled; it was first climbed in 1829, a clue. And the highest peak in Crete is Mt. IDA. Two very popular geographical features are Mauna KEA and Mauna LOA, active volcanoes on Hawaii Island, which appear about equally. Suggestion: write in the "A" and let a crossing word determine the first two letters. One puzzle informed its solvers that Mauna Kea is the highest mountain in the world, if measured from its base under the ocean to its peak in the sky. Other volcanoes you might come across are PELEE, in northern Martinique; OSSA, in Thessaly; and ASO, which has five cones (and is the largest), in Japan. Mt. Vesuvius, on the Bay of Naples, is frequently used as a clue for POMPEII.

Less frequent than mountains in puzzles are *deserts*, the most frequent being the SAHARA (which includes its eastern portion, the NUBIAN Desert, in Sudan). Another is the Sahara's neighbor to the south, the semi-arid SAHEL. The SINAI in Egypt is also popular, as well as the NEGEV in Israel and the GOBI in Mongolia.

If the word "map" is in a clue, the answer is often a contraction for "road," such as AVE, BLVD, HWY, RTE, etc. And RAND McNally has been an answer. Some other map-related answers are INSET, SCALE, LEGEND, TERR (territory), ALT (altitude), MTS (mountains), and ELEV (elevation). Two popular map-related answers are ISLE and ISLET, and sometimes the uncommon AIT appears, namely, a very small island. Infrequently, like "ait," are KEY and CAY. All of these are usually clued by "Dot on a map," "Dot in an atlas," "Dot in the ocean," etc.

A tricky clue you will see now and then is "East of ___, on a map," the blank being the name of a city. The answer is RIGHT, since maps are two-dimensional, and a place east of another is to the "right" of it. Likewise, "West of ___, on a map" is LEFT. Another trick is something like "East of Ecuador," where the solution is ESTE, Spanish for "east." And sometimes the clue is "West of ___," where the blank is a city. For this you may need to know the birthplace of MAE West (Brooklyn, NY) or ADAM West, who played Batman (Walla Walla, WA).

Popular U.S. cities are AMES, Iowa, seat of Iowa State University, sometimes clued as being near Des Moines; OCALA, Florida; OREM, Utah, clued as being near Provo or west of the Provo River; ORONO, Maine (a college town named after a Penobscot chief); OMAHA, Nebraska (on the Missouri River, and where the Union Pacific Railroad started); ALMA, Wisconsin; and EDINA, a suburb of Minneapolis.

Two other clued cities are ADA and ENID, Oklahoma, where the latter has been clued by Vance Air Force Base, Phillips University, the Queen Wheat City, a Cherokee Strip city, and the seat of Garfield County. Both Ada and Enid are on the Chisholm Trail, another clue. Oklahoma is sometimes clued by "Sooner" or "Sooner state." The first capital of Oklahoma, GUTHRIE, has also been in a puzzle. If "Four Corners state" is the clue, the answer nearly always is UTAH; the others that meet at this point are Colorado, Arizona, and New Mexico, the only place in the U.S. where this occurs.

As to *rivers* in puzzles, the longest river in France is the LOIRE, the longest in Spain is the EBRO (which runs past Logroño and Zaragoza), the longest in Scotland is the TAY, and the longest in Switzerland is the AAR(E), which flows through the capital, BERN(E), into the Rhine; in ancient times, the Aar was known as the Obringa (which fact would not be here if it had not been in a puzzle). A river in Scotland that pops up in puzzles is the DEE; Aberdeen is usually in the clue. Another Scottish river is the CLYDE, which flows through Glasgow. In Ireland, the LIFFEY flows through Dublin.

Three rivers beginning with "Y" are the YALU in China, the YONNE in France, and the YSER in Belgium and northern France. The Yser is often clued with "Flanders" or as "strategic World War I river" or as "North Sea feeder." Another North Sea feeder is the WESER, once clued as related to the Pied Piper of Hamelin. And a "Baltic Sea feeder" is the ODER, which separates Germany and Poland and has been clued as flowing through Silesia. Close in construction to the Oder (and more popular) is the EDER, which flows through Hesse in central Germany; it flows into the FULDA. (The Eder is not to be confused with EGER, which is a city in Hungary.) The German city of ULM is sometimes clued by its location on the Danube, the second longest river in Europe.

Other popular rivers in Europe are the ELBE (Hamburg or Dresden a clue), the ARNO in Florence and Pisa (it is also clued by "Tuscany"), which flows into the Ligurian Sea, the TIBER, which flows through Rome, the OISE in Belgium and France, and the ISERE, which runs through Grenoble from the Savoy Alps. The Isère is a tributary of the Rhône, and the latter has been a clue for ARLES, AVIGNON, and GENEVA. Another tributary of the Rhône is the SAONE, which joins it at Lyon. The EURE is at Chartres, in France.

The AIRE, a major river in Yorkshire, flows through Leeds and runs into the OUSE; and the LEA meets the Thames at London. Another river that shows up is the ORNE, which flows through the Normandy city of Caen, and is usually clued as such; a second clue for the Orne is "D-Day river." Orne is also the name of a department in France. Near Caen, the VIRE flows through St Lô (see "French" section for the World War II towns and beaches). And a city that is clued as "World War I battle site" is often YPRES.

Another popular river is the URAL, third longest in Europe, which runs through ORSK and flows into the Caspian Sea. (As mentioned above, Ural is also the name of a mountain range.) Close in construction is the ARAL River, which also flows into the Caspian. If another Russian river is ever needed, it is usually the VOLGA, the longest in Europe, and also flowing into the Caspian.

The NEVA is typically clued by either St. Petersburg or by the fact that it flows into the Gulf of Finland. Yet another Russian river in puzzles is the AMUR, which defines the Russian border with China. The OKA River, south of Moscow and a tributary of the Volga, has been clued by the city of Orel; and then there is the LENA, a river in Siberia. The

INDUS is the longest in Pakistan, and flows into the Arabian Sea. But beware of "Rivers" in a clue, as the answer may not relate to rivers at all, but to the comedienne, Joan Rivers, or to the artist, Larry Rivers, or to someone else having the name.

Then there are *lakes* and *seas*. One of the most popular is the ARAL Sea (sometimes referred to as a lake), which has been shrinking since 1960, which has high salinity, and which has lost over 75% of its surface area (three clues), between Uzbekistan and Kazakhstan ("stan" is Persian for "country"). The Sea of AZOV, south of Russia and Ukraine, has also appeared. If a clue concerns the world's oldest, deepest lake, the answer is Lake BAIKAL, in Russia. And the longest lake in the world is Lake Tanganyika. The ROSS Sea in Antarctica is named for an English explorer, Sir James Clark Ross, and Lake ITASKA is the source of the Mississippi River. You may also come across the word TARN, a small mountain lake, typically glacial.

PORTS is usually the answer when two cities are listed as a clue, without any other clarifiers; examples are the clues "New York and Baltimore" or "San Francisco and San Diego." And SEAS is usually the answer when two bodies of water (disguised) are the clue, such as "Red and Black" or "Red and Dead." The giveaway in the "seas" clues is that the final word in the clue is capitalized. Speaking of the DEADSEA, it is sometimes clued as the lowest place on the surface of the earth. And, of course, the clue "Blue and White" can refer to the NILE, since the Blue Nile and the White Nile join at Khartoum, in Sudan, to form the longest river in the world.

To close this section, three geographic names do not seem to fit any of the categories above. One is IONIA, an ancient coastal region of Asia Minor, now in Turkey. Also in Asia Minor, "Acre" is a tricky place when found in a clue: it has several variant spellings, but puzzle makers expect you to know that it is a city in ISRAEL (sometimes ISR), not a measure of land area. The third of these is Rapa Nui, the natives' name for EASTER Island.

Miscellaneous Subjects

The subjects below are grouped arbitrarily under this heading, but they are just as common in crosswords as those found in the preceding sections.

Typography and Editors' Marks

Clues for typographical answers sometimes include the words "proof," "marginal note," or "ms," which is the abbreviation for a manuscript (plural "mss"); the last is sometimes also an entry (MSS). A manuscript of large dimensions is a FOLIO (about 15 inches high). Half a LEAF is a PAGE and 500 leaves (or sheets) constitute a REAM. A left-hand page is VERSO and a right-hand page is RECTO. Corrections to or retractions in books and other publications are called ERRATA. *Typeface* refers to the full range of type of the same design. Some typefaces have SERIFS, which are occasionally clued as "ascenders" or "descenders" or as "fine lines." On occasion, their opposite, sans serif, has appeared: SANSSERIF. *Font* refers to a complete set of type of one size and face. Within these are various *styles*, such as ROMAN, ITALIC, BOLD, etc.

Two common typefaces on typewriters are PICA and ELITE, and they show up in crosswords. The latter can be tricky if in a clue. Two other typefaces are ARIEL and COURIER, both with more vowels than consonants. If a clue hints at small type, AGATE may be the answer, as an agate is about 5½ points (a point is about 1/72nd of an inch). Editors' marks are many, but for puzzles, the most frequent answers are DELE (delete or remove or take out, and "strike out" is a favorite clue) and STET (undo the change or instruction). A CARET (^) is used to make an insertion and dash lengths are EMS and ENS, with "em" being longer than "en." Sometimes these become EMDASH and ENDASH in puzzles.

As for diacritical marks, a TILDE is that wavy mark over a letter, as in the Spanish word, "niño"; a VIRGULE is a slash, as in "and/or"; a circumflex is a small, arrow-shaped symbol over a letter, such as in the French word, "âme"; an UMLAUT is a pair of dots above a letter, such as in the German word, "über"; and a CEDILLA is a small, hook-like symbol under a letter, such as in the French word, "reçu." A pronunciation symbol, the MACRON, has also appeared; it is the horizontal line over a vowel to indicate a long sound, as the "a" in "cake."

The word TYPO was encountered only a few times, and the rare OBELUS (plural OBELI), or dagger sign, but once. Who in the world would know that? Sometimes you will come across "galley," which is the sheet of paper (or proof) that editors write their revisions and corrections on. The word "dummy" has also appeared in a clue; it is a layout or mock-up, showing what the final product might look like.

Card Games and Chess

Bridge and poker are the most popular card games in crosswords. For bridge, the positions NORTH, EAST, SOUTH, and WEST (defender's seat) sometimes appear as answers. Some others have been GRANDSLAM, SCOREPAD, TRUMP, DUMMY, SLAM, HONORS, SET (to defeat), RENEGE, REVOKE, and FINESSE. In bridge, you are VOID if you have no cards of a particular suit. The clue "According to . . ." results in HOYLE, but the names of the bridge experts Charles H. GOREN and ELY Culbertson appear, too, as does the bridge analyst and columnist, ALAN Truscott. Goren has been clued by his book, *Winning Bridge Made Easy*, and Culbertson as founder of *The Bridge World*, a magazine.

In poker, terms like "cut," "deal," "stake," "raise," "stay," "call" (raises and calls are BETS), "bluff," "fold," "stud," and "pot" (or "kitty") are usually clues, with ANTE being a very common answer; HIT and HITME (hit me) have also occurred, as has SEE, as in "I'll see you." A poor poker hand is a RUNT. Terms in common to both bridge and poker are "bid," "rebid," "deal," "hand," "suit," "deuce," "trey," "open," and "pass." IMIN (I'm in) and IPASS (I pass) were both entries, as were WHIST, a forerunner of bridge, and EUCHRE, which also uses trumps. STU Ungar ("the Kid") has been in crosswords; he was one of the greatest poker and gin rummy players. The poker expert, Phil IVEY, also appears and GABE Kaplan was host of the TV series "High Stakes Poker."

Pinochle made several appearances, where the clues "combo" and "combination" resulted in MELD as an answer ("meld" applies to canasta, too). In one puzzle, it helped to know that a low card in pinochle is NINE. GIN is sometimes an answer for "Card-table exclamation" or similar clue in gin rummy, and a shutout in that game is SCHNEIDER. Starters in rummy are UPCARDS. A form of rummy is CANASTA (which has four jokers, a clue).

UNO is the exclamation in the game of the same name when only one card is left; it has been clued as a family card game. On one occasion you had to know that Uno has skip and reverse cards and on another that there are 108 cards in a specially printed deck. The French card game of

MILLE Bornes also uses a special deck, which has hazard, remedy, safety, and distance cards. A card game that uses 32 cards (sevens through aces) is SKAT, and it is popular in Germany; another clue is that it is played by three people. *Note*: Skat is not to be confused with the American card game, Scat.

Another game with 32 cards (also sevens through aces) is ECARTE (Écarté). An old card game of Spanish origin, also played by three people (four can play, but the dealer sits out), is OMBER (or OMBRE or HOMBRE), played with 40 cards. Another card game is FARO (or Pharoah), which can have any number of players, or "punters"; it uses a regular 52-card deck and requires a bank. And an American card game is SPADES.

In blackjack, or "21," if you have a score greater than 21, you are OVER or BUST. (Be careful of the clue "Blackjack" all by itself, though, because in British slang a blackjack is a COSH, which has also appeared several times.) A blackjack natural is ACETEN (ace-ten). Also in a puzzle has been the name of Edward O. THORP, clued by his book, *Beat the Dealer*. You may encounter the word PAM, which is the jack of clubs, the highest trump in certain games of LOO.

A PIP is the mark on a card indicating its number and/or suit, such as spade (maximum number of pips is 10). And in crosswords, you are expected to know that one king and two jacks each have one eye. Speaking of jacks, a NOB is a jack of the same suit as the card turned up by the starter in cribbage, a game for two to four players. A boxcar means "6" on a die and to STAND means not to take a card.

The most common chess clue and answer are "castle" and its synonym, ROOK. ("Castle" is also a verb, whereby the king and rook simultaneously move in a specific way.) The *pieces* in chess are the king, queen, two bishops, two knights, and two rooks, making a total of eight for each side; there are also eight *pawns* for each side. DRAW has been an entry, for when one cannot make CHECKMATE, and GAMBIT is an opening maneuver.

On occasion, a puzzle will ask for "___neighbor," where the blank is a chess piece. The bishops stand to either side of the king and queen, and the knights are between the bishops and rooks, which are on the end. The name of the chess analyst Shelby LYMAN has appeared, as well as the chess masters YURI Averbakh, Mikhail Botvinnick, Max EUWE, and Mikhail TAL. Japanese chess is SHOGI.

Travel and Transportation

This subject is generally limited to abbreviations used in air travel. Commonly used airport symbols are LAX (Los Angeles), JFK (New York), LGA (La Guardia), and SFO (San Francisco). Chicago's airport, OHARE (once Orchard Field Airport, a clue), and its symbol, ORD, appear now and then. ORD is also the entry for a military base near Monterey, California, which was decommissioned in 1994. The schedule-related transportation entries are ARR (arrival), DEP (departure), ETA (estimated time of arrival), and ETD (estimated time of departure). The entry is nearly always ETA, due to its two vowels, so it is usually safe to pencil that in. Other terms are SKED, an abbreviation for "schedule," and TBA (to be announced).

Although the Concorde has been phased out of service, the abbreviation SST (for "supersonic transport") will, no doubt, long remain, as it is a popular answer in crosswords, as is one of Paris's airports, ORLY. Airlines are also included on occasion and, like the Concorde, need not necessarily be operating any longer; entries have included the former BOAC, PANAM, and TWA. But the most popular in crosswords is ELAL, sometimes clued by "1948," when it began service. Back near the ground, a common answer is ELL or ELS (for elevated transport lines). This can be clued in so many ways: "high lines," "tracks in the air," "raised transports," etc.

This section would not be complete without the eight three-letter compass points. Clockwise from the north, these are: NNE, ENE, ESE, SSE, SSW, WSW, WNW, and NNW. Obviously, ENE and ESE are the most popular, due to their two vowels.

Nautical Terms

Most nautical terms in puzzles relate to a boat (or ship), which can be referred to as SHE. And the term HER, the possessive form of "she," applies to things related to a ship, such as "her hull." The front of a boat is referred to as the BOW, which contains the curved upright beam called the STEM, which in turn forms part of the PROW ("bow" and "prow" are often used interchangeably). When puzzle makers are having a particularly bad day, they might insert SNY, which is a shipbuilding term that refers to the upward curve of the edge of a ship's plank, especially toward the bow or the stern. (You will not likely find this word in a desk dictionary, but it has appeared in puzzles.)

The back of the boat is the STERN. To go toward the bow is to go FORWARD and to go toward the stern is to go AFT (or ASTERN or ABAFT). The terms FORE and AFT are commonly used to refer to front and rear directions on a boat. To go up on deck is to go TOPSIDE and to go inside is to go BELOW, or below deck; in one puzzle, the inside of a ship was called the HOLD, and in another, the BELLY. A word close in construction is BELAY, meaning to fasten or make secure, such as a line. If you thought SNY was tricky, how about ORLOP? At least five puzzle makers had the nerve to include this term, which is the lowest deck on a ship having at least four decks, usually a military ship (they usually omit the part about the four decks); the BILGE is the lowest inner part of a ship's hull. Right is STARBOARD, left is PORT or LARBOARD, and either side of a boat can be ABEAM, that is, crosswise to the hull.

A boat is built up from a HULL, underneath of which is the KEEL. The term THWART has occurred, which is a horizontal structural piece that can even be a seat in a small craft, such as a canoe or dinghy. A HAWSE (or hawsehole or cat hole) is an opening for the HAWSER, a heavy-duty line such as an anchor cable. And WALE has appeared; it is a hull plank. A SPAR on a sailboat is any pole that supports the rigging; examples of a spar are the MAST, BOOM, YARD, YARDARM, SPRIT, and BOWSPRIT. And STAYS are cables, usually of wire, that hold the mast. The term BIBB was once an entry: it is a support bracket on the mast.

A BITT is a vertical deck post to secure lines or cables, and an EARING is a short reefing line. A THOLE is actually a thole pin; an oar fits between two such pins on the GUNWALE, which is the upper edge of the side of a boat. A DAVIT is a small crane over the side of a ship, such as to lower a lifeboat. Those strings of fabric on sails, which indicate wind direction, are TELLTALES, and have also appeared.

The side of a boat away from the wind, or weather, is said to be ALEE (or in the LEE of the boat); its opposite is AWEATHER. The word "alee" is extremely popular in crosswords and is sometimes clued by "Helm position." And HELM has been an entry for "Pilot's place" or "Wheel of a boat." AMAIN means "at full speed" and APEAK means that a vessel is in a vertical position (or nearly so). The answer BECALMED has appeared; a sailboat is becalmed when there is no wind. A TACK is a heading for a sailboat and the adjective YARE means responsive, or easily handled.

HEAVE and its past tense, HOVE, have several meanings, one of which is to haul up by means of a rope, line, or cable. If an anchor is just clear of the bottom, it is ATRIP (or aweigh); this arcane fact, at least to a landlubber, was in a Wednesday *Times* puzzle (Saturday might have been more appropriate). And then there is HEAVEHO (Heave Ho!), the command to pull hard on a rope, line, or cable.

The calls or shouts of AHOY (a greeting or a term used to attract attention) and AVAST (to stop whatever you are doing) are sometimes related to the "Popeye" comic strip (see "Comics" above); two other clues to these entries may include "aye" and "mate" (or "matey"). Even AYEAYE has appeared, as in "Aye, aye, sir." A BOSUN or BOSN (bos'n) is an officer or deck chief on a naval ship, who reports to the captain (cap'n). A "captain's mast" is a naval disciplinary hearing. A coxswain (or simply COX in puzzles) is the person in a crew who sits in the stern, steers the boat, and coordinates the rowers. The sailor's distress signal, SOS, is a frequent answer (it is also the brand name of a scouring pad, not unknown in puzzles); less so is MAYDAY.

The clues "mariner," "sea dog," "sailor," or "old salt" usually result in TAR or GOB or SWAB(BY) or LIMEY (British). It helps to know that GROG is a sailor's drink made from rum diluted with water and that the mariner's patron is St. ELMO, at least in puzzles. Other patrons of mariners are the 4th century Nicholas of Myra, in Greece, St. Brandon the navigator, and St. Clement. (St. Nicholas is kept quite busy, as he is also the patron of archery, thieves, merchants, pawnbrokers, students, and children.)

More nautical terms are as follows: PINNACE, a ship's boat; PUNT, an open, flat-bottomed boat, usually poled; DORY, a small, shallow-draft boat with high sides and a narrow transom, once clued as "V-shaped"; PIROGUE, a canoe made from a hollowed tree trunk; AVISO, a dispatch boat; LIGHTER, a large, flat-bottomed barge; KEDGE, a light anchor; PAINTER, a line attached to the bow; and COLORS, the flag identifying a ship's country of origin. Only a landlubber would pull on a rope or line instead of a SHEET when adjusting a sail.

Clock-time on a boat is announced by bells, and in one puzzle it helped to know that eight bells is NOON. (But eight bells can also be 4:00 or 8:00 or midnight.) The long-range navigation aid LORAN appears in puzzles; speed is measured in KNOTS and distance in

LEAGUES. Depth is measured in FATHOMS, a length of 1.8288 meters, or about six feet. Clues for a nautical answer are often something like "___, at sea." Speaking of the sea, a very common crossword answer is ASEA if the clue points to sailing or traveling by water. ATSEA (at sea), nearly as popular in crosswords, is often a metaphorical answer for "lost," "confused," "bemused," "clueless," "baffled," "puzzled," "perplexed," "flummoxed," "discombobulated," "bewildered," "befuddled," or "nonplused."

Mathematics and Geometry

A term that sometimes occurs comes from trigonometry; that is the SINE function. Of the other five trig functions (cosine, tangent, cotangent, secant, and cosecant), three have appeared in puzzles. (For the trig-challenged, the sine is the ratio of the length of the side of a right triangle opposite one of the acute angles to the length of the hypotenuse.)

For geometry, the elements of a circle are sometimes employed, such as ARC, CHORD (a line that connects two points on a circle), and RADIUS (plural RADII). For other curved figures, such as ellipsoids, parabolas, and such, the terms FOCUS and its plural, FOCI, are used. A TORUS (plural TORI) has also been in puzzles, clued by its donut shape as well as by the shape of bagels, inner tubes, and Cheerios. The most popular term is AREA (length times width), which can be clued in so many ways. It has helped to know that the term for a plane angle is THETA, or T; this has been clued by "Trig symbol."

On one occasion, the word APOTHEM was an answer; this is a regular polygon's short radius, the perpendicular distance from the center to any of its sides. On another, it helped to know that an equal-sided figure is an ISOGON. LEMMA occurred twice; it is a proposition or a "helping theorem," or part of a proof, in geometry. Three short Latin words are also related to proofs in geometry; these are ERGO, ERAT, and QUOD (see "Latin" section above).

The famous Greek mathematician EUCLID has served as both clue and answer with respect to geometry. Five other mathematicians have appeared in puzzles: (1) Leonhard EULER, author of *Elements of Algebra*, who is usually clued as being Swiss, and to whom we owe the e-function, the law of quadratic reciprocity, much of the basic notation in mathematics, including integral calculus, and the PHI function, (2) Pierre de FERMAT, usually clued as being French or by his famous "last theorem," which was not proved until more than 350 years later, (3) John von NEUMANN, one of the greatest mathematicians in modern history, who was involved in nuclear physics, (4) John NAPIER, the inventor of logarithms, who was a Scot, and (5) Paul ERDOS, known especially for number theory and combinatorics, who has been clued as Hungarian.

For algebra, a single term appears quite regularly. Its clues relate to "high" or "infinite" in amount or degree or to being the last of a series, and the answer is NTH (as in "nth degree"). For calculus, the only clue and answer have been "calculus symbol" and SIGMA (the Greek letter Σ). It is the sign for summation. Square roots and cube roots have been in puzzles, but infrequently; on one occasion, 3 was compared to 27, the answer being CUBEROOT, and on another, it was necessary to square a number, that is, multiply it by itself. It is helpful to know that there are an x-axis and a y-axis in two-dimensional graphs plus a z-axis in three-dimensional ones. An example for an entry in crosswords is XAXIS (x-axis).

Prime numbers have been encountered, where the answer is usually the next in a series; the first few prime numbers are 2, 3, 5, 7, 11, 13, 17, and 19. These are defined as positive integers not divisible without a remainder by any positive integer other than itself and one; the series is infinite. Because letters, not numbers, are needed in puzzles, the answer will be in Roman numerals. Examples for squares and cubes are "4 squared" = XVI and "3 cubed" = XXVII. An example for prime numbers is "Prime number following 13," which is XVII. Then there is the Fibonacci sequence, named after Leonardo Fibonacci, where each successive number is equal to the sum of the two preceding numbers. The first few Fibonacci numbers are 1, 1, 2, 3, 5, 8, 13, etc. This sequence was brought to the attention of the public in *The da Vinci Code*, a novel by Dan Brown. And ALIQUOT, an exact proper divisor, would not be here if it were not in a puzzle.

Sometimes a ratio-related clue appears, based on a:b::c:d, that is, "a" is to "b" as "c" is to "d." Answers are COLON and ISTO (is to). PHI represents the golden ratio (golden mean, golden section, or divine proportion), which is 1.618; it is named for the Greek sculptor, Phidias. From fractions, LCD, or lowest common denominator, has appeared. (It could also stand for "liquid crystal display.") Lastly, do not be misled into thinking that the word "digit" or "digits" in a clue refers to a number or numbers, as these terms usually refer to FINGER(S) or TOE(S).

Metric System

Although puzzle solvers may be familiar with the meter-kilogram-second system to measure length, mass, and time, three terms used in puzzles may not immediately come to mind: CENTARE, a square meter; ARE, an area of 100 square meters; and STERE, a cubic meter. A metric ton is 1,000 kilograms, and is referred to as a TONNE. Going down in size, the reductions in the metric system are "deci" (1/10th), "centi" (1/100th), "milli" (1/1,000th), and "micro" (1/1,000,000th); the term for the last is MICRON, one millionth of a meter. With the increasing speed of computer chips, the multiples go even lower than "micro," such as "nano," "pico," "femto," and "atto." And going up the scale, they are "deka" (x10), "hecto" (x100), "kilo" (x1,000), "mega" (x1,000,000), "giga" (x1,000,000,000), and "tera" (x1,000,000,000,000). A newspaper article in October 2009 referred to a petabyte, 1,000 times as large as a terabyte.

Noble Gases and Other Elements

The noble, rare, nonreactive, or inert gases (listed with their symbols and atomic numbers) are (He) helium (2), (Ne) neon (10), (Ar) argon (18), (Kr) krypton (36), (Xe) xenon (54), and (Rn) radon (86). Helium is sometimes clued as relating to balloons, neon to signs or advertising, argon to radio tubes or light bulbs, and xenon to television tubes, strobe lights, and flash gas. In addition to the noble gases, puzzles sometimes require the names of other elements. The first 30 of these are listed below, along with their symbols and atomic numbers:

Hydrogen H (1)	Sulfur S (16)
Helium He (2)	Chlorine Cl (17)
Lithium Li (3)	Argon Ar (18)
Beryllium Be (4)	Potassium K (19)
Boron B (5)	Calcium Ca (20)
Carbon C (6)	Scandium Sc (21)
Nitrogen N (7)	Titanium Ti (22)
Oxygen O (8)	Vanadium V (23)
Fluorine F (9)	Chromium Cr (24)
Neon Ne (10)	Manganese Mn (25)
Sodium Na (11)	Iron Fe (26)
Magnesium Mg (12)	Cobalt Co (27)
Aluminum Al (13)	Nickel Ni (28)
Silicon Si (14)	Copper Cu (29)
Phosphorus P (15)	Zinc Zn (30)

Other Scientific Terms

Scientific terms appear in crosswords, and a few are listed here. The six most common are ION, ERG, JOULE, DYNE, ENOL, and ESTER. An ion is an atom or group of atoms that has acquired a net electric charge by gaining or losing one or more electrons. An erg is a unit of work; there are 10 million ergs in a joule. A dyne is a unit of force related to acceleration of mass, and is a fraction (1/100,000th) of a NEWTON (symbol N in physics).

Enols and esters are organic compounds; an enol has been clued as being a double-bonded carbon atom and an ester is aromatic and used in perfumes. (The etymology of the word "ester" is related to vinegar, though, hardly a fragrant odor.) Since they have a different number of letters, more explanation here is probably not necessary. "Oily ester" and "used in soaps" are usually clues for OLEATE.

AZOLES are yet another class of organic compounds, as are AMINO acids, often clued by the term "protein" or "nitrogen compound." Two other terms from organic chemistry that occur are AMIDE and AMINE. If you come across a clue containing the word "ammonia" or the chemical radical NH_2, the answer could well be amide or amine. Several letter combinations for chemical suffixes are IDE, ITE, ATE, ANE (for hydrocarbons), ASE (for enzymes), and OSE (for sugars). A chemical *prefix* that occurs is OXY.

An OHM is a unit of electrical resistance, while its reverse, MHO, was the name formerly given to a unit of electrical conductance, now known as a SIEMENS (after Ernst Werner von Siemens). The ohm is named for Georg Simon Ohm, a German physicist. Some other electrical terms that occur are AMPERE (or AMP), VOLT, and WATT, a volt-ampere. An ampere (for André-Marie Ampère) is a unit of current, a volt (for Alessandro Volta) is a unit of electric potential, and a watt (for James Watt) is a unit of power. A FARAD (for Michael Faraday) (symbol F) is a unit of electrical capacitance and a GAUSS (for Karl Friedrich Gauss) is a unit of magnetic flux density.

Another "electrical" entry is ACDC; clues usually refer to the Australian rock band of the name (AC/DC), but occasionally to electricity. The letter combinations AC and DC stand for alternating current and direct current. Concerning the "AC" part, this might be the place to introduce Nikola Tesla, the Serbian-born American physicist who discovered its principles. Like the gauss above, the TESLA (symbol T) is a unit of magnetic flux density. His first and last names are used in both clues and answers. He and Thomas Alva Edison were contemporaries; Edison promoted direct current for household use, but Tesla prevailed, as we all know. (And now, Tesla is the name of a car.) Then there is the REM, for measuring doses of ionizing radiation. In Europe and Asia, the SIEVERT is used; it equals 100 rem. The RAD, a unit of energy absorbed from ionizing radiation, has been replaced by the GRAY, but not yet in puzzles.

The terms VHF (very high frequency) and UHF (ultra high frequency) are also found in puzzles. The clues are usually a frequency of 30-300 MHz for the former and 300-3,000 MHz for the latter. Two other terms are THERM and BTU, or British thermal unit; a BTU is 1,055 joules (see above) and a therm is a unit of heat equal to 100,000 BTUs.

Then there are LUX, a unit of illumination; LUMEN, a measure of light flux; BEL, a unit of sound; SONE, a unit of perceived loudness; RHO, the symbol for density; ETA, the symbol for viscosity; TAU, the symbol for torque; and MIL, a measure of thickness (.001 inch), such as the diameter of a wire. A MINIM is $1/60^{th}$ of a DRAM, a weight equal to $1/16^{th}$ of an ounce in the U.S. Customary System and $1/8^{th}$ of an ounce as a unit of apothecary weight.

On occasion, usually in more difficult puzzles, the chemical elements and their symbols will be clues and answers. Some of these are mentioned above under "Noble Gases and Other Elements"; the most popular of these pairings is Fe in a clue and IRON as the answer. Although there are now 115 elements (as of August 2013), puzzles generally limit themselves to iron and to Sn for TIN, Na for SODIUM, Si for SILICON, Ag for SILVER, and Au for GOLD. The only molecule that comes up in puzzles is NaCl, the chemical symbol for sodium chloride, or table salt.

When puzzle makers want to be even more ornery, they might insert EPACT in a puzzle (in fact, they have). Who would know what such a word means? It is the solar-lunar time differential, or the time required to bring the solar calendar into agreement with the lunar calendar.

In addition to the scientists above, only one appears again and again in puzzles, and that is the Italian-born American, Enrico Fermi (both his first and last names in both clues and answers). He received a Nobel Prize for Physics in 1938 (another clue) and is known especially for the first controlled nuclear chain reaction; this was in 1942 at the University of Chicago (both sometimes clues). Later he was a consultant at Los Alamos National Laboratory.

Another scientist who received the prize (in 1918) was MAX Planck; he made many contributions to theoretical physics, but is especially known for his discovery of quantum physics. Another recipient of the prize (in 1922) was the Danish physicist NIELS Bohr, who worked on the atomic bomb at Los Alamos. If Archimedes is in a clue, the answer is usually his apocryphal expression, EUREKA. The Danish astronomer Tycho Brahe appears in puzzles, too, with one of his names the clue and the other the solution.

Computers, Software, and the Web

Related to hardware, the following have appeared: CPU, VDT, LCD, CRT, MOUSE, IBM (or "Big Blue" in clues), NEC (the Japanese computer giant), COMPAQ, DELL, MAC, IMAC (and "Apple" in clues). If "Jobs" is the first word in a clue, it will likely refer to the late Steve Jobs, the cofounder of Apple. In one puzzle we learned that he and Bill Gates, of Microsoft, were ADOPTED.

Some of the computer functions and keys that have been encountered are ALT, DEL, CTRL, UNDO, SAVE, UNZIP, and ESC. Speaking of ESC (escape), this has been the answer for "Neighbor of F1" and "Corner key," so puzzle makers assume that one can visualize the keyboard. And a clue for ALT is "Key near space bar."

On several occasions, it helped to recall that ENIAC (Electronic Numerical Integrator and Computer, sometimes referred to as the "Great Brain") was a pioneering computer at the University of Pennsylvania in the 1940s (it was announced and received a patent in 1946). UNIVAC (Universal Automatic Computer) also appears in puzzles, with its three vowels. It was the first commercial computer produced in the U.S., and was delivered in 1951.

As mentioned in the section on "Movies" above, the mainframe computer in the movie "2001: A Space Odyssey" was named HAL 9000, sometimes clued as a tyrant or a villain. Two home computers that occur in puzzles are the ATARI and the Commodore AMIGA. The basic unit of information in a computer is a BIT, which has only two values, 0 or 1, thus the term "binary." These bits are sequenced into a BYTE, usually a multiple of eight bits; this byte is operated on as a unit by the computer. Byte multiples are the familiar kilo-, mega-, and giga-, etc. One of many storage devices is a ZIPDRIVE.

Software terms have been RAM (and DRAM), ROM (and CDROM), MENU (and POPUPMENU), ICON, SCREENSAVER,

DESKTOP, ASCII, FIREWALL, APP(S) and APPLET(S), DEBUG, BITMAP, BETA (a software prototype), and MACRO ("shortcut" in a clue). Video games are software, and quite common is ATARI (mentioned above), often clued as "Video (or arcade) game pioneer"; one of Atari's first offerings was PONG (Atari also makes video game consoles). MYST is a computer game set on an island and SEGA is a Japanese video game software producer.

Apple's IPOD, ITUNES, IBOX, IPHONE, IPAD, and IBOOKS appear now and then, as do Microsoft's XBOX and ZUNE. The author has not yet come across Microsoft's E-readers, such as Kin One or Kin Two, which are no longer in production, or Amazon's Kindle readers or the Kobo (an anagram of "book") or Barnes & Noble's Nook. Neither have social media made inroads into puzzles the author has solved: Facebook, Twitter, Flickr, YouTube, Myspace, LinkedIn, Buzz, Foursquare, Tumblr, or others.

Microsoft gave WINDOW a new meaning, and now VISTA has one. SKYPE, the voice-over-internet protocol (VOIP) service started by eBay, is now owned by Microsoft. Two useful terms with three vowels are UPLOAD and DOWNLOAD. Even program file suffixes, such as EXE, make their way into puzzles.

There are many NETIZENS now, and internet terms have overtaken hardware and software terms in puzzles, namely, entries such as SITE and WEBSITE, WEBCAST, WEBINAR (an on-line class), SURF and SURFING, CHAT (and CHATROOM), EMAIL, ENOTE, ECARD, EVITE (an invitation), ELOAN, QMAIL, XMAIL, DOTCOM, SPAM, ADWARE, MEME, VIRUS, WEB, BLOG (a web log, or online diary). It is helpful to know that one POSTS a blog.

To get ONLINE there are LOGIN or LOGON; the result of an on-line search is a HIT; then there are MODEM, WIFI (Wi-Fi network), HTTP (hypertext transfer protocol) and HTTPS (with encryption), HTML (hypertext markup language), URL (universal resource locator), DSL (digital subscriber line), ISP (internet service provider, or portal) such as AOL, MSN, or Earthlink, SERVER, USERID, USERNAME, and various protocols, such as TELMET. As for browsers, they go from one of the first, MOSAIC, to MOZILLA Firefox, NETSCAPE, OPERA, Apple SAFARI, Google CHROME, and others. For more such information, consult the on-line computer dictionary and internet search engine "Webopedia."

The various URL suffixes are popular, too, among them COM, EDU, GOV, NET, and ORG. To mail a message, you press SEND, and to get off the internet, you must, of course, LOGOFF or LOGOUT. On-line purchasing and selling terms are ETAIL, EBAY, ECASH, ELOAN, EWALLET, and ETICKET, and one can access USENET, EBOOKs, EZINEs, and EMAGs such as SLATE and the UTNE Reader. There are many digital book file extensions, but the only one to appear in a puzzle was EPUB. Popular search engines in crosswords are AMAZON, GOOGLE, and YAHOO, with their many vowels. And then there is NETTV (net TV).

Chat-room (or cyberchat) abbreviations are many and varied, but the only ones of interest to puzzle solvers are those without numbers. Some of these are BTW (By the way), DIKU (Do I know you?), FTR (For the record), FWIW (For what it's worth), GAL (Get a life), GGN (Gotta go now), GIAR (Give it a rest), ILU (I love you), JJA (Just joking around), RUOK (Are you OK?), OMG (Oh, my God), SETE (Smiling ear to ear), SUP (What's up?), WAM (Wait a minute), and slightly different, LOL (Laugh on line). Related to the last, LOL, are EMOTICONs, many using various keyboard-generated symbols, such as a SMILEYFACE. These have been collectively referred to as cyberhumor.

Computer languages appear infrequently, but answers that have appeared are ADA, BASIC, COBOL, FORTRAN, JAVA, and PASCAL, and there are many others. ADA, based on PASCAL, commemorates a person, whose full name was Lady Augusta Ada Byron King, the Countess of Lovelace. She is sometimes clued as Lord Byron's daughter, as the "Enchantress of Numbers," or as a mathematician.

Operating systems are found in puzzles, and UNIX (developed at Bell Labs and used since 1969, two clues) is the most common, followed by DOS (and MSDOS, released in 1982, a clue) and WINDOWS, mentioned above. The start-up sound of Windows 95 has been a clue for Brian ENO and the background color of Windows 98 is TEAL. Apple's operating system, iOS, is a natural for crosswords. ANDROID is a Linux-based operating system purchased by Google in 2005 (but DROID is a commercial line of smart phones). Related to smart phones are PDAs, or personal digital assistants. The spreadsheets LOTUS and EXCEL have also appeared. The longest word encountered was WORKSTATION, but the most popular answer is short: USER.

Currency

As mentioned in the "Strategy" section, clues for money or currency are bread, dough, do-re-mi, scratch, clams, dineros, cabbage, lettuce (and kale in one puzzle), lucre, moola or moolah, gelt, jack, green (and long green), wampum, and shekels. The word "tender" or "capital" in a clue also often refers to money.

Specifically for U.S. dollars (USD has occurred several times), $1 is a CLAM, BUCK, SIMOLEON, or SMACKER, $5 is a FIN or a FIVER or a FIVESPOT, (ABEs have also appeared, for the president on their face), $10 is a TENSPOT, TENNER, or a SAWBUCK, and 10 sawbucks is a CNOTE, CSPOT, Benjamin (for Benjamin Franklin), or $100 bill, sometimes clued as "Big bill" or "100 smackers" or something similar. A DNOTE (D-note) is a $500 bill and a GNOTE (G-note) or a GRAND is $1,000 (a GNOTE has been clued as "Thou"); another slang word for that sum is GEE. And a thousand grand (or 1,000 gees) is a MIL ($1 million).

When puzzle makers use one of the above terms in a clue, it usually means that the entry will also be a slang term; for example, "20 fins" in a clue could result in CNOTE. On a lower scale, two BITS are a quarter. And if you do not want to use currency, you can always use PLASTIC. (Yes, that was in a puzzle, too.)

Even though the EURO (€) has replaced many European currencies since 2002, puzzles still contain the old terms. Even coins that were old years ago appear in puzzles, for example, the Roman DENARI, the FARTHING, the TUPPENCE (or two pence), the gold DUCAT and DOUBLOON, the Dutch DOIT, the French DENIER, SOU, and ECU (the last was minted under Louis XI, a clue), the Roman SESTERCE, the medieval STER (or British penny), the Italian SCUDO, and the not-so-old German PFENNIG. For the former Italian LIRA (sing.) and LIRE (pl.), both are used as answers, so the best bet is to write the first three letters, and let the intersecting word determine the fourth and final letter.

Cities are usually the clue and the type of currency the entry, for example, "Moscow money" and RUBLE (and 100 KOPECKS equal a ruble). Other currencies that appear are the Mexican and Cuban PESO (the peso is also used in several other Central and South American countries), the Panamanian BALBOA, the Haitian GOURDE, the Ecuadoran SUCRE, and the Peruvian SOL.

Others are the former German MARK, the former French FRANC, the current British POUND (STERLING is also used), the Albanian LEK, the Romanian LEU, the Thai BAHT, the Cambodian RIEL, the Japanese YEN, the Chinese YUAN, the Laotian KIP, the North and South Korean WON, the RUPEE of India, Pakistan, Mauritius, Nepal, and other countries, the Nigerian NAIRA, the LEONE of Sierra Leone, the South African RAND, and the Iranian, Yemeni, and Omani RIAL.

The DINAR is the name of the currency in many countries of the world, including Iraq, Jordan, Kuwait, Algeria, and Tunisia (not to be confused, however, with the dinar that is 1/100th of a RIAL in Iran). The Israeli currency is the SHEQEL (sometimes SHEKEL in puzzles), the Czech Republic and Slovakia use the KORUNA, Saudi Arabia and Qatar use the RIYAL, Sweden and Iceland use the KRONA, and Norway and Denmark use the KRONE (plural KRONER). This rather short list of currencies that have been found in puzzles is but a fraction of the total of the world's currencies. If you have a six-letter answer and do not know the currency, try DOLLAR, as the term is used in over 30 countries. Several puzzles needed the words SWAG and PELF, stolen money or loot, and AGIO, a currency exchange fee (which is mentioned later in the glossary). And a TALENT is a unit of money used in the Bible.

Schools, Colleges, and Universities

Popular names in crosswords are ELON, a university in North Carolina; IONA, a college in New Rochelle, N.Y.; and ETON, the famous English boarding school in Berkshire, clued as being on the Thames, being a rival of Harrow, or being Ian Fleming's school (and James Bond's, or 007's, and even Captain Cook's), having been founded by Henry VI in 1440, or being across the river from Windsor. Eton is a type of collar as well as a jacket and Eton blue is a color.

The most popular university is YALE, where a student or alumnus or alumna is known as an ELI or a YALIE, and the Yale cheer is BOOLA ("Boola, Boola"). Yale references are sometimes slightly disguised by a clue containing "Skull and Bones," "Bulldogs," "New Haven," or "Connecticut." And it helps to know that Mr. Yale's first name was ELIHU and that the first name of the founder of Cornell was EZRA. Others named Elihu in puzzles have been the U.S. diplomats Elihu Root (Nobel Peace Prize, 1912) and Elihu Washburne. But YALE is also the answer for a type of lock. Harvard, whose motto is VERITAS, is sometimes clued by the word "crimson." But if you should come across the Crimson Tide, it refers to the University of Alabama football team.

As mentioned in the strategy section, if the word "Brown" is the first word in a clue, it can refer to the university. Some other institutions with ambiguous names are Auburn, Bard, Bishop, Butler, Rice, and Temple. The Welsh name, Bryn Mawr, pops up now and then; it refers to a college in southeastern Pennsylvania. Of the two words, one is the clue and one the answer. And colleges and universities are often the solution for sports-related clues, especially UCLA (see the "Sports" section above). A frequent clue-answer combination is Iowa State University and its location, in AMES. One puzzle let us know that OHIOSTATE has the world's largest brass band. And keep in mind that pre-college is known as ELHI (El-Hi, or Elementary-High School) in crosswords, with the clue usually "K-12."

Native Peoples

Of the hundreds of tribal names of the native peoples of North America, puzzles are usually limited to those of four or five letters, although some have three letters; examples of the last are FOX, KAW, OTO (Nebraska, the plains, the Midwest, or buffalo hunters are clues), SAC, UTE (Utah or Colorado or the west are clues), and ZIA. Some of the four-letter names are CREE (Canada and some of its provinces are clues), CROW, ERIE, HOPI, IOWA, KIUA, OTOE, PIMA, POMO, SAUK, TANO, TAOS, TEWA (and TIWA and TOWA, too), YANA (northern California often a clue), YUMA, and ZUNI.

Some five-letter tribes are ACOMA, ALEUT (Cyrillic alphabet sometimes a clue), CADDO, CARIB, CREEK, HAIDA, HURON, INUIT, JEMEZ, KIOWA, LUMMI (Washington State a clue), METIS, MIAMI, NAMBE, OMAHA, OSAGE, PONCA, SIOUX, SUPAI, YAQUI, YUKON, and YUPIC.

Longer names are also answers, and some of those having six letters are APACHE, CAYUSE, DAKOTA, ESKIMO, LAGUNA, LAKOTA, LENAPE, MANDAN, MOHAWK, NAVAJO, OGLALA, OJIBWE, ONEIDA, OTTAWA, PAIUTE, PAWNEE, SALISH, SANDIA, SANTEE, SENECA, TACOMA, WASHOE, and YOKUTS.

Some seven-letter names are ARAPAHO, ARIKARA, CHILEAT, CHOCTAW, COCHITI, INUPIAT, ONTARIO, POLACCA, SHAWNEE, TLINGIT, TUSUQUE, WICHITA, and YAVAPAI, and some eight-letter names are ARAPAHOE (once clued by "many tattoos"), CHEROKEE, CHEYENNE, CHIPPEWA, COMANCHE (Southern plains a clue), DELAWARE, HUALAPAI, IROQUOIS, KICKAPOO, MARICOPA, MISSOURI, MUSCOGEE, NEZPERCE (Nez Perce), SEMINOLE, SHOSHONE, and UMATILLA. If you should come across the word "Anasazi," it refers to an American Indian culture in the southwest U.S. that existed until about 1300 C.E. Many of their pueblos still exist.

Olio

The subjects below are gathered together because they are similar in their number of letters and other ways, such as meaning or sound.

Age, era, and *eon* (sometimes *aeon*): Because all have three letters, it is sometimes difficult to determine from a clue which one is wanted. For what it's worth, in geology an AGE is shorter than an ERA, which is shorter than an EON. In geology, an eon is the longest in time, and contains two or more eras. In order of short to long, ages make up epochs, which are part of periods, which are part of eras, which are part of eons. In spite of the foregoing, English usage does not seem to make such fine distinctions, so a guess might be as good as trying to figure out what is wanted, unless a specific age in human history is the answer, as in BRONZE, IRON, STONE, etc. An answer for natural history has been ICEAGE, in the Pleistocene Epoch, useful for its four vowels.

Axel, axle, and *axil*: The most common of these in crosswords is AXEL, an ice-skating maneuver, usually elicited by the name of a skater in combination with "leap," as in "___ leap." (Another leap is a LUTZ, and a type of spin is a CAMEL.) An AXLE is the shaft on which wheels rotate, as on a bicycle or car. An AXIL is the angle between the upper surface of a plant part, such as a branch, and its stem. (The related "axilla" is Latin for "armpit," also found in a puzzle.)

Caret, carat, and *karat*: A CARET is a proofreading symbol for making an insertion (see "Typography and Editors' Marks" above); a CARAT is a unit of weight (200 milligrams, or about three grains) for precious stones; and a KARAT is a measure of the proportion of pure gold in an alloy. If you should come across "1-24" in a clue, it may refer to karats.

Oleo, olio, and *olla*: OLEO is an abbreviation for "oleomargarine," a butter substitute. Clues often contain the words "stick," "spread," or "refrigerator"; sometimes the clue is "Dairy-case buy" or "Tub in the fridge." An OLIO is a hodgepodge or assortment or miscellany or potpourri or pastiche or gallimaufry, a collection of this and that, a medley, mixture, mixed bag, grab bag, jumble, stew, salmagundi, mélange, or mishmash. An OLLA, which is a Spanish word pronounced "oya," is an earthenware pot or jar having a wide mouth. It is also a spicy stew that is cooked in such a pot (short for "olla podrida"). Ollas have a LIP and, often, EARS, which also occur in puzzles.

Initials

Initials are typically limited to the following persons, who need no introduction:

AES—Adlai E. (Evans) Stevenson
DDE—Dwight D. (David) Eisenhower
EAP—Edgar Allan Poe
FDR—Franklin D. (Delano) Roosevelt
FLW—Frank Lloyd Wright
GBS—George Bernard Shaw
HHH—Hubert H. (Horatio) Humphrey
HST—Harry S. (no middle name) Truman
JFK—John F. (Fitzgerald) Kennedy
RLS—Robert Louis Stevenson
TAE—Thomas A. (Alva) Edison
TSE—T.S. (Thomas Stearns) Eliot
YSL—Yves Saint Laurent

A Glossary of Special Words

The nearly 70 words listed below do not fit any of the earlier categories, but are listed here because many of them appear in puzzles with some frequency. Anyone who does crosswords regularly will recognize nearly all of them and know what they mean. If you are new to puzzles, you might want to memorize them or simply keep this list handy. It is not intended to take the place of or to compare with lists in crossword books—lists such as "100 most frequent words" and such. In this volume, most or all of those words will be found in the sections to which they apply, such as ETA in "Greek" and ELIA in "Literature."

ABRA—mouth of a canyon
ABU—in Arabic, slang for head of a family
ACTA—recorded proceedings
ADIT—mine entrance, access, or passage
AGIO—currency changer's fee, premium paid to exchange currency
AGLET—a sheath, such as a plastic one on the end of a shoelace; sometimes defined as "ornamental"
AGNATE—paternally related
ALAR—an apple pesticide banned in 1989
AMAH—Oriental nursemaid
AMBO—pulpit, lectern
ANA—a collection of items reflecting the character of a person or place, an anecdotal collection
ANI—tropical American bird related to the cuckoo, sometimes clued as a blackbird or tickbird
ANIL—indigo plant or the blue dye from it
ANILE—old-womanish
ANOA—a small (or dwarf) buffalo of Celebes and the Philippines, but in puzzles is often called a Celebes or Indonesian ox
ANTA—masonry support, such as a pilaster
ARETE—narrow, sharp mountain ridge
ARIL—seed coat, cover, or sheath
ARISTA—bristlelike part of grains and grasses (see awn); also an American record company
ARUM—in puzzles, usually refers to the calla lily family
AWN—bristlelike appendage on many grasses (see arista); clues often include "beard"
ATRA—a brand of Gillette razor
BNAI (b'nai)—son of, in Hebrew
DADO—carpenter's groove
DIRK—a long dagger
EDDO—certain taro plant or its tuber
EFT—an immature newt
ELAND—African antelope
ENATE—maternally related
EPEE—fencing sword (with no cutting edge)
ERN(E)—white-tailed sea eagle
ESKER—a long, narrow glacial ridge of coarse gravel

ESNE—among the Anglo-Saxons, a domestic slave, sometimes clued as "feudal slave" or "serf"
ETUI—ornamental or decorative box or case for holding small articles such as pins and needles
FIRN—an old granular snowfield
GANEF (or GONIF)—Yiddish for thief, rascal, or scoundrel
IBN—"son of" in Arabic
ILEX—holly
IZAR—Moslem woman's garb
KEA—a mountain-dwelling New Zealand parrot
KNAR—a knob or burl in wood or a tree
LIANE—a climbing, woody, usually tropical vine
MERL(E)—an old-world blackbird
MOTT(E)—a small stand of trees on a prairie
NEB—bird's beak (NIB an alteration)
OCA—a perennial of the high Andes, with edible tubers, sometimes clued in puzzles as wood sorrel
ODA—room in a harem
ORANT—praying female figure
ORDO—Roman Catholic church calendar
ORLE—in heraldry, a border on a shield
ORRIS—a fragrant iris root used in cosmetics and perfumes
ORT—a small scrap or leaving of food
OSAR (plural of OS)—ridges (from Old Norse); see ESKER
OSIER—willow, especially one used in basketry
PERI—in Persian mythology, a beautiful and benevolent fairy
SABOT—a wooden shoe
SEPOY—an Indian employed as a British soldier
SERAC—glacial ridge, pointed mass of ice in a glacier
SKEAN—a double-edged dagger once used in Scotland and Ireland
SNEE—old name for a dagger
SRI—a polite form of address on the Indian subcontinent, a Hindu honorific
STOMA—botanical pore
STRIA—a thin, narrow groove or channel
TESTA—hard seed covering
TOR—high rock or pile of rocks on top of a hill
TUN—large cask or vat for liquids, especially wine
UMBO—a boss or knob in the center of a shield
WOLD—a chain of treeless rolling hills

You may want to add more words to this list as you come across them in puzzles, either on this page or at the back of the book.

For some reason, clerical garments find their way into puzzles, too. Some that have occurred are ALB, a priest's long, white, linen robe, AMICE, a scarf of white linen, BIRETTA or BERETTA, a cap worn by Roman Catholic clergy, CHASUBLE, a long sleeveless garment worn over the alb, COPE, another long vestment worn over the alb or surplice, COTTA, a short surplice, FANON, an embroidered band attached to the left wrist, ORALE, a striped, scarf-like vestment worn by the pope over the alb (and the most popular in puzzles), and RABAT, a clerical cloth covering the shirt front.

Others are STOLE, a long scarf worn over the left shoulder or both shoulders, TIPPET, just about any adornment that hangs down in front, TUNICLE, a short vestment worn over the alb, MOZZETTA, an elbow-length cape, MITRE, a liturgical headdress, and ZUCCHETTO, an ecclesiastical skullcap. Speaking of the pope, the most popular name for popes in puzzles is LEO, of which there were 13 (often a clue): LEOI (called "the Great") to LEOXIII. By the way, Leo I met Attila the Hun in 452 C.E., which has been a clue. ADRIAN and PAOLO (or PAUL) were the names of six popes, URBAN was the name of eight, PIUS the name of 12, and GREGORY the name of 16.

British Words

Similar to the conventions for foreign languages, clues sometimes include cities or counties (shires), such as Leeds, Liverpool, or Devonshire, followed by the U.S. version of the noun. On occasion, the clue will be "___, on the Thames." The entry will be a British version of the clue, for example, a can is a TIN, an elevator is a LIFT, a delivery truck is a LORRY, a lock-up is a GAOL, a line you wait in is a QUEUE, a fireplace is an INGLE, a chunk is a WODGE, hors d'oeuvres are STARTERS, dessert is AFTERS, potato chips are CRISPS, and oleo is MARGE.

A crib is a COT, a diaper is a NAPPIE, a bandage is a PLASTER, gasoline is PETROL, a tire is a TYRE, the hood of a car is the BONNET, the trunk of a car is the BOOT, a fabric dealer is a DRAPER, sneakers are TRAINERS, a raincoat is a MAC (for mackintosh), a sailor is a LIMEY, a NOB is a fat cat (a wealthy person), a SWOT is a nerd, the TV is the TUBE or the TELLY, and an afternoon TV program might be a CHATSHOW (chat show).

The British contraction LTD (Ltd. or Limited), which is akin to our "Corp." ("Corporation"), turns up in puzzles. Then there are interjections, especially as in the old comics, such as GOR, ROT, BOSH (and TOSH), ZOUNDS, BYJOVE ("By Jove!"), ISAY ("I say!"), EGAD(S), GADZOOKS, BALDERDASH, BOTHERATION, and FIDDLESTICKS. To get from one place to another, you can take the TUBE (London's subway) or the TRAM; this is a reminder of PRAM, a baby carriage. A BLOKE is a fellow or chap, and in addressing a man, one might say GUV or, more familiarly, MATE. PIPPIP (Pip-Pip) was once in a puzzle; it simply means "Good-bye."

Other cases are words that change their endings from ER to RE, such as NITRE for niter (saltpeter), METRE for meter, LITRE for liter, LUSTRE for luster, THEATRE for theater, and CENTRE for center. A gram is a GRAMME and a clue is a CLEW. Then there are words that change from our "z" to their "s," such as RASE for raze. A clue for this might be "Tear down, British-style." Another common one is their "ou" for our "o," as in "colour" and "color" as well as "honour" and "honor." To make a telephone call is to RINGUP (ring up). Fourteen pounds is a STONE, crazy is DAFT or BARMY, precious is TWEE, to smooch is to SNOG, and the letter Z (zee) as spoken is ZED.

Quite easy once you realize what is needed are the Cockney pronunciations that omit the initial "h," such as ELLO for hello, ELP for help, ENRY for Henry, ERE for here, OLE for hole, and OPE for hope; these are often clued by "East End." Pounds and quids are synonymous, as are WCs in clues and LOOs and LAVs in entries. A common term in puzzles is OBE (O.B.E.), an honor granted by the queen; it stands for "Order of the British Empire."

Scottish Words

These are clued as those above, with a place, such as Aberdeen, Dundee, or Lothian, as well as with poets, as in "___, to Robert Burns." Another poetic reference to Scotland is Caledonia. Also, the terms "bagpipes," "clan," "highlands," and "bonny" or "bonnie" are often in clues. Some of the answers are NAE for no and not, GAE for go, GIE for give, HAE for have, SNA for snow, ANE for one, TWA for two, WEE for little, SMA for small, LEAL for faithful, EME for uncle, AWE for lake or river, TASS for goblet, SYNE for ago, and ORRA for odd.

The only proper names that have appeared were IAN for John and LIAM for William. A BRAE is a hillside, a STRATH is a valley, a LOCH is a lake (NESS and LOMOND are rather common), a LAIRD is a landowner, TREWS are trousers, a THANE is a lord, a BAIRN is a child, and then there are lads and lasses or laddies and lassies. TAMS are made of WOOL and the Scot's emblem is the THISTLE flower.

Hawaiian Words and Places

Two popular words in this category are ALOHA and LUAU. A shorter one is UKE, sometimes clued as "Banjo cousin" or "Guitar cousin." Hawaiian words have lots of vowels, making them a natural for crosswords. Just look at some of Hawaii's islands as a case in point: KAUAI, LANAI, MAUI, MOLOKAI, and OAHU. (Lanai is not only the name of a city and an island, but it also means "courtyard" or "veranda," usually the clue.) Oahu is sometimes clued as "Waikiki's island" or "Diamond Head island," and is called the "gathering place." The largest and southernmost island is HAWAII and the largest city on any island is HONOLULU, on the island of Oahu.

There is in Honolulu a 1.8-square-mile area called AIEA, which has been clued by "H-1," a route designation in Hawaii. (H-2 and H-3 have also been in puzzles.) Honolulu's IOLANI Palace has been in crosswords, as has the ALOHA Tower. A port on the so-called "big island" of Hawaii is HILO.

A very popular word in puzzles is LEI, the wreath of flowers worn around the neck; it is usually clued as "Wahine wear" or "Wahine's gift." (And May 1 is Lei Day.) The pikake, a fragrant jasmine, is one of these flowers, and can be a clue for "lei." Some other words are HULA, the dance itself as well as an adjective for the skirt worn at the dance; NENE, the state bird, a rare (and endangered) gray-brown wild goose related to the Canada goose; POI, a food made from the tuber of the taro, often clued as "Luau appetizer" (and it helps to know that roast pig is also eaten at luaus); AHI (yellow fin tuna); WAHINE, girl; MAHALO, thank you; LEHUA, the state flower; AVA, a certain drink; LOA, long; MUUMUU, a dress; KONA, leeward or dry side of the island; and KAHUNA, wizard or medicine man.

Lists

The limited selection of lists provided below seems practical for a handbook of this sort, inasmuch as many reference works would serve the purpose. The lists below were selected for their relevance to the author's experience in solving crosswords.

Rulers of England and Their Dates of Accession

Two types of clues usually elicit one of the names below for an answer. These are (1) when a date is given and (2) when a name is given that precedes or follows the desired entry. An example of the first might be the clue "18th century English king," the answer being one of the three Georges in that period, with the number of squares determining which one. An example of the second might be the clue "Follower of Queen Victoria," with the answer being EDWARDVII.

From as early as about 510 C.E., there was a king of Wessex, which is in southwest England; his name was Cerdic. Egbert became king of the West Saxons in 802, and from the date of 828 or 829, some sources consider him the first king of England. Alfred the Great of Wessex (871) and his son Edward the Elder (899) used the title "King of the Anglo-Saxons"; some sources consider Alfred the first true king of England. Athelstan ("the Glorious") took the title Rex Anglorum in 924. He was followed by at least 12 rulers until 1066, when William I defeated Harold II at Hastings, beginning nearly 90 years of Norman rule. It was not until 1154 that Henry II took the title Rex Angliae, or King of England. Beginning with that date, the rulers of England are listed below.

House of Plantagenet

Henry II of Anjou, Curtmantle	1154
Richard I, the Lionheart	1189
John I, Lackland	1199
Henry III	1216
Edward I, Longshanks	1272
Edward II	1307
Edward III	1327
Richard II	1377

House of Lancaster

Henry IV, Bolingbroke	1399
Henry V	1413
Henry VI (first reign)	1422

House of York

| Edward IV | 1461 |

House of Lancaster (restored)

| Henry VI (second reign) | 1470 |

House of York (restored)

Edward IV (2nd reign)	1471
Edward V	1483 (April)
Richard III, Crookback	1483 (June)

House of Tudor

Henry VII, Tudor	1485
Henry VIII*	1509
Edward VI	1547
Mary I, Tudor ("Bloody Mary")	1553
Elizabeth I	1558

House of Stuart

| James I (James VI of Scotland) | 1603 |
| Charles I | 1625 |

(The office of King was formally abolished on February 7, 1649. The interregnum, from that date until May 29, 1660, is known as the Commonwealth, or Protectorate, when Oliver Cromwell, and then his son, Richard, were dictators as Lord Protector of the Commonwealth.)

House of Stuart, restored

Charles II	1660
James II (James VII of Scotland)	1685
William III and Mary II** (joint)	1689
Anne	1702

House of Hanover

George I	1714
George II	1727
George III	1760
George IV	1811 regency
	1820 crowned
William IV	1830
Victoria	1837

House of Saxe-Coburg and Gotha

Edward VII	1901
George V	1910 (during his reign, on July 17, 1917, name of house changed to . . .)

House of Windsor

Edward VIII	1936 (January)
George VI	1936(December)
Elizabeth II	1952

*Crosswords sometimes include one of the many wives (queens consort) of King Henry VIII. They were as follows:

Catherine of Aragon
Anne Boleyn
Jane Seymour
Anne of Cleves
Catherine Howard
Catherine Paar

**Queen Mary II died in May 1694, leaving William III to rule alone.

U.S. Presidents and Their Dates in Office

George Washington	1789-1797
John Adams	1797-1801
Thomas Jefferson	1801-1809
James Madison	1809-1817
James Monroe	1817-1825
John Quincy Adams	1825-1829
Andrew Jackson	1829-1837
Martin Van Buren	1837-1841
William Henry Harrison	1841
John Tyler	1841-1845
James K. (Knox) Polk	1845-1849
Zachary Taylor	1849-1850
Millard Fillmore	1850-1853
Franklin Pierce	1853-1857
James Buchanan	1857-1861
Abraham Lincoln	1861-1865
Andrew Johnson	1865-1869
(Hiram) Ulysses S. (Simpson) Grant	1869-1877
Rutherford B. (Birchard) Hayes	1877-1881
James A. (Abram) Garfield	1881

Chester A. (Alan) Arthur	1881-1885
(Stephen) Grover Cleveland	1885-1889 (1st term)
Benjamin Harrison	1889-1893
(Stephen) Grover Cleveland	1893-1897 (2nd term)
William McKinley	1897-1901
Theodore Roosevelt	1901-1909
William Howard Taft	1909-1913
(Thomas) Woodrow Wilson	1913-1921
Warren G. (Gamaliel) Harding	1921-1923
Calvin Coolidge	1923-1929
Herbert (Clark) Hoover	1929-1933
Franklin D. (Delano) Roosevelt	1933-1945
Harry S[.] [NMN] Truman	1945-1953
Dwight D. (David) Eisenhower (Ike)	1953-1961
John F. (Fitzgerald) Kennedy	1961-1963
Lyndon B. (Baines) Johnson	1963-1969
Richard M. (Milhous) Nixon	1969-1974
Gerald R. (Rudolph) Ford	1974-1977
Jimmy (James Earl, Jr.) Carter	1977-1981
Ronald (Wilson) Reagan	1981-1989
George H.W. (Herbert Walker) Bush	1989-1993
Bill (William Jefferson) Clinton	1993-2001
George W. (Walker) Bush	2001-2009
Barack (Hussein) Obama	2009-

States and Their Capitals

Alabama (AL)	Montgomery
Alaska (AK)	Juneau
Arizona (AZ)	Phoenix
Arkansas (AR)	Little Rock

California (CA)	Sacramento
Colorado (CO)	Denver
Connecticut (CT)	Hartford
Delaware (DE)	Dover
Florida (FL)	Tallahassee
Georgia (GA)	Atlanta
Hawaii (HI)	Honolulu
Idaho (ID)	Boise
Illinois (IL)	Springfield
Indiana (IN)	Indianapolis
Iowa (IA)	Des Moines
Kansas (KS)	Topeka
Kentucky (KY)	Frankfort
Louisiana (LA)	Baton Rouge
Maine (ME)	Augusta
Maryland (MD)	Annapolis
Massachusetts (MA)	Boston
Michigan (MI)	Lansing
Minnesota (MN)	St. Paul
Mississippi (MS)	Jackson
Missouri (MO)	Jefferson City
Montana (MT)	Helena
Nebraska (NE)	Lincoln
Nevada (NV)	Carson City
New Hampshire (NH)	Concord
New Jersey (NJ)	Trenton
New Mexico (NM)	Santa Fe
New York (NY)	Albany
North Carolina (NC)	Raleigh
North Dakota (ND)	Bismarck
Ohio (OH)	Columbus
Oklahoma (OK)	Oklahoma City

Oregon (OR)	Salem
Pennsylvania (PA)	Harrisburg
Rhode Island (RI)	Providence
South Carolina (SC)	Columbia
South Dakota (SD)	Pierre
Tennessee (TN)	Nashville
Texas (TX)	Austin
Utah (UT)	Salt Lake City
Vermont (VT)	Montpelier
Virginia (VA)	Richmond
Washington (WA)	Olympia
West Virginia (WV)	Charleston
Wisconsin (WI)	Madison
Wyoming (WY)	Cheyenne

Birthstones

Clues eliciting birthstones typically include a month, such as "May birthstone," but regardless of birthstones, the most popular gem in crosswords is the OPAL. Some sources list birthstones by month, while others list them by star sign. (See "Signs of the Zodiac," immediately below.) In addition to this difference, the stones vary according to source. The list below was compiled from various sources, and includes both modern and traditional stones, since a puzzle may need any of them. Besides modern birthstones, there are "mystical" (or Tibetan) and "ayurvedic" birthstones (from Indian medicine).

January	garnet
February	amethyst, hyacinth, pearl
March	aquamarine, bloodstone, jasper
April	diamond, sapphire
May	emerald, agate

June	pearl, alexandrite, turquoise, agate, cat's eye
July	ruby, turquoise, onyx
August	peridot, sardonyx, carnation, topaz, moonstone
September	sapphire, crysolite
October	opal, pink tourmaline, aquamarine
November	topaz, citrine, pearl
December	turquoise, tarzanite, zircon, lapis lazuli, blue topaz, bloodstone, ruby

Signs of the Zodiac

The dates associated with the signs of the zodiac vary slightly, depending on the source. This should be of little concern to puzzle solvers, since the clue typically elicits the sign associated with the *greater* part of the month to which it applies. The most popular of these are ARIES and LEO.

January 20 or 21–February 18 or 19	Aquarius	(water bearer)
February 19 or 20–March 20	Pisces	(fish)
March 21–April 19 or 20	Aries	(ram)
April 20 or 21–May 20 or 21	Taurus	(bull)
May 21 or 22–June 20 or 21	Gemini	(twins)
June 21 or 22–July 22	Cancer	(crab)
July 23–August 22 or 23	Leo	(lion)
August 23 or 24–September 22 or 23	Virgo	(virgin)
September 23 or 24–October 22 or 23	Libra	(scales)
October 23 or 24–November 21 or 22	Scorpio	(scorpion)
November 22 or 23–December 21	Sagittarius	(archer)
December 22–January 19 or 20	Capricorn	(goat)

U.S. Military Officer Ranks

Army, Marines, and Air Force   *Navy and Coast Guard*

Second Lieutenant   Ensign
First Lieutenant   Lieutenant Junior Grade
Captain   Lieutenant
Major   Lieutenant Commander
Lieutenant Colonel   Commander
Colonel   Captain
Brigadier General   Rear Admiral (lower half)
Major General   Rear Admiral (upper half)
Lieutenant General   Vice Admiral
General   Admiral

(For other ranks, see www.milnet.com.)

Hebrew Alphabet

The 22 symbols of the Hebrew alphabet must be transliterated for non-Hebrew speakers to pronounce them. Depending on who is doing the transliterating (and for whom), the representation of the symbols will vary, as can be seen below. This variation should not present too much of a problem to the crossword solver, as the number of squares will determine which variant of the transliterated symbol is needed. Typically, the clue will be something like "First letter of the Hebrew alphabet." It is therefore obvious which of the variants (in this case, "alef" or "aleph") is the one to be used for the puzzle. These will be found below.

alef or aleph	lamed or lamedh
bet, beth, vet, or beit	mem
gimel or gimmel	nun
dalet or daleth	samekh, samech, or samex
hey, hei, he, or heh	ayin
vav or waw	pey, pe, pei, or fe
zayin	tsade, tsadik, zadi, or sadhe
het, xet, heth, or chet	qof, qoph, kof, or kuf
tet, teth, or teit	resh or reish
yod, yodh, or yud	shin or sin
kaf, kaph, or xaf	tav or taw

Hebrew Months

Clues eliciting a Hebrew month usually are simple, with the clue being one month and the entry the one before or after it or the clue being, say, "Twelfth Hebrew month." There is a distinction between the *civil* month and the *religious* month, but puzzle clues typically assume the former. Accordingly, the list below begins the calendar with the first *civil* month. If for some reason, the *religious* month is needed, simply begin the year with the seventh civil month, namely, Nisan, and end it with Adar. Incidentally, the Jewish New Year 5774 began on September 4, 2013. The Hebrew months are listed below.

Tishri or Tishrei (Rosh Hashanah month)
Heshvan or Cheshvan or Marhesvan
Kislew or Kislev
Tebet or Tevet or Teveth or Chislev
Sebat or Shvat or Shevat or Shebat or Sebat
Adar (Purim month, popular in crosswords)
Nisan or Nissan (Seder or Passover month)
Iyyar or Iyar
Siwan or Sivan
Tammuz or Thammuz or Tamuz
Ab or Av
Elul (popular in crosswords)

Note: Several other lists will be found in the sections of the handbook to which they relate. Examples of these are: (1) in the "Foreign Languages" section, words and phrases in French, Spanish, Italian, Latin, German, and Greek, (2) in the "Latin" section, the first ten cardinal numbers in Latin, Italian, Spanish, and French, as well as the first 14 Roman emperors, (3) in the "German" section, the cardinal numbers through 12, (4) in the "Greek" section, the 24 letters of the alphabet, (5) in the "Mythology" section, two lists of characters, (6) in "The Old Testament" section, its 39 books, (7) in the "Classical Music" section, various tempos as well as composers, conductors, and performers, (8) in the "Sports" section, baseball, football, basketball, hockey, and tennis players, as well as golfers and boxers, (9) in the "Entertainment" section, actors and actresses, as well as some popular TV shows and their characters, (10) in the "Art and Architecture" section, artists, (11) in the "Noble Gases and Other Elements" section, the six noble gases and their symbols and atomic numbers plus the first 30 elements and their symbols and atomic numbers, (12) in the "Native Peoples" section, the names of nearly 100 tribes, (13) in the "Initials" section, some popular initials and their possessors, and (14) in "A Glossary of Special Words," over 60 favorites of puzzle makers.

In addition to the above lists, you will also find, in the "Mathematics" section, the six trigonometric functions, and in the "Currency" section, various currencies of the world that have appeared in crosswords. ✦

Made in United States
North Haven, CT
22 December 2023

46385332R00138